S0-AJZ-813

Gopher Sketchbook

BY AL PĀPAS, JR.

NODIN PRESS
Minneapolis

ISBN 0-931714-41-9

Nodin Press, a division of Micauber's, Inc.
525 North Third Street
Minneapolis, MN 55401

Printed in U.S.A., at Gopher State Litho, Minneapolis, MN

Dedication

MY FIRST MEMORY OF SPORTS WAS GOPHER FOOTBALL. I WAS PLAYING ON THE FLOOR AT MY FATHER'S FEET WHILE HE LISTENED TO A GAME ON THE RADIO.

DAD HAD PLAYED STARTING LEFT END FOR BERNIE BIERMAN IN BIERMAN'S FIRST GAME AS HEAD COACH FOR MINNESOTA. SINCE LEFT END WAS LISTED FIRST ON THE ROSTER, IT MADE HIM THE FIRST GOPHER OF THE "GOLDEN ERA." A LEG INJURY AT A PRACTICE ENDED HIS CAREER. THIS HAPPENED BEFORE HE COULD PLAY ENOUGH TIME TO QUALIFY FOR AN "M." THE RULES WERE CHANGED THE FOLLOWING YEAR. THE NEW RULES WOULD HAVE QUALIFIED HIM, BUT HE WAS NOT ABLE TO RETURN TO GET IT. HE WAS SORELY DISAPPOINTED.

DAD TOOK ME TO SEE MY FIRST GAME AND THE GOOSE BUMPS WOULD SWELL ON HIS ARMS AS THEY PLAYED THE "MINNESOTA ROUSER." IT SOON DID THE SAME FOR ME.

AT A YOUNG AGE MY FATHER TOOK ILL WITH CANCER. HIS DOCTOR, BILL PROFFITT, WAS ONE OF HIS FOOTBALL BUDDIES. PROFFITT DREW UP A PETITION TO GET DAD THAT ELUSIVE "M." IT WAS PRESENTED TO HIM SHORTLY BEFORE HIS DEATH. HE WAS THRILLED TO GET IT. FROM TIME TO TIME HE WOULD ASK MY MOTHER TO PLACE THE "M" ON HIS CHEST. IN HIS WEAKENED CONDITION HE WOULD GLIDE HIS FINGERS OVER IT IN A CARESS.

AFTER HE WAS GONE MY MOTHER CONTINUED FOLLOWING THE MAROON AND GOLD ON RADIO AT TOP VOLUME. SHE FILLED ME IN ON EVEN MORE GOPHER LORE. NO TEAM OR SPORT HAS MEANT AS MUCH TO ME. THIS SKETCHBOOK IS OFFERED IN THE NAMES OF MY PARENTS... AL & BEA PAPAS.

Roster of Contents

Pregame Introduction

THE ROOTS OF FOOTBALL HISTORY SINK DEEP INTO THE SOIL OF MINNESOTA. THIS BOOK DEALS MOSTLY WITH MINNESOTA'S GREATEST INDIVIDUALS AND SEEKS TO BE AS COMPLETE AS POSSIBLE IN PORTRAYING ALL THEIR LIKENESSES UNDER ONE COVER.

THERE ARE THOSE WHO CAME TO FULL BLOOM AND THERE ARE THOSE WHO WERE SEEDLINGS THAT WENT ON TO GREATNESS ELSEWHERE. SOME HAVE BEEN FORGOTTEN OVER TIME AND ARE HERE RECALLED TO THE PLACE OF HONOR THEY DESERVE.

STILL THEY ARE BUT A BRANCH OF THE MIGHTY TREE OF OVER 1500 LETTERMEN WHO HAVE ADORNED THE COLORFUL MAROON AND GOLD LEAVES OF AUTUMN.

ALL-AMERICAN SELECTIONS STARTED IN 1889 AS THE IDEA OF YALE GRAD WALTER CAMP. SUCH SELECTIONS WERE LATER MADE BY OTHER FOLLOWERS OF THE GAME, TOO, BUT WERE NOT ACCEPTED WITH AS MUCH AUTHORITY.

EASTERN TEAMS WERE AT THE CENTER OF THE GAME IN THOSE DAYS AND SO CAMP DIDN'T ALWAYS NOTICE DESERVING PLAYERS FROM THE WEST. MANY GOPHERS BECAME ALL-AMERICANS AND EVEN CONSENSUS ALL-AMERICANS. A LESSER NUMBER BECAME FAMOUS FOR MAKING THE CAMP TEAM. ALL ARE RECOGNIZED WITHIN THIS BOOK.

CUSTOMS, RULES AND PEOPLE FROM OTHER FACETS OF THE GAME ARE ALSO REMEMBERED. DIAGRAMS OF SOME OF THE MOST HISTORIC GAMES ARE SHOWN. THE KEY TO THEM CAN BE FOUND AT THE RIGHT.

THESE PAGES SERVE AS A BRIEF DOCUMENT TO THE CONTRIBUTIONS AND GREATNESS OF UNIVERSITY OF MINNESOTA INDIVIDUALS TO THE SPORT OF FOOTBALL AND TO THE U OF M.

Key for Game Charts

POINT OF FUMBLE OR INTERCEPTION		X
INCOMPLETE PASS		IP
TOUCHBACK		TB.
BALL BROUGHT OUT FROM TOUCHBACK	....	
PUNT OR KICK	— — — — —	
RUNNING YARDAGE	————————	
PASSING YARDAGE	- - - - - - - - - -	
PENALTY YARDAGE	++++++++++++	
LOOSE BALL	~~~~~~~~	
	MINNESOTA	OPPONENT
TOUCHDOWN	TD. (open)	TD. (filled)
FIELD GOAL	FG. (open)	FG. (filled)
SAFETY	S (open)	S (filled)
DOWN AND DIRECTION OF PLAY	▷1 ▷2 ▷3 ▷4	◀4 ◀3 ◀2 ◀1

(POINT OF ARROW IS FORWARD PROGRESS)

1887 TEAM
BACK: ARTHUR MANN, WILLIAM WILLARD, FRED MANN, EDMUND ALLEN, WALTER HEFFELFINGER, HAL WATSON, HENRY MORRIS
FRONT: ALONZO MEADS, WILLIAM HOYT, PAUL GOODE, ALFRED PILLSBURY, JOHN CORLISS, JOHN HAYDEN

The Starting Lineup

PLAYERS, IN THE BEGINING, COULD BE RECRUITED FROM OUTSIDE OF THE CAMPUS. WALTER "PUDGE" HEFFELFINGER WAS ONE OF THEM. HE WAS A HIGH SCHOOL STUDENT FROM MINNEAPOLIS CENTRAL WHEN HE JOINED SOME FANS TO SEE THE GOPHERS OFF FOR AN AWAY GAME. THE TEAM WAS IN NEED OF ANOTHER PLAYER WHEN CAPTAIN PILLSBURY NOTICED THE STRAPPING LAD. "PUDGE" WAS INVITED TO COME ALONG AND SO HE JOINED THE TEAM.

HEFFELFINGER EVENTUALLY WENT TO COLLEGE AT YALE. WHILE THERE HE WAS SELECTED TO BE ON THE FIRST EVER ALL-AMERICAN TEAM. HE REPEATED THE DISTINCTION THE FOLLOWING TWO YEARS AND HAS MADE MOST OF THE ALL-TIME TEAMS SINCE.

AS AN EARLY INNOVATOR OF THE GAME, HE WAS THE FIRST GUARD TO LEAVE HIS POSITION AND RUN INTERFERENCE FOR THE BALL CARRIER. HE ALSO INVENTED THE SHIN GUARDS AND WAS THE FIRST FOOTBALL PLAYER TO EVER SIGN A PRO CONTRACT. HE DID THIS IN 1892 AT $500 TO PLAY FOR ONE GAME.

UPON RETURNING HOME HE AGAIN TOOK UP THE MAROON AND GOLD COLORS. IN 1895 HE SERVED AS MINNESOTA'S PAID COACH. AFTER THAT HE HELPED PART TIME WITHOUT PAY FOR 15 YEARS. YOU COULD ALSO FIND HIM PLAYING AGAINST MINNESOTA ON AN EX-COLLEGIAN TEAM TO TEST THE GOPHERS' METTLE.

HEFFELFINGER'S LAST GAME WAS IN A 1933 CHARITY CONTEST IN MINNEAPOLIS. AT AGE 65 HE FINALLY TOOK HIMSELF OUT OF THE ACTION FOR NOT BEING TOUGH ENOUGH. HIS PLAYING DAYS SPANNED 50 YEARS AND HE WAS, OF COURSE, ENSHRINED IN THE FOOTBALL HALL OF FAME.

John William Adams

JOHN ADAMS PLAYED CENTER FOR THE GOPHERS FROM 1881 TO 1886.

IN 1882 HE COMPETED IN MINNESOTA'S FIRST INTERCOLLEGIATE GAME AND WAS AMONG THE FIRST "M" LETTERMEN. THE FOLLOWING YEAR HE SERVED AS TEAM CAPTAIN.

HE WAS THE INVENTOR OF THE EXPRESSION "SKI-U-MAH."

HIS FOOTBALL DAYS WEREN'T OVER AFTER HE LEFT MINNESOTA. AS SHOWN IN THIS DRAWING HE WENT ON TO PLAY IN THE EAST FOR THE UNIVERSITY OF PENNSYLVANIA.

IN 1891 THIS GOPHER BECAME PENNSYLVANIA'S FIRST ALL-AMERICAN.

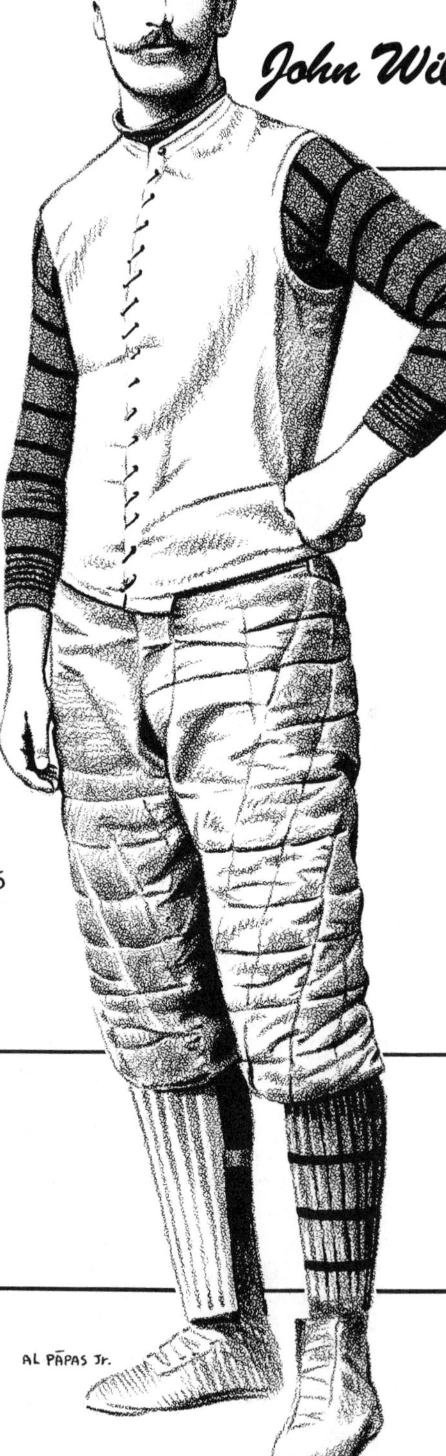

Alf Pillsbury

HIS NAME MAY SOUND FAMILIAR BECAUSE HE WAS OF THE PILLSBURY MILLS FAMILY. HIS FATHER WAS JOHN S. PILLSBURY, THE "FATHER OF THE UNIVERSITY" AND FORMER GOVERNOR OF THE STATE.

"PILLY" WAS THE EARLIEST GOPHER STANDOUT. HE PLAYED QUARTER (QUARTERBACK) AND ON THE RUSH LINE. HIS CAREER LASTED EIGHT YEARS WHILE SERVING AS CAPTAIN DURING 1887 AND 1889.

PILLSBURY'S GREATEST CONTRIBUTION MAY HAVE BEEN IN CHANGING MINNESOTA FROM THE SOCCER TO RUGBY STYLE OF GAME. THIS HE DID IN 1886 DUE TO HIS INFLUENCE OF OWNING THE ONLY BALL IN TOWN!

Thomas Peebles

BECAUSE HE HAD JUST ARRIVED FROM PRINCETON, WHERE HE LEARNED KNOWLEDGE OF HOW THE GAME WAS PLAYED, THOMAS PEEBLES WAS ASKED BY THE UNIVERSITY PLAYERS TO HELP THEM OUT. THE PROFESSOR OF MENTAL AND MORAL PHILOSOPHY THUS BECAME MINNESOTA'S FIRST FOOTBALL COACH IN 1883.

DURING THE FIRST GAME HE ALSO SERVED AS REFEREE. THIS CAME ABOUT AS A COMPROMISE WHEN CARLETON WAS CHALLENGED OVER THEIR ROSTER AND THEIR WANTING TO PLAY RUGBY STYLE.

PEEBLES LIKED THE SOCCER STYLE OF PLAY BUT THE RUGBY STYLE GAINED FAVOR UNDER SECOND "COACHER" FRED JONES.

Fredrick S. Jones

PEEBLES AND JONES CREATED INTEREST BY DIVIDING THE MINNESOTA TEAM UP AND PLAYING ONE ANOTHER. IF PEEBLES' SIDE SCORED HE WOULD HOLLER OUT FOR PRINCETON. IF JONES' TEAM SCORED HE WOULD CHEER FOR HIS ALMA MATER, YALE.

JONES TOOK A KEEN INTEREST IN THE GAME. HIS GUIDING HAND EARNED HIM THE TITLE "FATHER OF MINNESOTA FOOTBALL."

AFTER HIS TIME AS COACH HE SERVED AS FACULTY REPRESENTATIVE ON THE ATHLETIC BOARD. HE WAS INSTRUMENTAL IN OBTAINING THE LAND FOR NORTHROP FIELD AND SIGNING DR. HENRY L. WILLIAMS AS COACH.

The Yale Connection

EDWARD W. MOULTON

AFTER FRED JONES STEPPED DOWN, MINNESOTA HAD GAME COACHES FOR ONE SEASON. FOLLOWING THAT, TOM ECK NOTCHED THE FIRST CHAMPIONSHIP FOR THE GOPHERS IN 1890.

MINNESOTA'S FIRST NATIVE-BORN COACH WAS EDWARD "DAD" MOULTON FROM MINNEAPOLIS. AT 14 HE ENLISTED IN THE FIRST MINNESOTA HEAVY ARTILLERY DURING THE CIVIL WAR. AFTER THAT, IN THE MID-1870'S, HE WAS KNOWN AS THE CHAMPION SPRINTER OF AMERICA. HE DID THIS PROFESSIONALLY AND IT LED HIM INTO BECOMING AN ATHLETIC TRAINER. HE MOSTLY KEPT THE GOPHERS IN GOOD PHYSICAL SHAPE RATHER THAN COACH THEM IN THE GAME.

THE TEAM CAPTAIN, IN THOSE DAYS, WOULD OFTEN DOUBLE UP AND BE MORE OF A COACH THAN THE COACH. THE SEASON AFTER MOULTON LEFT, MINNESOTA HAD NO COACH AT ALL AND WENT UNDEFEATED.

ALEXANDER N. JERREMS

IF IT WASN'T THE CAPTAIN RUNNING THE SHOW, IT MIGHT BE A RECENTLY "RETIRED" PLAYER WHO WAS WELL-RESPECTED. SINCE THE "GREAT" ONES WERE FROM THE EAST, THE GOPHERS HEAVILY RELIED ON YALE GRADS AND ADOPTED THEIR STYLE OF PLAY.

"WALLIE" WINTER CAME ALONG AFTER HAVING BEEN AN ALL-AMERICAN TACKLE AT YALE. HE WAS CONSIDERED MINNESOTA'S FIRST "REAL" COACH. HE WORKED HIS PLAYERS HARD AND WOULD, FOR A FEW DAYS BEFORE GAMES, PUT HIS TEAM THROUGH RUGGED SCRIMMAGES. THE PLAYERS CONSIDERED THE ACTUAL GAMES AS BREATHERS COMPARED TO THE SCRIMMAGES IN 1893.

THOMAS COCHRANE, JR., AGAIN FROM YALE, CAME NEXT. THE PROGRAM WAS SUFFERING FINANCIALLY, SO HE GAVE A LECTURE TO RAISE FUNDS. IT WAS CALLED "FOOTBALL AS PLAYED IN THE EAST." HE STAYED FOR ONLY ONE YEAR.

"PUDGE" HEFFELFINGER RETURNED HOME FROM YALE TO SERVE FOR THE NEXT SEASON. "DAD" MOULTON ALSO RETURNED AS TRAINER AFTER A STINT AT MICHIGAN.

NEXT TO TAKE HIS TURN WAS ALEX JERREMS. HE WAS BORN IN SYDNEY, AUSTRALIA, BUT GREW UP IN CHICAGO. HE MOSTLY LEARNED THE GAME AT YALE WHILE PLAYING BACKFIELD POSITIONS.

JACK MINDS

THE YALE CONNECTION ENDED TEMPORARILY WITH THE ARRIVAL OF JACK MINDS. HE HAD BEEN AN ALL-AMERICAN FULLBACK AT PENNSYLVANIA, WITH A REPUTATION AS A KICKER.

IN 1899 A COUPLE OF MINNESOTA ALUMNI DECIDED TO GIVE CO-COACHING A TRY AND THEIR TEAM ENDED UP LAST IN THE CONFERENCE.

THE TIME FINALLY CAME WHEN MINNESOTA LANDED DR. HENRY WILLIAMS AS ITS FIRST FULL-TIME SALARIED COACH. HE GOT A THREE-YEAR CONTRACT FOR $2,500, STARTING IN 1900.

WILLIAMS PREVIOUSLY HAD PLAYED BALL WITH HEFFELFINGER AT YALE. AFTER THAT HE ASSISTED ARMY IN THEIR FIRST VICTORY OVER NAVY. HE COMMUNICATED WITH THE CADETS BY MAIL. THEY LEARNED HIS NEW THEORY OF PLAY THIS WAY AND WENT OUT AND WON. HE WOULD BECOME MINNESOTA'S WINNINGEST COACH.

John Harrison

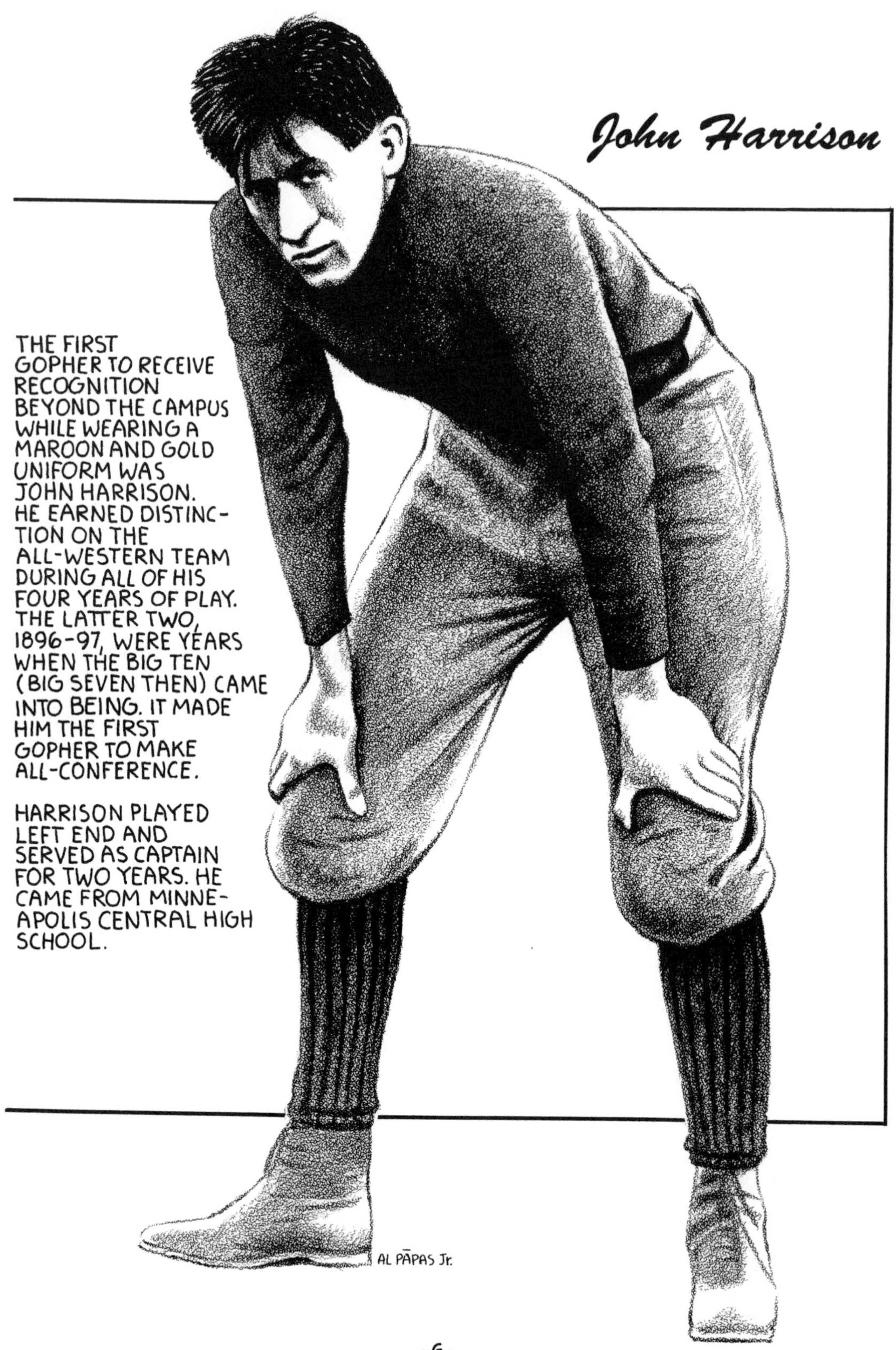

THE FIRST GOPHER TO RECEIVE RECOGNITION BEYOND THE CAMPUS WHILE WEARING A MAROON AND GOLD UNIFORM WAS JOHN HARRISON. HE EARNED DISTINCTION ON THE ALL-WESTERN TEAM DURING ALL OF HIS FOUR YEARS OF PLAY. THE LATTER TWO, 1896-97, WERE YEARS WHEN THE BIG TEN (BIG SEVEN THEN) CAME INTO BEING. IT MADE HIM THE FIRST GOPHER TO MAKE ALL-CONFERENCE.

HARRISON PLAYED LEFT END AND SERVED AS CAPTAIN FOR TWO YEARS. HE CAME FROM MINNEAPOLIS CENTRAL HIGH SCHOOL.

"Johnny" Campbell Lt. Edwin Glenn

A TACTIC BY PRINCETON PLAYERS IN THE FIRST COLLEGIATE GAME WAS TO USE THE BLOOD-CHILLING REBEL YELL LEFT OVER FROM THE CIVIL WAR. THEY WOULD USE IT AT STRATEGIC MOMENTS TO GAIN A PSYCHOLOGICAL EDGE. THIS GOT THEM UNNECESSARILY WINDED, HOWEVER, SO THEY GOT SCHOOLMATES ON THE SIDELINES TO DO THE YELLING FOR THEM. IT RESULTED IN CHEERING AT GAMES, WHICH EVENTUALLY EVOLVED INTO FANCY YELLS AND ROUSING SONGS. THE FIRST SPECIFIC CROWD CHANT WAS THE "LOCOMOTIVE" CHEER AT PRINCETON. THESE CHEERS WOULD BE STARTED BY ANYONE IN THE CROWD.

IN 1892 LT. EDWIN GLENN DEVELOPED THE ORGANIZED "ROOTERS" WHICH WAS UNIQUE TO MINNESOTA. THE PROFESSOR OF MILITARY SCIENCE AND TACTICS STARTED WITH ABOUT 20 FAITHFUL, WHO WOULD FOLLOW THE GOPHERS WHEREVER THEY PLAYED, TO LEND A VOCAL HAND.

ANOTHER MINNESOTA INVENTION, CHEERLEADING, WAS CREATED BY "JOHNNY" CAMPBELL ON NOVEMBER 12, 1898. THIS POPULAR IDEA SPREAD THROUGHOUT FOOTBALLDOM AS WELL AS INTO OTHER SPORTS. IN LATER YEARS CAMPBELL LED A CONTINGENT KNOWN AS THE SOUTH ST. PAUL "HOOK 'EM COWS." THEIR VOCAL AND COWBELL RINGING VOLUME WERE WELL-REPRESENTED AT GOPHER GAMES. HE DIDN'T MISS A HOME GAME FOR 42 YEARS.

Dr. Henry L. Williams

THIS HALL OF FAMER WAS ONE OF HIS ERA'S GREATEST OFFENSIVE COACHES. HIS PLAYS WERE CLEVER AND ILLUSIVE, CENTERING ON POWER AND SPEED. HE INVENTED THE MINNESOTA SHIFT, WHICH HAD DRAMATIC EFFECT ON THE GAME.

AS A MEMBER OF THE N.C.A.A. RULES COMMITTEE HE WAS THE FIRST TO PROPOSE LEGALIZATION OF THE FORWARD PASS.

GIL DOBIE PLAYED QUARTERBACK IN 1900-01. HE WAS AT HIS BEST ON DEFENSE AND RETURNING PUNTS.

AT THE END OF HIS PLAYING DAYS HE STUCK AROUND TO ASSIST UNDER HENRY WILLIAMS. HE HAD FOUND HIS NICHE IN COACHING, WHERE HE WOULD CONTINUE ON TO THE HALL OF FAME.

SOME OF THE STOPS ALONG THE WAY FOR "GLOOMY GIL" WERE NORTH DAKOTA, WASHINGTON, NAVY, CORNELL AND BOSTON COLLEGE.

HE COACHED HIS WHOLE WASHINGTON CAREER (1908-16) WITHOUT SUFFERING A DEFEAT. WASHINGTON STILL HOLDS THE ALL-TIME COLLEGIATE UNDEFEATED STRING OF 63 GAMES. THE RECORD 59-0-4 WAS MADE FROM 1907-17. SANDWICHED BETWEEN TIES WERE 39 VICTORIES IN A ROW... THE SECOND-LONGEST WIN STRING IN COLLEGE HISTORY.

AT CORNELL HE WENT THREE YEARS WITH A PERFECT WINNING RECORD. TWO OF THOSE YEARS WERE BACK-TO-BACK NATIONAL CHAMPIONSHIPS IN 1921 AND 22.

Gilmore Dobie

IN HIS 33 YEARS OF COACHING, DOBIE COMPILED A 180-45-15 MARK WITH A .781 WINNING PERCENTAGE.

Champions of the West

IT WAS HALLOWEEN, 1903. THE POINT-A-MINUTE MEN FROM MICHIGAN HAD COME TO GOPHERLAND WITH THEIR TRICKS AND TREATS. THEY WERE DEFENDING THEIR TITLE AS "CHAMPIONS OF THE WEST." INDEED, THEY WERE CHAMPIONS OF THE ENTIRE NATION! THEY HADN'T LOST A GAME IN THREE SEASONS. THE YEAR BEFORE THEY HAD THROTTLED STANFORD IN THE FIRST-EVER ROSE BOWL GAME 49-0. THEIR BIG GUN WAS THE IMMORTAL WILLIE HESTON. HE WOULD EVENTUALLY FINISH HIS FOUR YEARS OF BALL IN 1904 WITH AN INCREDIBLE 93 TOUCHDOWNS.

MICHIGAN COACH, FIELDING YOST, HAD VISITED TWO WEEKS BEFORE TO PERSONALLY SCOUT THE GOPHERS. WHEN HE RETURNED TO MICHIGAN HE PROMPTLY TOLD FOUR PLAYERS TO PRACTICE THEIR PUNTING. UP UNTIL THEN, MICHIGAN HAD NOT PUNTED ALL YEAR. TEAM SESSIONS WERE TOUGH BECAUSE OF THEIR RESPECT FOR THE MINNESOTANS. MICHIGAN'S STRENGTH WAS IN THEIR PHYSICAL CONDITIONING. THEY WERE INJURY-FREE AND THEIR TEAMWORK WAS CONSIDERED PERFECTION.

MINNESOTA HAD ALSO PREPARED FOR THE GREAT BATTLE. HIGH-SCORING GAMES WERE COMMON IN THIS ERA. ONCE A BALL CARRIER FOUGHT PAST THE LINE OF SCRIMMAGE HE WAS, MORE OR LESS, FREE TO THE GOAL LINE. TO STOP THIS, COACH WILLIAMS (WITH THE HELP OF PUDGE HEFFELFINGER) INVENTED THE SEVEN MAN DEFENSIVE LINE. FOUR MEN WOULD PLAY AS DEFENSIVE BACKS TO BOX IN HESTON. MINNESOTA'S GREATNESS WAS ITS SPEED AND PHYSICAL STRENGTH. THEY WERE, HOWEVER, NOT IN AS GOOD PHYSICAL CONDITION AS WAS MICHIGAN. THERE WAS DOUBT AS TO WHETHER SOME PLAYERS WOULD START. THE ODDS WERE 10-8 FOR MICHIGAN.

FANS GOT READY FOR THE GAME, TOO. SOME BOYS WERE ARRESTED AND FINED TWO DOLLARS BY A ST. PAUL MAGISTRATE. THEY HAD BEEN APPREHENDED FOR "PRACTICING" THE "SKI-U-MAH" YELL AT A NIGHTLY HOUR. THERE WAS A GREAT RALLY PUT ON BY THE MEDIC ROOTING CLUB. 2000 STUDENTS ALSO ATTENDED A "MONSTER" BONFIRE WHICH WAS LIT ON THE DRILL GROUNDS. FANS CAME FROM ALL OVER THE REGION AND FROM AS FAR AWAY AS NEW YORK. CONFIDENCE WAS INTENSE ON BOTH SIDES.

GAME DAY CAME WITH PERFECT INDIAN SUMMER WEATHER. EXCITED FANS WERE FILLING NORTHROP FIELD SIX HOURS BEFORE KICKOFF TIME. THOSE WHO COULDN'T GET IN CLUNG TO TELEGRAPH AND TELEPHONE POLES TO SEE. THE LIMBS OF TREES WERE SPROUTING PEOPLE. ALL AVAILABLE HOUSE TOPS WERE CROWDED. KIDS STOOD ON BARRELS IN WAGONS, WITH HOPES OF GETTING A VIEW.

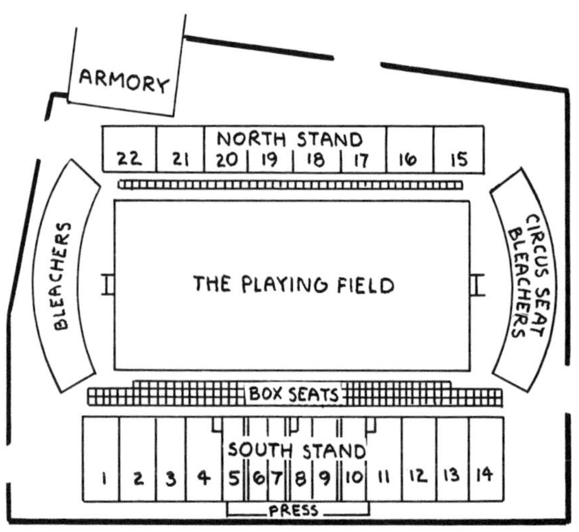

◀ THE "NEW" NORTHROP FIELD

THE CROWD WAS WELL-DECORATED IN MAROON AND GOLD. THE MEDICAL STUDENTS PARADED ONTO THE FIELD GUIDING A DONKEY AND PIG DRESSED IN MINNESOTA COLORS. MICHIGAN COLORS WERE TIED TO THEIR TAILS. THE "ORGANIZED" AND "UNORGANIZED" ROOTERS VIED FOR THE MOST NOISE. THE GIRLS' MEGAPHONE BRIGADE WAS SAID TO HAVE MADE AS MUCH, IF NOT MORE, NOISE AS ANY. THE WHOLE NATION LOOKED UPON THE BANKS OF THE MISSISSIPPI FOR AN EPIC CONTEST FEATURING MINNESOTA'S GREATEST TEAM TO DATE.

THE FIRST HALF WENT TO MINNESOTA ALTHOUGH THERE WAS NO SCORING. IT WAS PLAYED MOSTLY IN MICHIGAN TERRITORY. MICHIGAN WOULD STIFFEN WHEN MINNESOTA WAS WITHIN RANGE TO SCORE. THE GOPHERS OUT-FIRST-DOWNED THE WOLVERINES 17-3.

IN THE SECOND HALF MICHIGAN'S CONDITIONING PAID OFF WITH A LONG MARCH OVER THE GOAL LINE. TIME WAS BECOMING A FACTOR IN THE SCHEDULED 70 MINUTE GAME. THE GAME, HOWEVER, WASN'T OVER YET...

Early Rules

SOME OF THE RULES OF THE GAME IN 1903 WERE AS FOLLOWS:

THE FIELD WAS 110 YARDS LONG AND THE KICKOFF WAS FROM THE 55 YARD LINE; A TEAM HAD TO ADVANCE THE BALL FIVE YARDS IN THREE TRIES TO MAKE A FIRST DOWN; THE SCORED-UPON TEAM HAD THE OPTION OF KICKING OR RECEIVING. BEFORE 1903 THE SCORED-UPON TEAM ALWAYS KICKED OFF.

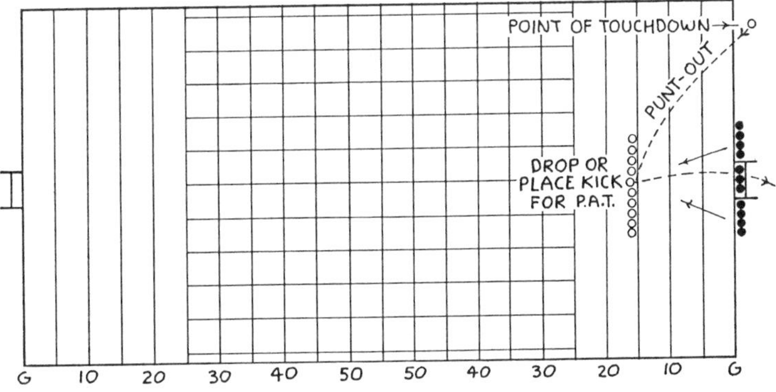

STARTING IN 1903 THE QUARTERBACK, WHO WAS FIRST TO RECEIVE THE BALL, COULD ADVANCE THE BALL BEYOND THE SCRIMMAGE LINE ONLY IF HE FIRST RAN FIVE YARDS TO THE LEFT OR RIGHT OF THE "SNAPPER-BACK." THIS TYPE ADVANCE WAS ONLY ALLOWED BETWEEN THE 25 YARD LINES. THE FIELD WAS DESIGNED IN A CHECKERBOARD PATTERN FOR THE SAKE OF THE REFEREE TO KEEP TRACK OF THIS LATERAL MOVEMENT.

ANOTHER NEW RULE ENDED ROUGHING OF THE PUNTER. PREVIOUSLY THE PUNTER COULD KICK AND SCAMPER DOWN FIELD TO PICK UP THE BALL AND ADVANCE IT AS IF THE PLAY HAD BEEN A RUN. TO PREVENT THIS, THE RECEIVING TEAM WOULD FLATTEN THE KICKER BEFORE HE COULD GET STARTED. NOW THE KICKER COULD NOT BE TOUCHED NOR COULD HE RECEIVE HIS OWN KICK.

A TOUCHDOWN WAS WORTH FIVE POINTS. THE SCORE COUNTED WHEN THE BALL WAS TOUCHED DOWN ON THE GROUND OR WHEN THE CARRIER WAS TACKLED PAST THE GOAL LINE. HE WOULD TRY TO PUT THE BALL AS CLOSE TO THE GOAL POSTS AS POSSIBLE BECAUSE THE POINT AFTER WAS ATTEMPTED 15 YARDS OUT FROM WHERE THE TOUCH-DOWN WAS MADE. SINCE THE POSTS WERE RIGHT ON THE GOAL LINE, TO SCORE NEAR THE SIDE OF THE FIELD OFFERED A HARD ANGLE FROM WHICH TO KICK THE POINT AFTER. GREAT STRUGGLES MIGHT OCCUR IN THE END ZONE FOR POSITION.

TO OVERCOME THESE BAD KICKING ANGLES A PUNT-OUT WAS ALLOWED. AN OFFENSIVE PLAYER WOULD TAKE THE BALL FROM THE POINT OF TOUCHDOWN AND PUNT IT TO A TEAMMATE BEYOND THE 15 YARD LINE IN FRONT OF THE GOAL-POSTS. THE RECEIVER WOULD PLACE OR DROP-KICK IT FOR THE SCORE. THE DEFENDERS WOULD LINE UP ON THE GOAL LINE AND TAKE OFF AT THE PUNT-OUT.

QUARTERBACK SIG HARRIS, OUT OF MINNEAPOLIS CENTRAL, WAS VALUED FOR HIS PUNTING AND PUNT RETURNS. HE WAS ALSO THE FINAL DEFENSIVE STOPPER ON WILLIE HESTON. ON ONE END RUN THE TWO COLLIDED AND WERE BOTH KNOCKED OUT. THEY WERE REVIVED AND CONTINUED PLAYING. AFTER THE MICHIGAN SCORE HARRIS RETURNED THE KICKOFF FOR 43 YARDS. IT WAS THE DAY'S MOST SPECTACULAR PLAY. IT GAVE MINNESOTA IMPORTANT FIELD POSITION.

HARRIS EVENTUALLY BECAME COACH OF THE GOPHER FRESHMEN SQUAD. BEFORE MICHIGAN GAMES HE WOULD GIVE THE VARSITY ROUSING SPEECHES TO SPUR THEM ON TO VICTORY.

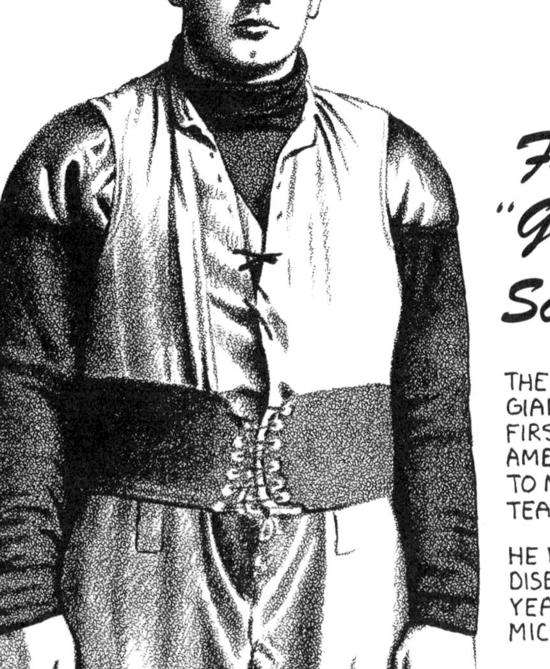

WITH MINUTES TO PLAY THE GOPHERS ROSE ABOVE THEIR FATIGUE TO FIGHT DOWN THE FIELD. A GREAT SPEARHEAD IN THE STRUGGLE WAS FRED SCHACHT.

SCHACHT WAS THE HEAVIEST LINEMAN FOR MINNESOTA AT 5'11" TALL AND 210 POUNDS. HE WORE A CORSET, MUCH TO THE DISGUST OF THE MICHIGAN COACH... BUT HE JUST WANTED TO LOOK GOOD.

LINEMEN WERE ALLOWED TO RUN WITH THE BALL, AND SO, FROM TACKLE, HE WAS THE TEAM'S BEST GROUND-GAINER. WITH HIS SPEED AND WEIGHT HE WOULD HIT THE LINE AND POUND OUT MANY OF THE MOST CRITICAL YARDS IN THE GOPHER'S TOUCHDOWN DRIVE.

Fred "Germany" Schacht

THE FERGUS FALLS GIANT BECAME MINNESOTA'S FIRST CONSENSUS ALL-AMERICAN. HE FAILED TO MAKE WALTER CAMP'S TEAM, THOUGH.

HE DIED OF BRIGHTS DISEASE JUST THREE YEARS AFTER THE MICHIGAN GAME.

AL PĀPAS Jr.

Ed Rogers
FINALLY, EGIL BOECKMANN CRACKED THE GOAL LINE. THE PUNT-OUT TRY WENT TO ED ROGERS. TWO WEEKS BEFORE, AGAINST IOWA, HE HAD KICKED 10 CONVERSIONS. THIS ONE WAS TO BE HIS BIGGEST. HE COOLLY DROP-KICKED IT THROUGH TO TIE THE GAME.
THERE WAS NOTHING TO HOLD THE JOYOUS FANS AS THEY FLOODED ONTO THE FIELD. A POLICEMAN GOT HIS RIBS BROKEN WHILE TRYING TO HOLD BACK THE BURSTING TIDE.
ROGERS AND THE MICHIGAN CAPTAIN AGREED TO END THE GAME RATHER THAN CLEAR THE HUMANITY OFF THE FIELD. THERE WERE ONLY A FEW MINUTES LEFT AND DARKNESS WAS SETTING IN, ANYWAY.
BEFORE BECOMING THE MINNESOTA CAPTAIN, ROGERS PLAYED SIX YEARS AT CARLISLE. HE WAS CAPTAIN THERE, TOO.
AFTER HIS PLAYING DAYS THE CHIPPEWA LEFT END FROM WALKER, MINNESOTA COACHED ST. THOMAS AND CARLISLE.
HE BECAME A MEMBER OF THE FOOTBALL HALL OF FAME.
AL PĀPAS Jr.

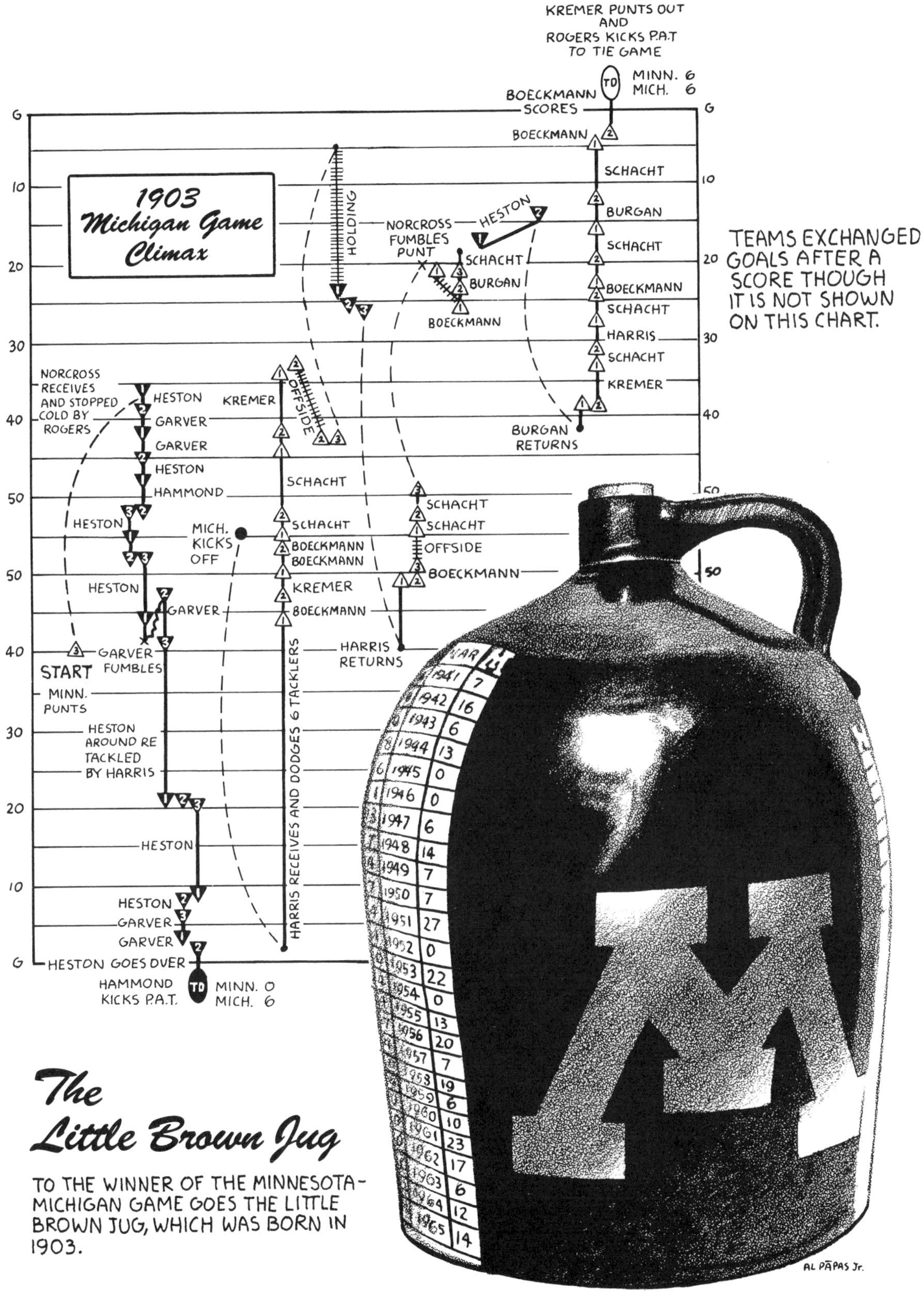

1903 Michigan Game Climax

KREMER PUNTS OUT AND ROGERS KICKS P.A.T TO TIE GAME

BOECKMANN SCORES — MINN. 6 MICH. 6

BOECKMANN
SCHACHT
BURGAN
SCHACHT
BOECKMANN
SCHACHT
HARRIS
SCHACHT
KREMER
BURGAN RETURNS

NORCROSS FUMBLES PUNT
HESTON
SCHACHT
BURGAN
BOECKMANN
HOLDING

KREMER
OFFSIDE
SCHACHT
SCHACHT
BOECKMANN
BOECKMANN
KREMER
BOECKMANN
HARRIS RECEIVES AND DODGES 6 TACKLERS
MICH. KICKS OFF

SCHACHT
SCHACHT
OFFSIDE
BOECKMANN
HARRIS RETURNS

NORCROSS RECEIVES AND STOPPED COLD BY ROGERS
HESTON
GARVER
GARVER
HESTON
HAMMOND
HESTON
HESTON
GARVER
START
GARVER FUMBLES
MINN. PUNTS
HESTON AROUND RE TACKLED BY HARRIS
HESTON
HESTON
GARVER
GARVER
HESTON GOES OVER
HAMMOND KICKS P.A.T. — MINN. 0 MICH. 6

TEAMS EXCHANGED GOALS AFTER A SCORE THOUGH IT IS NOT SHOWN ON THIS CHART.

YEAR	
1941	7
1942	16
1943	6
1944	13
1945	0
1946	0
1947	6
1948	14
1949	7
1950	7
1951	27
1952	0
1953	22
1954	0
1955	13
1956	20
1957	7
1958	19
1959	6
1960	10
1961	23
1962	17
1963	6
1964	12
1965	14

AL PAPAS Jr.

The Little Brown Jug

TO THE WINNER OF THE MINNESOTA-MICHIGAN GAME GOES THE LITTLE BROWN JUG, WHICH WAS BORN IN 1903.

THE GREAT MINNESOTA-MICHIGAN GAME OF 1903 WAS OVER, BUT NOT THE EXCITEMENT. YOU WOULD THINK THE LATE MINNEAPOLIS AMERICAN LEAGUE BASEBALL TEAM OF 1901 HAD RETURNED AND WON A WORLD SERIES OR SOMETHING. CONSIDERING THE OPPOSITION, A TIE WAS AS GOOD AS A WIN THIS DAY. THE GOPHERS WERE BEING PROCLAIMED THE NEW "CHAMPIONS OF THE WEST."

ALTHOUGH STREET CARS WERE LINED UP FOR BLOCKS TO CARRY THE LIVELY THRONG FROM THE GAME, MOST ENDED UP WALKING. IT WAS TWO MILES TO DOWNTOWN AND ITS CELEBRATIONS. COULD SUCH EXCITEMENT EVER HAPPEN AGAIN?

THE FRIENDLY MOB SNAKED DOWN THE STREETS BY ZIG-ZAGGING FROM ONE SIDE TO THE OTHER. RIDES WERE GIVEN IN WHEEL BARROWS WHETHER PEOPLE WANTED TO BE PASSENGERS OR NOT. THEATERS WERE PUNCTUATED BETWEEN ACTS WITH CRIES OF "SKI-U-MAH!" A POLICEMAN CONFISCATED A RICKETY OLD WAGON THAT FANS WERE PULLING ALL OVER DOWNTOWN. AN AUTO DRIVER WAS LASSOED AND ALMOST PULLED FROM HIS VEHICLE BEFORE HE COULD STOP IT.

MOST OF THE ACTION WAS ON NICOLLET, BETWEEN WASHINGTON AND 7TH STREET. ANYTHING TO MAKE NOISE WAS USED. THE STREETS AND SIDEWALKS WERE JAMMED. HALLOWEEN TRICKS WERE PULLED ON MICHIGAN FANS WHO WERE UNWISE ENOUGH TO RIDICULE THE GOPHERS. THERE WERE STILL THOUSANDS IN THE STREETS AT 2 A.M.

A GOOD TIME WAS HAD BY ALL.

IN SPITE OF THE JOY, SOME BAD FEELINGS ALSO CAME OUT. MICHIGAN HAD THOUGHT MINNESOTA PLAYED OVERLY-ROUGH. MINNESOTA ACCUSED THE MICHIGAN COACH OF GIVING SIGNALS TO HIS QUARTERBACK FROM THE SIDELINES. IT TOOK A WEEK FOR BOTH SIDES TO CALM DOWN.

NOT GIVING UP COMPLETELY, MICHIGAN MADE A CHALLENGE TO HAVE A POST-SEASON GAME TO CONCLUSIVELY DECIDE THE CHAMPIONSHIP. MINNESOTA REFUSED BECAUSE THERE WAS NO PRECEDENT FOR SUCH A THING.

We'll cheer for Minnesota,
for the old Maroon and Gold.

We'll cheer for Minnesota
in our coffins when we're cold.

And when we're up in heaven
we'll yell to Ski-u-mah!

But if we go the other way
we'll give 'em Sis-boom-ah!

(ADAPTED FROM 1904 SONG)

IT WAS THE CUSTOM OF TRAVELING TEAMS TO BRING THEIR OWN WATER TO GAMES. THIS IS WHAT MICHIGAN DID IN 1903.

COACH YOST HAD HIS STUDENT MANAGER, TOMMY ROBERTS, GO TO A DOWNTOWN MINNEAPOLIS VARIETY STORE TO PURCHASE A WATER CONTAINER. HE BOUGHT A GRAY FIVE GALLON JUG FOR 35 CENTS.

THE JUG SAT BY THE MICHIGAN BENCH DURING THE GREAT STRUGGLE, BUT WAS LATER FORGOTTEN IN THE TEAM

Oscar Munson

DRESSING ROOM. TWO DAYS AFTER THE GAME, CUSTODIAN OSCAR MUNSON FOUND AND BROUGHT IT TO THE DIRECTOR OF PHYSICAL EDUCATION, DR. LOUIS COOKE.

IN HIS SCANDINAVIAN ACCENT MUNSON SAID, "LOOK DOC, JOST LEFT HIS YUG." COOK REPLIED, "IF YOST WANTS IT, LET HIM COME AND GET IT."

COOKE PAINTED "MICHIGAN JUG, CAPTURED BY OSCAR," ON IT AS SHOWN ABOVE. HE THEN HUNG IT ON A HOOK ABOVE HIS OWN DESK WHERE IT STAYED FOR SIX YEARS.

IN 1909 THE TWO TEAMS MET AGAIN. CAPTAIN JOHN McGOVERN SUGGESTED TO THE MICHIGAN CAPTAIN THAT THE JUG BE A GAME TROPHY. MICHIGAN AGREED AND PROMPTLY WON IT OVER.

IT WASN'T UNTIL 1919, AT ANN ARBOR, THAT MINNESOTA WON IT BACK. AFTER THE VICTORY, THE JUG WAS FOUND CHAINED TO THE FLOOR OF THE SCHOOL GYMNASIUM TROPHY ROOM.

YOST SUGGESTED THE TEAMS PAINT THEIR SCHOOL COLORS ON IT. EVENTUALLY IT ENDED UP AS IT IS TODAY, WITH GAME SCORES AND THE MINNESOTA M ON ONE SIDE, AND THE MICHIGAN M ON THE OTHER.

Dr. Louis Cooke

"MOSE" STRATHERN, FROM HASTINGS, WAS TEAM CAPTAIN AND ALL-AMERICAN CENTER IN 1904. HIS SQUAD WENT 13-0-0 WHILE PILING UP 725 POINTS. THIS STANDS SECOND ONLY TO HARVARD'S ALL-TIME RECORD OF 765 POINTS IN 1886.
Moses Strathern
AL PĀPAS Jr.

Bobby Marshall

ANOTHER HALL OF FAMER WAS SIX FOOT AND LANKY-LIMBED BOBBY MARSHALL. HE PLAYED AT BOTH RIGHT AND LEFT END AND WAS A PLACE KICKER.

IN THE 1903 MICHIGAN GAME HE SERVED AS A RESERVE IN HIS FIRST REAL VARSITY STINT. THE RESERVES WERE HEROIC IN THE CLOSING MOMENTS.

IN 1906 HE KICKED THE WINNING FIELD GOAL OF 40 YARDS AGAINST CHICAGO. IT DETERMINED THE CONFERENCE TITLE.

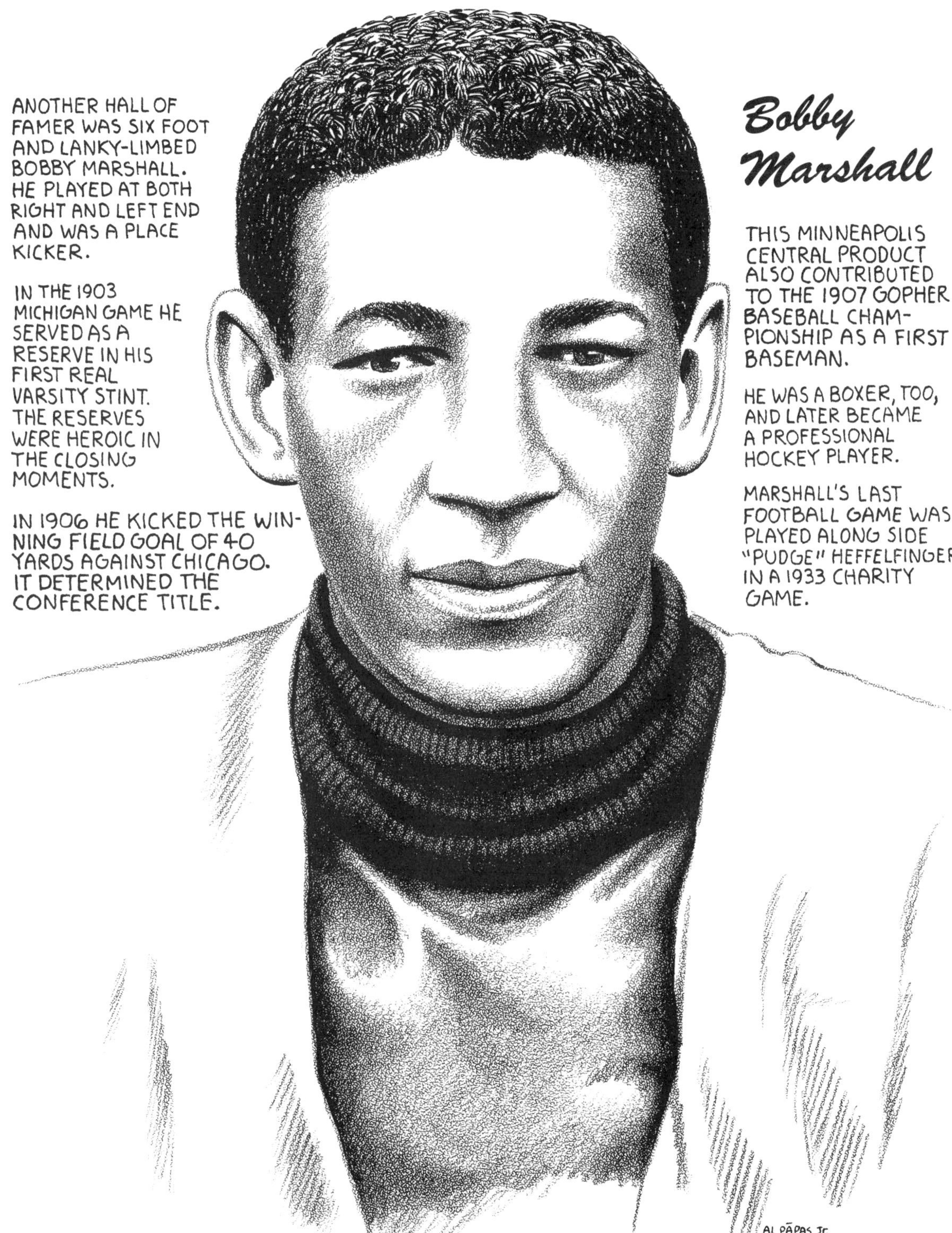

THIS MINNEAPOLIS CENTRAL PRODUCT ALSO CONTRIBUTED TO THE 1907 GOPHER BASEBALL CHAMPIONSHIP AS A FIRST BASEMAN.

HE WAS A BOXER, TOO, AND LATER BECAME A PROFESSIONAL HOCKEY PLAYER.

MARSHALL'S LAST FOOTBALL GAME WAS PLAYED ALONG SIDE "PUDGE" HEFFELFINGER IN A 1933 CHARITY GAME.

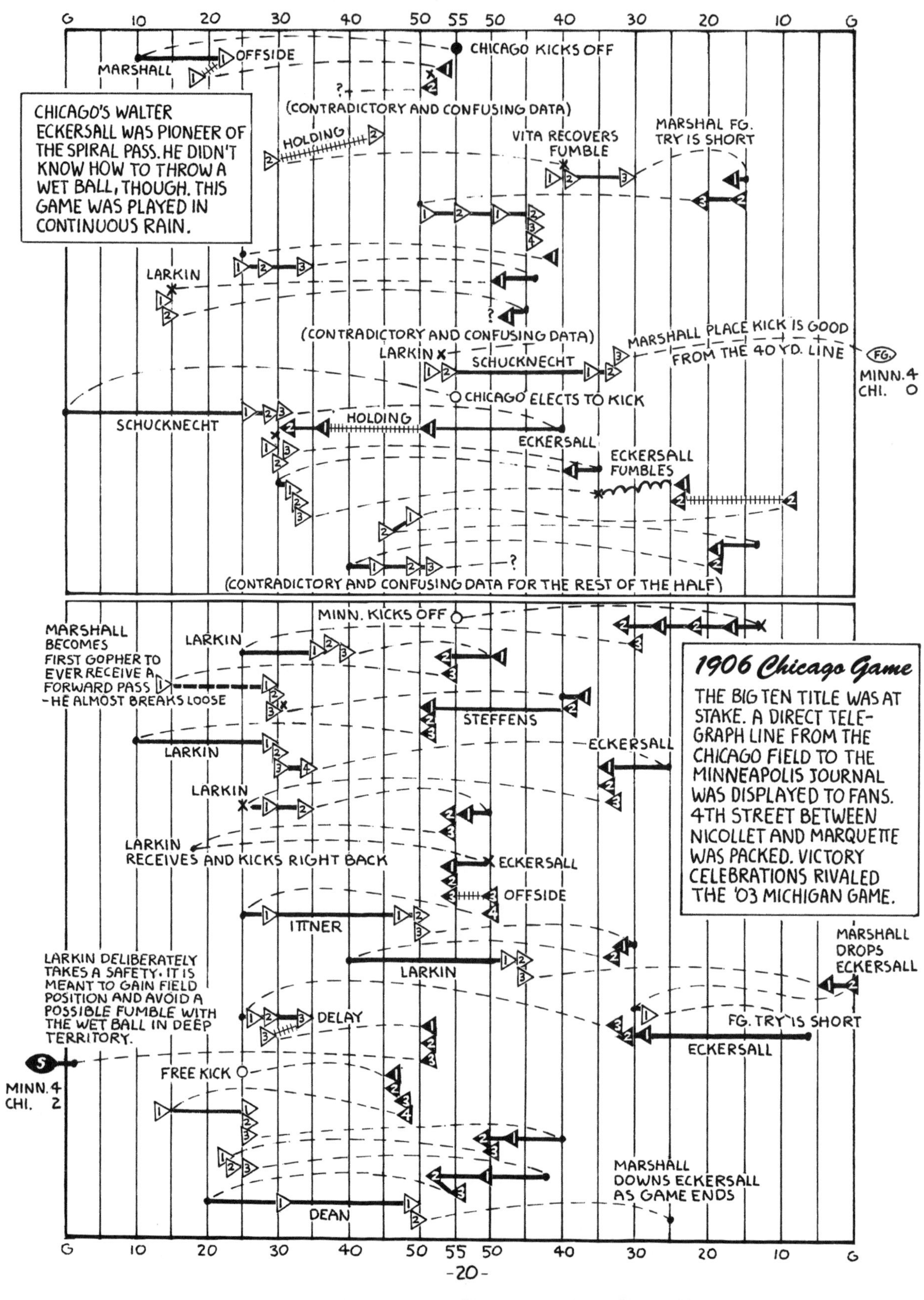

G 10 20 30 40 50 55 50 40 30 20 10 G
CHICAGO KICKS OFF
OFFSIDE
MARSHALL
?
(CONTRADICTORY AND CONFUSING DATA)
CHICAGO'S WALTER ECKERSALL WAS PIONEER OF THE SPIRAL PASS. HE DIDN'T KNOW HOW TO THROW A WET BALL, THOUGH. THIS GAME WAS PLAYED IN CONTINUOUS RAIN.
HOLDING
VITA RECOVERS FUMBLE
MARSHAL FG. TRY IS SHORT
LARKIN
?
(CONTRADICTORY AND CONFUSING DATA)
MARSHALL PLACE KICK IS GOOD FROM THE 40 YD. LINE
FG.
LARKIN
SCHUCKNECHT
MINN. 4
CHI. 0
CHICAGO ELECTS TO KICK
SCHUCKNECHT
HOLDING
ECKERSALL
ECKERSALL FUMBLES
?
(CONTRADICTORY AND CONFUSING DATA FOR THE REST OF THE HALF)
MINN. KICKS OFF
MARSHALL BECOMES FIRST GOPHER TO EVER RECEIVE A FORWARD PASS - HE ALMOST BREAKS LOOSE
LARKIN
1906 Chicago Game
THE BIG TEN TITLE WAS AT STAKE. A DIRECT TELEGRAPH LINE FROM THE CHICAGO FIELD TO THE MINNEAPOLIS JOURNAL WAS DISPLAYED TO FANS. 4TH STREET BETWEEN NICOLLET AND MARQUETTE WAS PACKED. VICTORY CELEBRATIONS RIVALED THE '03 MICHIGAN GAME.
STEFFENS
LARKIN
ECKERSALL
LARKIN
LARKIN RECEIVES AND KICKS RIGHT BACK
ECKERSALL
OFFSIDE
ITTNER
MARSHALL DROPS ECKERSALL
LARKIN
LARKIN DELIBERATELY TAKES A SAFETY. IT IS MEANT TO GAIN FIELD POSITION AND AVOID A POSSIBLE FUMBLE WITH THE WET BALL IN DEEP TERRITORY.
DELAY
FG. TRY IS SHORT
ECKERSALL
S
MINN. 4
CHI. 2
FREE KICK
MARSHALL DOWNS ECKERSALL AS GAME ENDS
DEAN
G 10 20 30 40 50 55 50 40 30 20 10 G

George Capron

"CAPE" WAS QUARTERBACK OF THE GOPHERS IN 1907. HE WAS AN ALL-AROUND ATHLETE FROM SHATTUCK WHO ALSO PLAYED BASKETBALL AND TRACK.

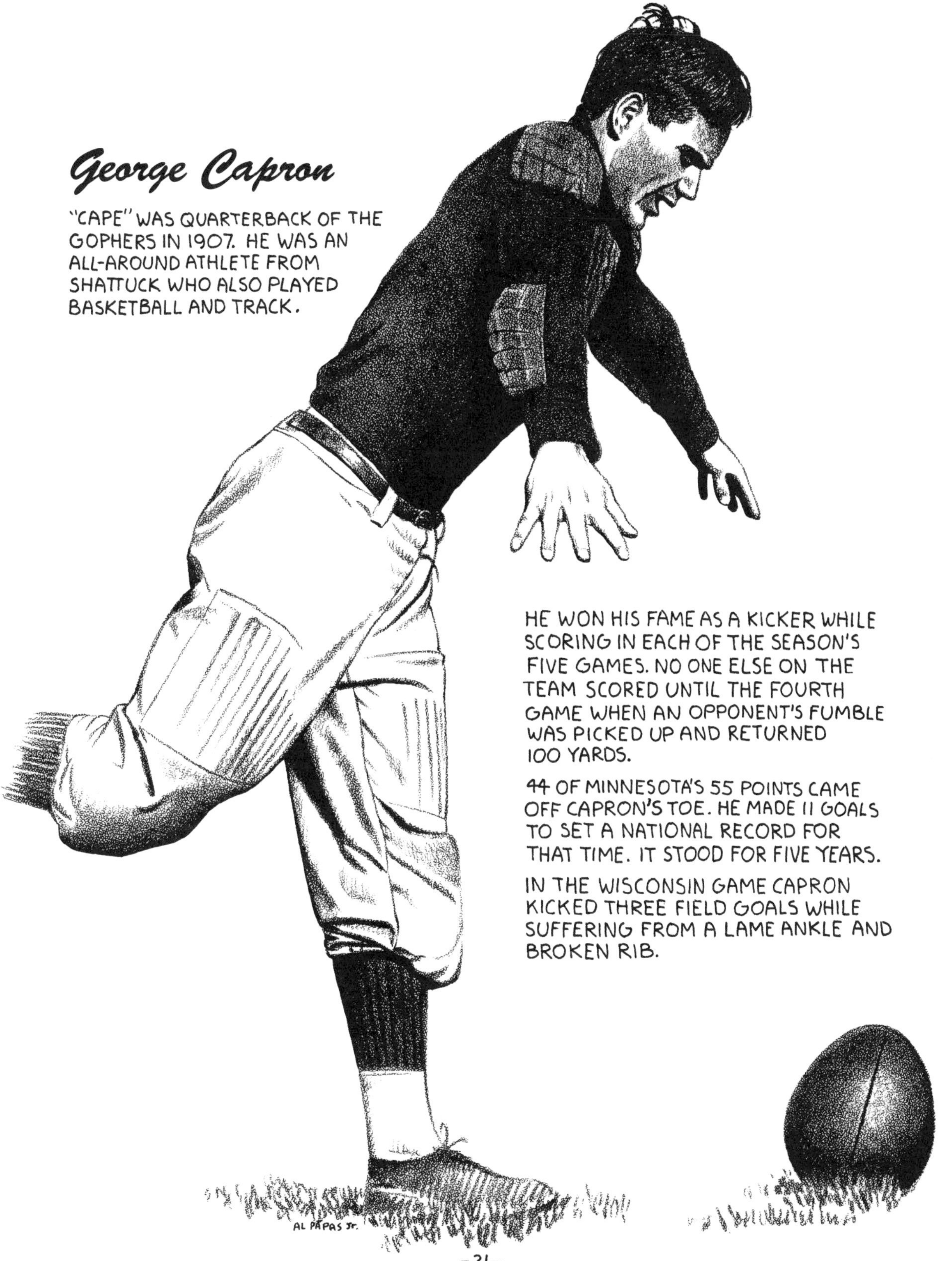

HE WON HIS FAME AS A KICKER WHILE SCORING IN EACH OF THE SEASON'S FIVE GAMES. NO ONE ELSE ON THE TEAM SCORED UNTIL THE FOURTH GAME WHEN AN OPPONENT'S FUMBLE WAS PICKED UP AND RETURNED 100 YARDS.

44 OF MINNESOTA'S 55 POINTS CAME OFF CAPRON'S TOE. HE MADE 11 GOALS TO SET A NATIONAL RECORD FOR THAT TIME. IT STOOD FOR FIVE YEARS.

IN THE WISCONSIN GAME CAPRON KICKED THREE FIELD GOALS WHILE SUFFERING FROM A LAME ANKLE AND BROKEN RIB.

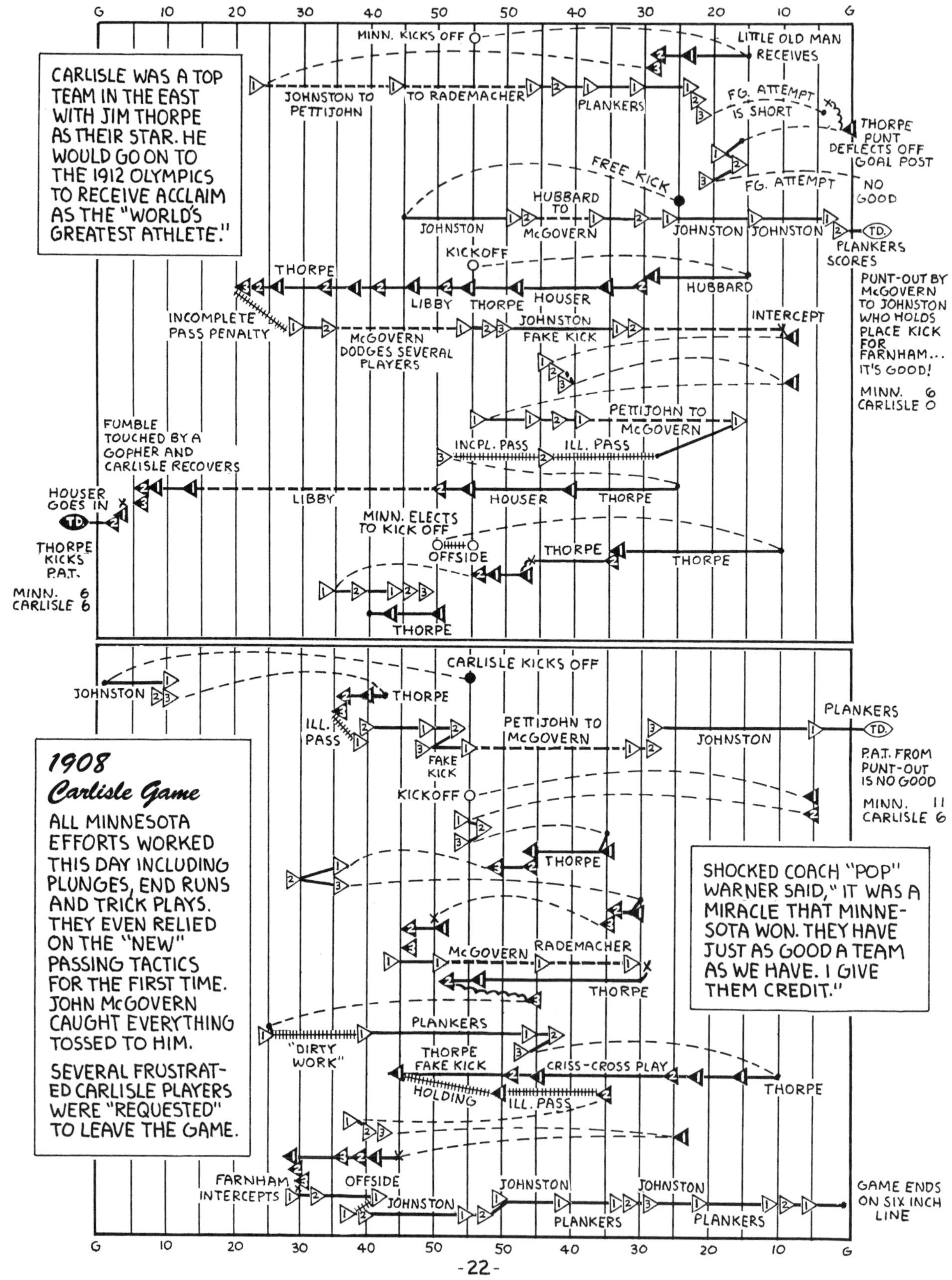

G 10 20 30 40 50 50 40 30 20 10 G
CARLISLE WAS A TOP TEAM IN THE EAST WITH JIM THORPE AS THEIR STAR. HE WOULD GO ON TO THE 1912 OLYMPICS TO RECEIVE ACCLAIM AS THE "WORLD'S GREATEST ATHLETE."
MINN. KICKS OFF
LITTLE OLD MAN RECEIVES
JOHNSTON TO PETTIJOHN
TO RADEMACHER
PLANKERS
FG. ATTEMPT IS SHORT
THORPE PUNT DEFLECTS OFF GOAL POST
FREE KICK
FG. ATTEMPT NO GOOD
HUBBARD TO McGOVERN
JOHNSTON
JOHNSTON
JOHNSTON
PLANKERS SCORES
KICKOFF
THORPE
LIBBY
THORPE
HOUSER
HUBBARD
PUNT-OUT BY McGOVERN TO JOHNSTON WHO HOLDS PLACE KICK FOR FARNHAM... IT'S GOOD!
MINN. 6
CARLISLE 0
INCOMPLETE PASS PENALTY
McGOVERN DODGES SEVERAL PLAYERS
JOHNSTON FAKE KICK
INTERCEPT
PETTIJOHN TO McGOVERN
FUMBLE TOUCHED BY A GOPHER AND CARLISLE RECOVERS
INCPL. PASS
ILL. PASS
HOUSER GOES IN
TD.
LIBBY
HOUSER
THORPE
MINN. ELECTS TO KICK OFF
THORPE KICKS P.A.T.
MINN. 6
CARLISLE 6
OFFSIDE
THORPE
THORPE
THORPE
CARLISLE KICKS OFF
JOHNSTON
THORPE
ILL. PASS
PETTIJOHN TO McGOVERN
FAKE KICK
JOHNSTON
PLANKERS
TD.
P.A.T. FROM PUNT-OUT IS NO GOOD
MINN. 11
CARLISLE 6
KICKOFF
1908 Carlisle Game
ALL MINNESOTA EFFORTS WORKED THIS DAY INCLUDING PLUNGES, END RUNS AND TRICK PLAYS. THEY EVEN RELIED ON THE "NEW" PASSING TACTICS FOR THE FIRST TIME. JOHN McGOVERN CAUGHT EVERYTHING TOSSED TO HIM.
SEVERAL FRUSTRATED CARLISLE PLAYERS WERE "REQUESTED" TO LEAVE THE GAME.
THORPE
SHOCKED COACH "POP" WARNER SAID, "IT WAS A MIRACLE THAT MINNESOTA WON. THEY HAVE JUST AS GOOD A TEAM AS WE HAVE. I GIVE THEM CREDIT."
McGOVERN
RADEMACHER
THORPE
PLANKERS
"DIRTY WORK"
THORPE FAKE KICK
CRISS-CROSS PLAY
THORPE
HOLDING
ILL. PASS
FARNHAM INTERCEPTS
OFFSIDE
JOHNSTON
JOHNSTON
JOHNSTON
PLANKERS
PLANKERS
GAME ENDS ON SIX INCH LINE

John McGovern

NOT ONLY DID JOHN McGOVERN BECOME A CONSENSUS ALL-AMERICAN IN 1909, HE WAS THE FIRST GOPHER TO MAKE WALTER CAMP'S ELEVEN.

AS QUARTERBACK, HAILING FROM ARLINGTON, MINNESOTA, HE WAS AN INSPIRING CAPTAIN WITH GREAT GENERAL-SHIP ABILITIES.

ON OFFENSE HE WAS SLICK IN THE OPEN FIELD. HE WAS SMALL, SQUATTY, PIANO-LEGGED BUT POWERFUL TO THE POINT OF NOT GOING DOWN UNTIL BURIED. TACKLERS MIGHT RIP OFF HIS LOWER JERSEY AS HE WOULD DUCK THROUGH THE LINE. ON ONE 55 YARD TOUCHDOWN RUN HE WAS TACKLED TWICE AND SHOOK LOOSE. WITH LEGALIZATION OF THE PASS HE BECAME THE TEAM'S BEST RECEIVER.

HE WAS ALSO A SUPERB DROP-KICKER IN THE YEAR SUCH A SCORE WAS LOWERED TO THREE POINTS. IT WAS PREVIOUSLY WORTH MORE TO PACIFY SOCCER-STYLE FANS OF THE GAME. Mc GOVERN FIGURED IN MANY VICTORIES BECAUSE OF HIS KICKING.

DEFENSIVELY HE TACKLED WITH DEADLY PRECISION AND WAS KNOWN TO SNATCH AN INTERCEPTION NOW AND THEN.

EXCEPT FOR ONE GAME, HE PLAYED EVERY MINUTE OF EVERY GAME FOR THREE YEARS. HE EVEN PLAYED WITH A BROKEN COLLAR BONE SUFFERED TOWARD THE END OF 1909.

HIS SHOULDER INJURY HAMPERED HIS ABILITY TO REPEAT AS ALL-AMERICAN IN 1910. IT DIDN'T STOP HIM AT ALL FROM ENTERING THE HALL OF FAME.

AL PĀPAS Jr.

James Walker

1910 WAS THE FIRST YEAR THE GAME WAS DIVIDED INTO QUARTERS INSTEAD OF HALVES AND MINNESOTA HAD ITS SECOND WALTER CAMP ALL-AMERICAN. THE MINNEAPOLITAN WAS FAST FOR HIS SIZE AND A TERROR ON DEFENSE, SMEARING THE OPPOSITION BEFORE THEY COULD GET SET UP.

IN THE FIRST GAME FOR WHICH THE LITTLE BROWN JUG WAS FOUGHT, IN 1909, HE SCORED ON A TACKLE ELIGIBLE PLAY. HE SERVED EVERY MINUTE ON THE FIELD OF ALL BUT ONE GAME FOR TWO YEARS.

IN HIS OLD AGE WALKER WAS STILL ANNOYED OVER A RULING NULLIFYING HIS BLOCKED KICK THAT TOUCHED A REFEREE. THE BALL WAS INCORRECTLY GIVEN TO MICHIGAN WHO USED THE ADVANTAGE TO WIN IN 1910.

Lisle Johnston

HE WAS BORN IN CRESCO, MINNESOTA.

MANY EXPERTS MENTIONED THIS GOPHER CAPTAIN AS ALL-AMERICAN FULLBACK IN 1910. HE PLAYED LEFT-HALF IN 1909.

NEBRASKA KEYED THEIR OFFENSE ON HIM TO STOP HIS FAMOUS LONG RUNS. HE WAS FINALLY TAKEN FROM THE GAME WITH A BROKEN LEG SUFFERED AT THE END OF A BRILLIANT DASH.

JOHNSTON PLAYED BASEBALL AND WAS THE WESTERN WRESTLING CHAMP FOR TWO YEARS.

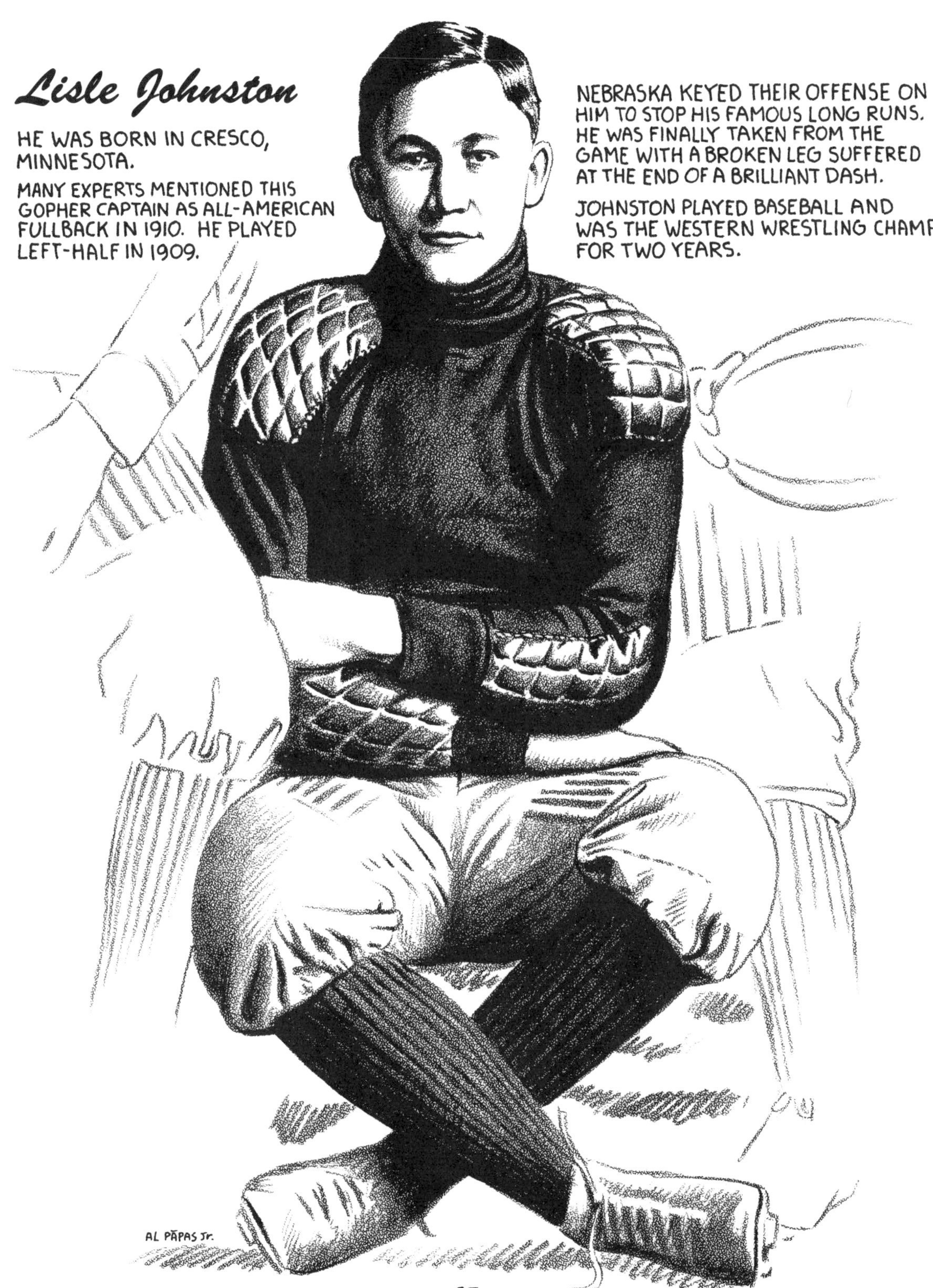

HE WAS ORIGINALLY FROM ST. CLOUD, BUT WENT TO HIGH SCHOOL AT NORTH ST. PAUL. WHILE IN HIGH SCHOOL HE PLAYED NO SPORTS.

Clark Shaughnessy

AT MINNESOTA HE PLAYED TACKLE AND FULLBACK. AS AN ALL-AMERICAN IN 1913 HE EXCELLED AS A KICKER WHILE ALSO BEING A PASS RECEIVER AND RUNNER.

IN THE 1912 IOWA GAME HE GRABBED THREE HAWKEYE FUMBLES. ONE OF THEM RESULTED IN A TOUCHDOWN.

HIS GREATEST ACHIEVEMENTS CAME AS A COACH FOR WHICH HE WAS NAMED TO THE HALL OF FAME.

HE COACHED TULANE, LOYOLA, CHICAGO, STANFORD, MARYLAND, PITTSBURGH AND THE L.A. RAMS.

WHILE AT CHICAGO ONE OF HIS PLAYERS WAS JAY BERWANGER, THE FIRST-EVER HEISMAN TROPHY WINNER.

SHAUGHNESSY STUDIED MILITARY TACTICS FOR FOOTBALL IDEAS. FROM THE GERMAN GENERAL HEINZ GUDERIAN, HE TOOK THE BLITZKRIEG TO INVENT THE MAN-IN-MOTION FOR THE T-FORMATION.

HE PERFECTED THE USE OF BRUSH BLOCKS TO ENHANCE HIS INVENTION'S SPEED AND DECEPTION. A 1700 WORD VOCABULARY WAS DEVISED THAT ONLY HIS PLAYERS COULD UNDERSTAND FOR FAST PLAY CALLING.

THE FIRST YEAR HE UNLEASHED HIS MAN-IN-MOTION HE WON THE NATIONAL TITLE. BETWEEN THE FINAL SEASON GAME AND VICTORY IN THE ROSE BOWL, HE TAUGHT HIS INVENTION TO THE CHICAGO BEARS WHO USED IT TO MOP UP THE WASHINGTON REDSKINS IN THE N.F.L. TITLE GAME.

CLARK SHAUGHNESSY REVOLUTIONIZED FOOTBALL WITH HIS MAN-IN-MOTION TO MAKE IT THE EXPLOSIVE AND EXCITING GAME IT IS TODAY.

THOUGH ORIGINALLY FROM MICHIGAN, HE MOVED TO MINNEAPOLIS WHERE HE WENT TO WEST HIGH.
WALTER ECKERSALL NAMED HIM TO HIS ALL-AMERICAN TEAM AS A GUARD IN 1915. WITH THE HELP OF DUNNIGAN'S EFFORTS THE GOPHERS WON THE BIG TEN TITLE THAT YEAR.
Merton Dunnigan
HE LATER RETURNED TO THE "U" AS AN ASSISTANT FOR COACH CLARENCE SPEARS.
AL PĀPAS JR.

Lorin Solon

HE THREW, RECEIVED AND RAN INTERFERENCE EXCEPTIONALLY WELL. IN 1913 HE RECEIVED ALL-AMERICAN RECOGNITION AT END. THE FOLLOWING YEAR HE BECAME A FULLBACK.

IN 1915, AGAINST IOWA STATE, HE CAUGHT SIX PASSES, RAN BACK KICKOFFS OF 60 AND 35 YARDS AND SCORED FOUR TOUCHDOWNS.

IN THE MIDDLE OF THE 1915 SEASON IT WAS LEARNED HE HAD PLAYED PRO BASEBALL FOR A TEAM IN MONTANA THE PREVIOUS SUMMER. NO OPPONENTS OBJECTED TO HIS CONTINUED PLAY BUT MINNESOTA AUTHORITIES DISQUALIFIED HIM. BERNIE BIERMAN TOOK OVER HIS POSITION AS TEAM CAPTAIN.

Bernie Bierman

SUCH A GREAT COACH WAS BERNIE BIERMAN THAT HIS ATHLETIC ABILITY IS SOMETIMES FORGOTTEN.

AS A CHILD HE GOT A BONE INFECTION IN HIS LEG. TO IMPROVE HIS CONDITION HE TOOK UP SPORTS. IN HIGH SCHOOL HE BECAME A STAR FOR A CHAMPION LITCHFIELD TEAM.

AT MINNESOTA HE PLAYED LEFT HALFBACK WHILE SOMETIMES SUBSTITUTING FOR CLARK SHAUGHNESSY AT FULLBACK. HE PLAYED LEFT END AS WELL.

HIS MOST OUTSTANDING SEASON WAS 1915, WHEN HE MADE ALL-AMERICAN DISTINCTION. HE ALSO WON THE CONFERENCE MEDAL FOR SCHOLASTIC AND ATHLETIC ACHIEVEMENT.

IN A GAME AGAINST WISCONSIN HE MANAGED TO INTERCEPT FOUR PASSES AND SCORE TWO TOUCHDOWNS.

BIERMAN LETTERED IN BASKETBALL AND TRACK, TOO. HE DID THE 100 YARDS IN TEN SECONDS AND THE 220 IN 22.5 SECONDS.

HE DIDN'T INTEND TO GO INTO COACHING AFTER LEAVING SCHOOL. IT WASN'T A PROMISING CAREER TO MAKE A LIVING. HE DID TRY ONE SEASON AT THE BUTTE, MONTANA HIGH SCHOOL, THOUGH. THEY WON THE STATE TITLE.

AFTER SERVING IN WORLD WAR I, HIS FRIEND, CLARK SHAUGHNESSY, ASKED HIM TO BE HIS ASSISTANT AT TULANE. EVENTUALLY BIERMAN TOOK OVER THE HEAD TULANE COACHING JOB HIMSELF.

HIS RECORD FOR THE GREEN WAVE BECAME 36-10-2, WHILE PRODUCING FOUR ALL-AMERICANS.

IN HIS FINAL SEASON, HIS TEAM ENDED UP BEING RATED SECOND IN THE NATION. HIS ONLY LOSS WAS TO NUMBER ONE RATED U.S.C. IN THE 1932 ROSE BOWL. THAT GAME ENDED AN 18 GAME WIN STRING.

MINNESOTA CALLED HIM HOME AND SOON HE WAS GREETED LIKE KING MIDAS, WHO TOUCHED THE CAMPUS TO BRING ON THE "GOLDEN ERA" OF MINNESOTA FOOTBALL.

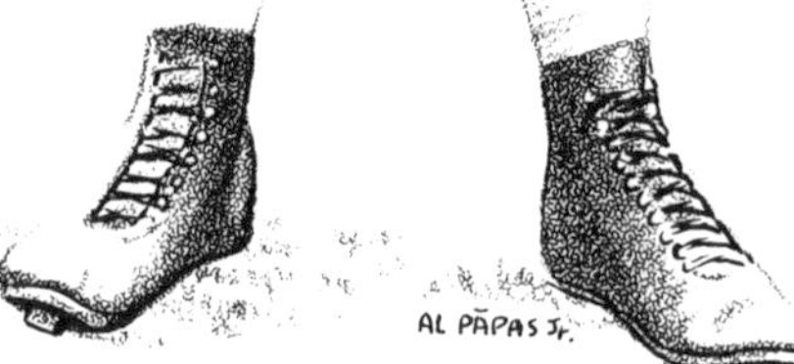

Bert Baston

FROM ST. LOUIS PARK CAME MINNESOTA'S FIRST TWO-TIME WALTER CAMP ALL-AMERICAN. IT WAS BERT BASTON IN 1915-16. THE LATTER YEAR HE WAS CONSENSUS.

HE WAS THE RECEIVER IN THE GAME'S FIRST GREAT PASSING COMBINATION, WITH "PUDGE" WYMAN ON THE TOSSING SIDE.

IT WAS SAID BASTON HAD LEGS LIKE STEEL SPRINGS AND WOULD SNATCH PASSES JUST OVER THE FINGERTIPS OF HIS OPPONENTS. THIS LEFT WING DID IT TWICE IN A FLOCK OF HAWKEYES IN 1916. SOMETIMES HE WOULD JUGGLE THE BALL WITH ONE HAND WHEN TWO WEREN'T CONVENIENT. HE HAD AN INSTINCT FOR GETTING IN THE OPEN WHEN HE TIRED OF CROWDS.

HE COULD CLEAR THE WAY FOR HIS BACKS AND ON DEFENSE WAS HARD TO TAKE OUT OF A PLAY.

ON A WISCONSIN KICKOFF HE ONCE RETURNED 85 YARDS FOR A SCORE WHILE MAKING THE LAST 30 IN RECORD TIME. HE MISTOOK A TEAMMATE'S SHADOW FOR A PURSUER.

HE COULD ALSO BE USED TO KICK CONVERSIONS.

IN 1954 HE WAS INDUCTED INTO THE HALL OF FAME.

OTHER HONORS CAME TO HIM ON OTHER FIELDS. SIX MONTHS AFTER LEAVING THE PLAYING GRIDIRON HE WAS TWICE WOUNDED ON THE BATTLEFIELDS OF WORLD WAR I. HE RECEIVED THE DISTINGUISHED SERVICE CROSS.

AT FRITZ CRISLER'S REQUEST HE RETURNED TO THE "U" IN 1930. HE CONTINUED TO HELP AS AN ASSISTANT UNDER HIS FORMER TEAMMATES BERNIE BIERMAN AND GEORGE HAUSER. FOR 20 YEARS HE SHAPED SOME OF MINNESOTA'S FINEST WINGS.

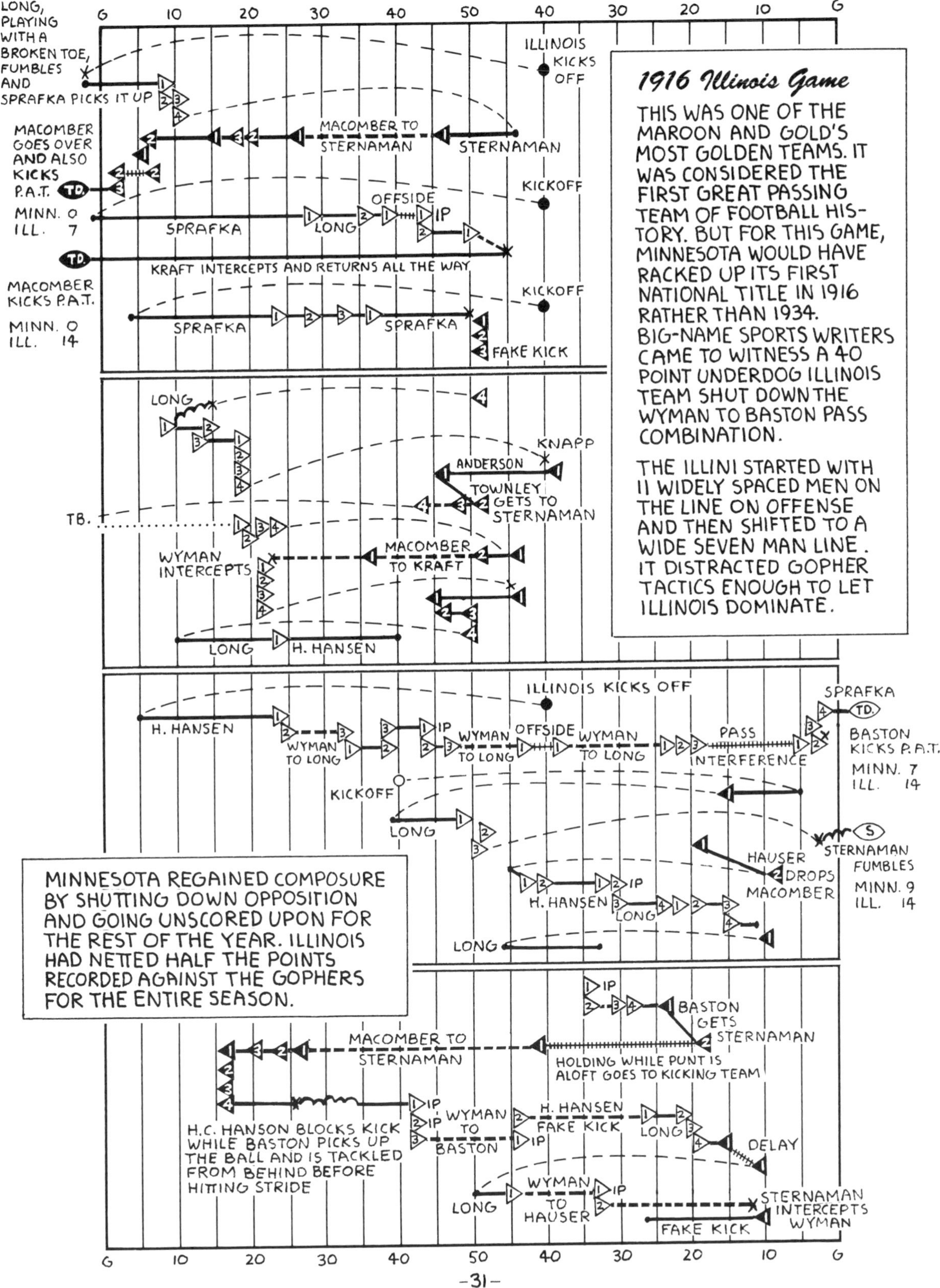
1916 Illinois Game
THIS WAS ONE OF THE MAROON AND GOLD'S MOST GOLDEN TEAMS. IT WAS CONSIDERED THE FIRST GREAT PASSING TEAM OF FOOTBALL HISTORY. BUT FOR THIS GAME, MINNESOTA WOULD HAVE RACKED UP ITS FIRST NATIONAL TITLE IN 1916 RATHER THAN 1934. BIG-NAME SPORTS WRITERS CAME TO WITNESS A 40 POINT UNDERDOG ILLINOIS TEAM SHUT DOWN THE WYMAN TO BASTON PASS COMBINATION.
THE ILLINI STARTED WITH 11 WIDELY SPACED MEN ON THE LINE ON OFFENSE AND THEN SHIFTED TO A WIDE SEVEN MAN LINE. IT DISTRACTED GOPHER TACTICS ENOUGH TO LET ILLINOIS DOMINATE.
MINNESOTA REGAINED COMPOSURE BY SHUTTING DOWN OPPOSITION AND GOING UNSCORED UPON FOR THE REST OF THE YEAR. ILLINOIS HAD NETTED HALF THE POINTS RECORDED AGAINST THE GOPHERS FOR THE ENTIRE SEASON.
G 10 20 30 40 50 40 30 20 10 G
LONG, PLAYING WITH A BROKEN TOE, FUMBLES AND SPRAFKA PICKS IT UP
ILLINOIS KICKS OFF
MACOMBER GOES OVER AND ALSO KICKS P.A.T.
MACOMBER TO STERNAMAN
STERNAMAN
TD
MINN. 0 ILL. 7
KICKOFF
SPRAFKA
OFFSIDE
LONG
IP
KRAFT INTERCEPTS AND RETURNS ALL THE WAY
MACOMBER KICKS P.A.T.
MINN. 0 ILL. 14
SPRAFKA
FAKE KICK
LONG
KNAPP
ANDERSON
TOWNLEY GETS TO STERNAMAN
TB.
WYMAN INTERCEPTS
MACOMBER TO KRAFT
LONG
H. HANSEN
ILLINOIS KICKS OFF
SPRAFKA
TD
H. HANSEN
WYMAN TO LONG
IP
WYMAN TO LONG
OFFSIDE
WYMAN TO LONG
PASS INTERFERENCE
BASTON KICKS P.A.T.
MINN. 7 ILL. 14
KICKOFF
LONG
S
STERNAMAN FUMBLES
HAUSER DROPS MACOMBER
H. HANSEN
IP
LONG
MINN. 9 ILL. 14
LONG
IP
BASTON GETS STERNAMAN
MACOMBER TO STERNAMAN
HOLDING WHILE PUNT IS ALOFT GOES TO KICKING TEAM
H.C. HANSON BLOCKS KICK WHILE BASTON PICKS UP THE BALL AND IS TACKLED FROM BEHIND BEFORE HITTING STRIDE
IP
IP
WYMAN TO BASTON
H. HANSEN
FAKE KICK
IP
LONG
DELAY
LONG
WYMAN TO HAUSER
IP
STERNAMAN INTERCEPTS WYMAN
FAKE KICK
G 10 20 30 40 50 40 30 20 10 G

WISCONSIN SEEMED TO BE HIS FAVORITE VICTIM. IN 1915 HE WAS THE GOPHERS ONLY CONSISTENT GROUND GAINER AGAINST THEM. THE FOLLOWING YEAR HE RETURNED A WISCONSIN PUNT 45 YARDS FOR A TOUCHDOWN AND FREQUENTLY MADE 15-20 YARD GAINS.
Claire "Shorty" Long
"SHORTY" LONG WAS AN OPEN FIELD RUNNER WHO CAME FROM MINNEAPOLIS. HE WAS AN ALL-AMERICAN QUARTERBACK ON THE GREAT 1916 TEAM.
AL PĀPAS Jr.

HAUSER CAME FROM CEDAR FALLS, IOWA TO BECOME A GOPHER ALL-AMERICAN IN 1917.

HE PLAYED RIGHT TACKLE AND WAS KNOWN TO BREAK UP MORE PLAYS IN THE TRENCHES THAN ANYONE ELSE. IN HIS SPARE MOMENTS HE MADE SACKS ON END RUNS, TOO.

HIS 1917 LINE ALLOWED ONLY ONE FIRST DOWN BY THE RUN ALL SEASON.

George Hauser

LINE COACHING TOOK HIM TO MINNESOTA, IOWA STATE, OHIO STATE AND BACK TO MINNESOTA. HE WAS CONSIDERED ONE OF THE BEST IN THE NATION. HE ALSO PUT IN A COUPLE OF YEARS AS HEAD COACH AT COLGATE, IN THE 1920'S, AND A FEW MORE AT MINNESOTA DURING WORLD WAR II.

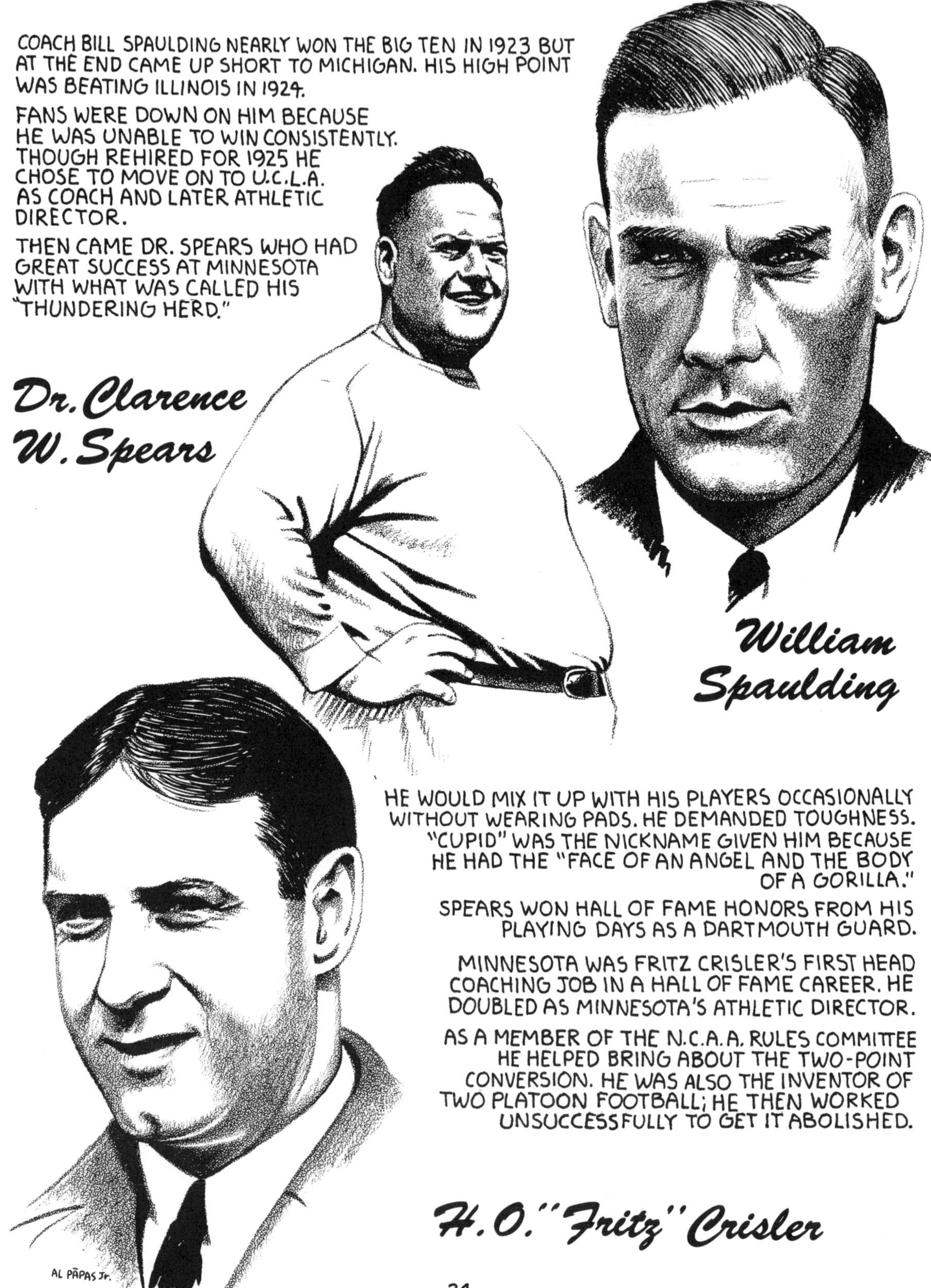
COACH BILL SPAULDING NEARLY WON THE BIG TEN IN 1923 BUT AT THE END CAME UP SHORT TO MICHIGAN. HIS HIGH POINT WAS BEATING ILLINOIS IN 1924.
FANS WERE DOWN ON HIM BECAUSE HE WAS UNABLE TO WIN CONSISTENTLY. THOUGH REHIRED FOR 1925 HE CHOSE TO MOVE ON TO U.C.L.A. AS COACH AND LATER ATHLETIC DIRECTOR.
THEN CAME DR. SPEARS WHO HAD GREAT SUCCESS AT MINNESOTA WITH WHAT WAS CALLED HIS "THUNDERING HERD."
Dr. Clarence W. Spears
William Spaulding
HE WOULD MIX IT UP WITH HIS PLAYERS OCCASIONALLY WITHOUT WEARING PADS. HE DEMANDED TOUGHNESS. "CUPID" WAS THE NICKNAME GIVEN HIM BECAUSE HE HAD THE "FACE OF AN ANGEL AND THE BODY OF A GORILLA."
SPEARS WON HALL OF FAME HONORS FROM HIS PLAYING DAYS AS A DARTMOUTH GUARD.
MINNESOTA WAS FRITZ CRISLER'S FIRST HEAD COACHING JOB IN A HALL OF FAME CAREER. HE DOUBLED AS MINNESOTA'S ATHLETIC DIRECTOR.
AS A MEMBER OF THE N.C.A.A. RULES COMMITTEE HE HELPED BRING ABOUT THE TWO-POINT CONVERSION. HE WAS ALSO THE INVENTOR OF TWO PLATOON FOOTBALL; HE THEN WORKED UNSUCCESSFULLY TO GET IT ABOLISHED.
H.O. "Fritz" Crisler
AL PĀPAS Jr.

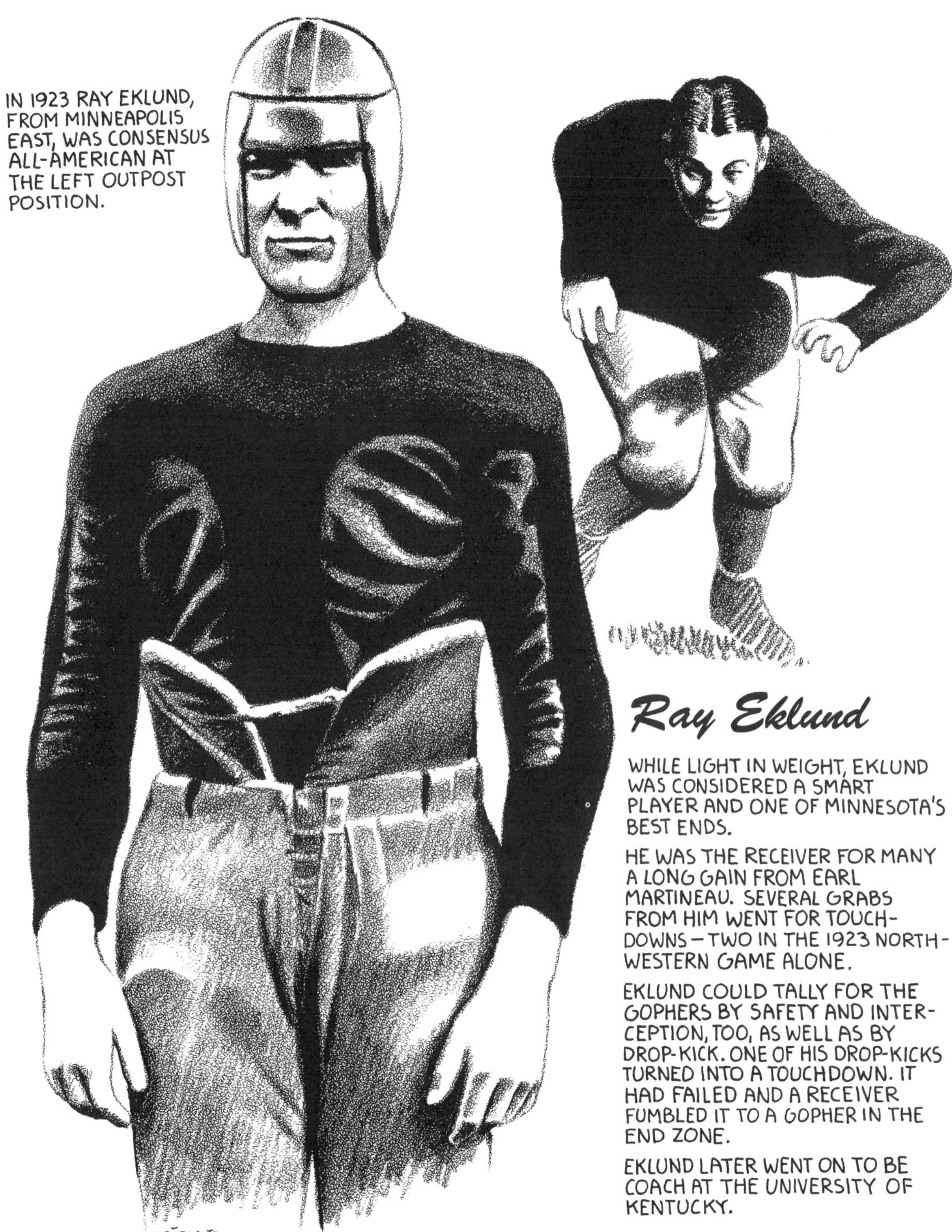

IN 1923 RAY EKLUND, FROM MINNEAPOLIS EAST, WAS CONSENSUS ALL-AMERICAN AT THE LEFT OUTPOST POSITION.

Ray Eklund

WHILE LIGHT IN WEIGHT, EKLUND WAS CONSIDERED A SMART PLAYER AND ONE OF MINNESOTA'S BEST ENDS.

HE WAS THE RECEIVER FOR MANY A LONG GAIN FROM EARL MARTINEAU. SEVERAL GRABS FROM HIM WENT FOR TOUCHDOWNS—TWO IN THE 1923 NORTHWESTERN GAME ALONE.

EKLUND COULD TALLY FOR THE GOPHERS BY SAFETY AND INTERCEPTION, TOO, AS WELL AS BY DROP-KICK. ONE OF HIS DROP-KICKS TURNED INTO A TOUCHDOWN. IT HAD FAILED AND A RECEIVER FUMBLED IT TO A GOPHER IN THE END ZONE.

EKLUND LATER WENT ON TO BE COACH AT THE UNIVERSITY OF KENTUCKY.

Earl Martineau

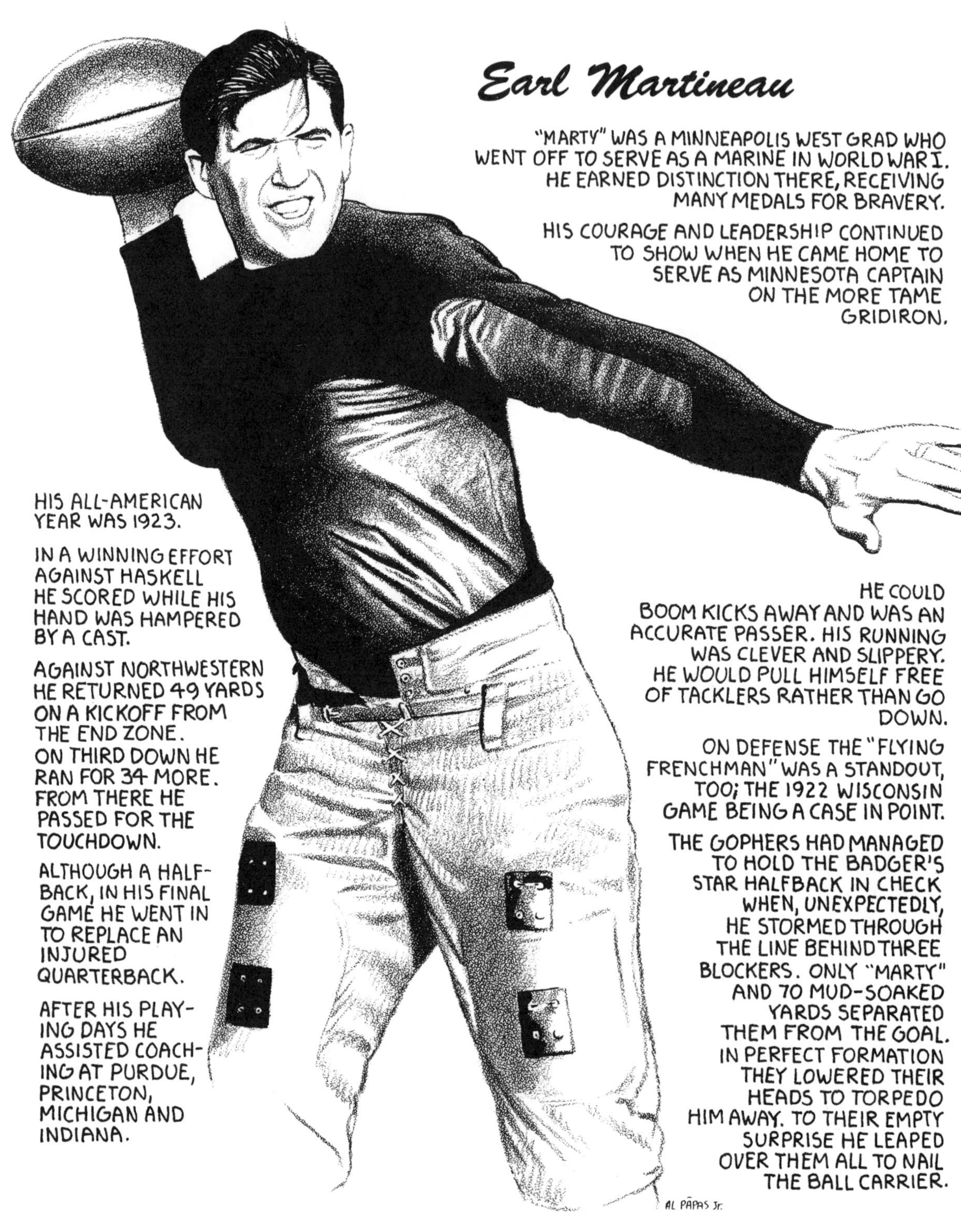

"MARTY" WAS A MINNEAPOLIS WEST GRAD WHO WENT OFF TO SERVE AS A MARINE IN WORLD WAR I. HE EARNED DISTINCTION THERE, RECEIVING MANY MEDALS FOR BRAVERY.

HIS COURAGE AND LEADERSHIP CONTINUED TO SHOW WHEN HE CAME HOME TO SERVE AS MINNESOTA CAPTAIN ON THE MORE TAME GRIDIRON.

HIS ALL-AMERICAN YEAR WAS 1923.

IN A WINNING EFFORT AGAINST HASKELL HE SCORED WHILE HIS HAND WAS HAMPERED BY A CAST.

AGAINST NORTHWESTERN HE RETURNED 49 YARDS ON A KICKOFF FROM THE END ZONE. ON THIRD DOWN HE RAN FOR 34 MORE. FROM THERE HE PASSED FOR THE TOUCHDOWN.

ALTHOUGH A HALFBACK, IN HIS FINAL GAME HE WENT IN TO REPLACE AN INJURED QUARTERBACK.

AFTER HIS PLAYING DAYS HE ASSISTED COACHING AT PURDUE, PRINCETON, MICHIGAN AND INDIANA.

HE COULD BOOM KICKS AWAY AND WAS AN ACCURATE PASSER. HIS RUNNING WAS CLEVER AND SLIPPERY. HE WOULD PULL HIMSELF FREE OF TACKLERS RATHER THAN GO DOWN.

ON DEFENSE THE "FLYING FRENCHMAN" WAS A STANDOUT, TOO; THE 1922 WISCONSIN GAME BEING A CASE IN POINT.

THE GOPHERS HAD MANAGED TO HOLD THE BADGER'S STAR HALFBACK IN CHECK WHEN, UNEXPECTEDLY, HE STORMED THROUGH THE LINE BEHIND THREE BLOCKERS. ONLY "MARTY" AND 70 MUD-SOAKED YARDS SEPARATED THEM FROM THE GOAL. IN PERFECT FORMATION THEY LOWERED THEIR HEADS TO TORPEDO HIM AWAY. TO THEIR EMPTY SURPRISE HE LEAPED OVER THEM ALL TO NAIL THE BALL CARRIER.

AL PĀPAS Jr.

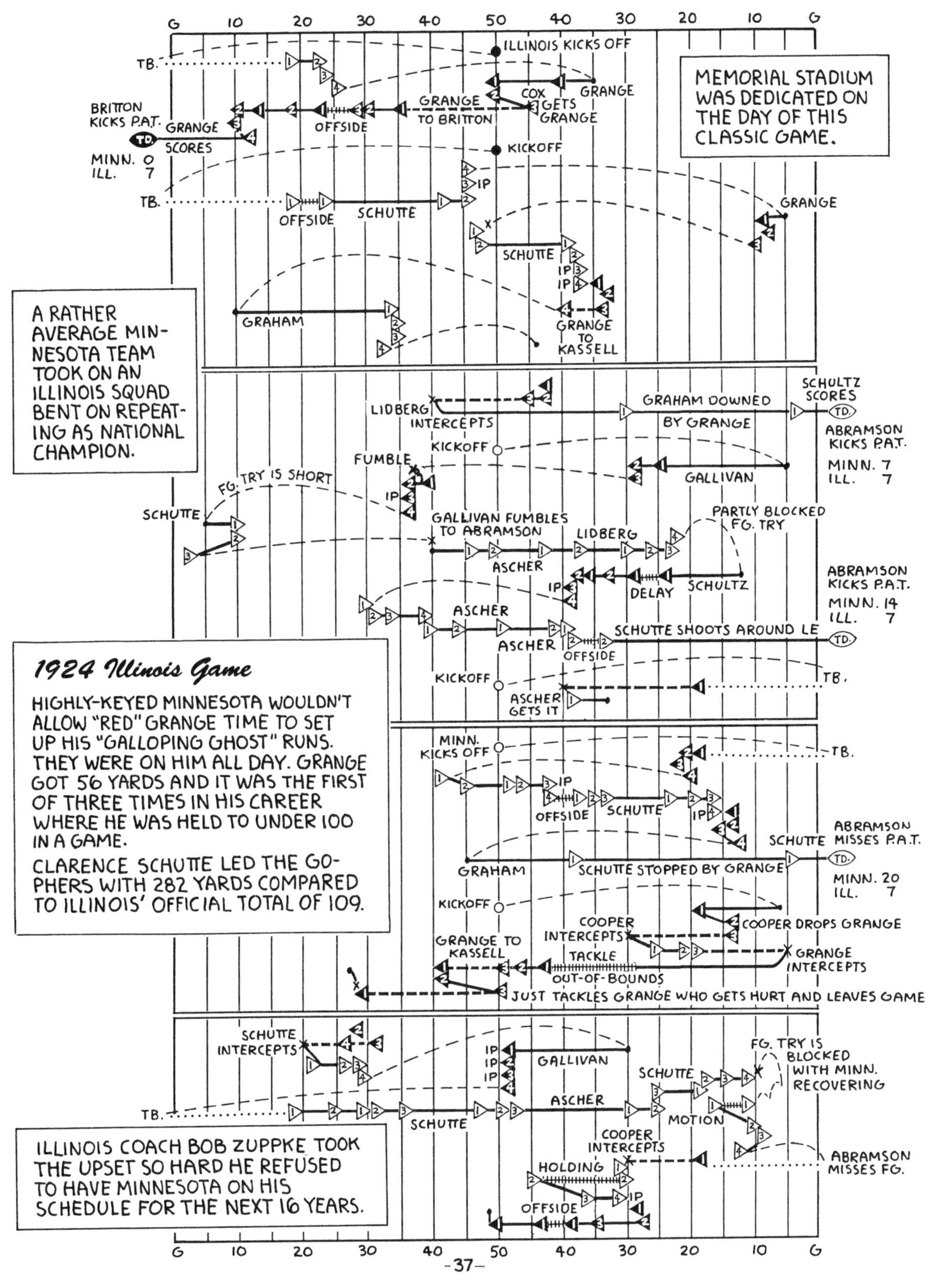

G 10 20 30 40 50 40 30 20 10 G
MEMORIAL STADIUM WAS DEDICATED ON THE DAY OF THIS CLASSIC GAME.
A RATHER AVERAGE MINNESOTA TEAM TOOK ON AN ILLINOIS SQUAD BENT ON REPEATING AS NATIONAL CHAMPION.
1924 Illinois Game
HIGHLY-KEYED MINNESOTA WOULDN'T ALLOW "RED" GRANGE TIME TO SET UP HIS "GALLOPING GHOST" RUNS. THEY WERE ON HIM ALL DAY. GRANGE GOT 56 YARDS AND IT WAS THE FIRST OF THREE TIMES IN HIS CAREER WHERE HE WAS HELD TO UNDER 100 IN A GAME.
CLARENCE SCHUTTE LED THE GOPHERS WITH 282 YARDS COMPARED TO ILLINOIS' OFFICIAL TOTAL OF 109.
ILLINOIS COACH BOB ZUPPKE TOOK THE UPSET SO HARD HE REFUSED TO HAVE MINNESOTA ON HIS SCHEDULE FOR THE NEXT 16 YEARS.
ILLINOIS KICKS OFF
TB.
GRANGE
COX GETS GRANGE
GRANGE TO BRITTON
OFFSIDE
BRITTON KICKS P.A.T.
GRANGE SCORES
TD.
MINN. 0
ILL. 7
KICKOFF
IP
OFFSIDE
SCHUTTE
SCHUTTE
GRAHAM
GRANGE TO KASSELL
LIDBERG INTERCEPTS
GRAHAM DOWNED BY GRANGE
SCHULTZ SCORES
ABRAMSON KICKS P.A.T.
MINN. 7
ILL. 7
FUMBLE
GALLIVAN
FG. TRY IS SHORT
GALLIVAN FUMBLES TO ABRAMSON
LIDBERG
PARTLY BLOCKED FG. TRY
ASCHER
DELAY
SCHULTZ
ABRAMSON KICKS P.A.T.
MINN. 14
ILL. 7
ASCHER
SCHUTTE SHOOTS AROUND LE
OFFSIDE
ASCHER GETS IT
MINN. KICKS OFF
SCHUTTE
ABRAMSON MISSES P.A.T.
SCHUTTE STOPPED BY GRANGE
MINN. 20
ILL. 7
COOPER INTERCEPTS
COOPER DROPS GRANGE
GRANGE TO KASSELL
TACKLE OUT-OF-BOUNDS
GRANGE INTERCEPTS
JUST TACKLES GRANGE WHO GETS HURT AND LEAVES GAME
SCHUTTE INTERCEPTS
FG. TRY IS BLOCKED WITH MINN. RECOVERING
MOTION
COOPER INTERCEPTS
HOLDING
ABRAMSON MISSES FG.

Harold Hanson

AFTER ARRIVING FROM STEWART, MINNESOTA, HANSON ASKED COACH SPEARS IF HE WAS "ALLOWED" TO GO OUT FOR FOOTBALL. HE HAD NEVER PLAYED THE GAME BEFORE.

WITH HIS 185 POUNDS AND SIX FOOT STATURE HE STARTED AS A BACK AND THEN MOVED TO THE LINE AS A LEFT GUARD. HE EARNED HIS ALL-AMERICAN HONORS THERE IN 1927.

AFTER WATCHING HIM IN ACTION KNUTE ROCKNE PRAISED HIM AS THE "BEST GUARD" HE HAD "EVER SEEN."

Herb Joesting

ON THE SAME DAY AFTER LEAVING THE HOSPITAL THE "OWATONNA THUNDERBOLT" STRUCK FOR 103 YARDS AGAINST IOWA.

HE ATTAINED CONSENSUS ALL-AMERICAN STATURE IN BOTH 1926 AND 27.

HE WAS LEAN AND SUPPLE, BUT HOW HE COULD POUND THAT LINE. THE HALL OF FAME FULLBACK WAS ONE OF THE GREATEST LINE PULVERIZERS OF HIS ERA. THROUGH STRAIGHT-AHEAD BRUTE STRENGTH HE TIED A BIG TEN SEASON RECORD OF 13 TOUCHDOWNS AND WAS ONLY A FEW YARDS SHORT OF THE BIG TEN RECORD FOR TOTAL YARDS GAINED.

HE SERVED HIS PROFESSIONAL DAYS WITH THE MINNEAPOLIS RED JACKETS, PHILADELPHIA YELLOW JACKETS AND THE CHICAGO BEARS.

PASSING WAS ANOTHER FINE QUALITY OF HIS. HE THREW WHAT MAY HAVE BEEN HISTORYS FIRST JUMP PASS IN THE 1927 NOTRE DAME GAME TO PRODUCE A BIG TOUCHDOWN.

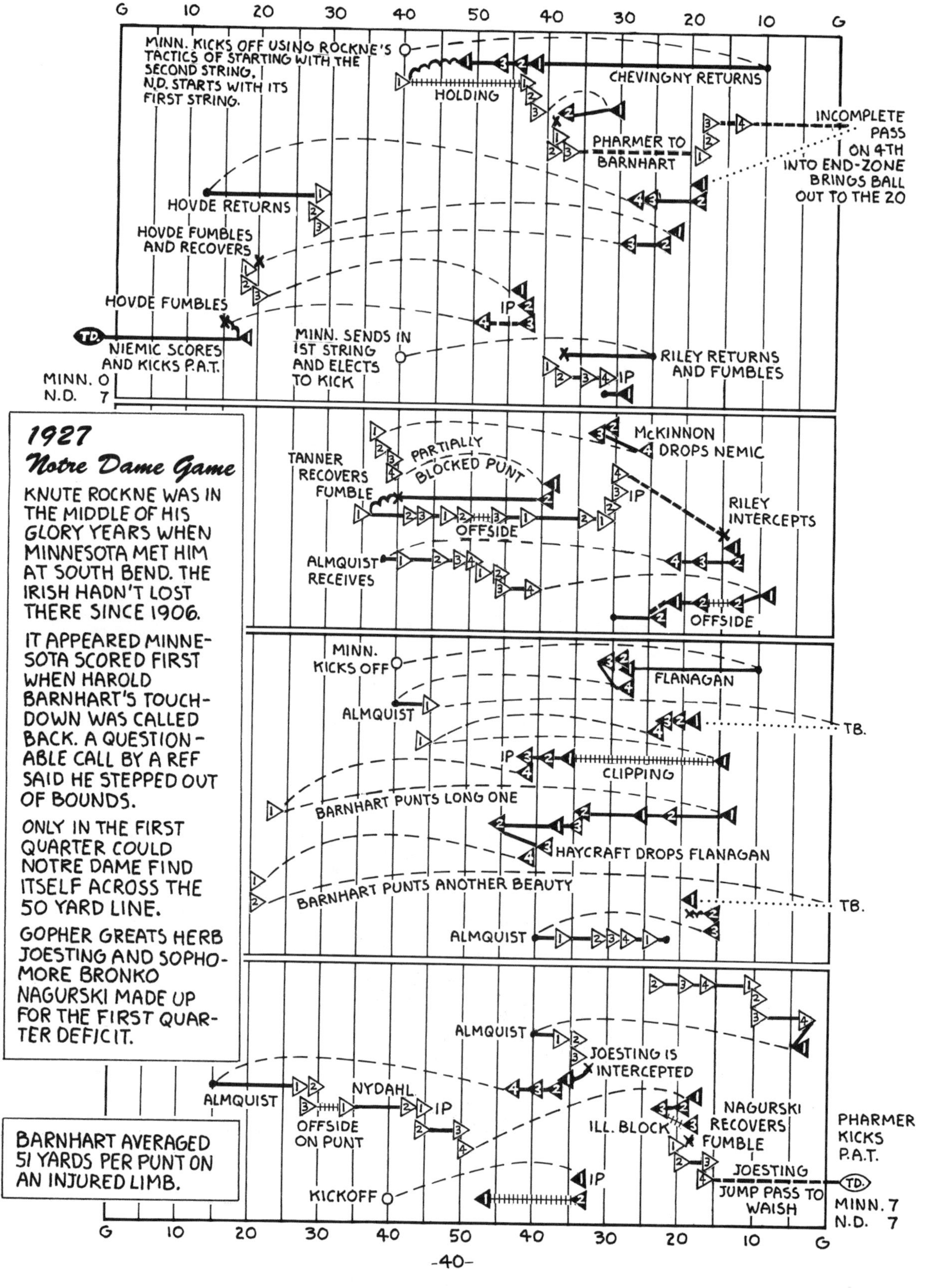
MINN. KICKS OFF USING ROCKNE'S TACTICS OF STARTING WITH THE SECOND STRING.
N.D. STARTS WITH ITS FIRST STRING.
HOLDING
CHEVINGNY RETURNS
INCOMPLETE PASS ON 4TH INTO END-ZONE BRINGS BALL OUT TO THE 20
PHARMER TO BARNHART
HOVDE RETURNS
HOVDE FUMBLES AND RECOVERS
HOVDE FUMBLES
IP
NIEMIC SCORES AND KICKS P.A.T.
MINN. SENDS IN 1ST STRING AND ELECTS TO KICK
RILEY RETURNS AND FUMBLES
IP
MINN. 0
N.D. 7
1927
Notre Dame Game
KNUTE ROCKNE WAS IN THE MIDDLE OF HIS GLORY YEARS WHEN MINNESOTA MET HIM AT SOUTH BEND. THE IRISH HADN'T LOST THERE SINCE 1906.
IT APPEARED MINNESOTA SCORED FIRST WHEN HAROLD BARNHART'S TOUCHDOWN WAS CALLED BACK. A QUESTIONABLE CALL BY A REF SAID HE STEPPED OUT OF BOUNDS.
ONLY IN THE FIRST QUARTER COULD NOTRE DAME FIND ITSELF ACROSS THE 50 YARD LINE.
GOPHER GREATS HERB JOESTING AND SOPHOMORE BRONKO NAGURSKI MADE UP FOR THE FIRST QUARTER DEFICIT.
McKINNON DROPS NEMIC
TANNER RECOVERS FUMBLE
PARTIALLY BLOCKED PUNT
IP
OFFSIDE
RILEY INTERCEPTS
ALMQUIST RECEIVES
OFFSIDE
MINN. KICKS OFF
FLANAGAN
ALMQUIST
TB.
IP
CLIPPING
BARNHART PUNTS LONG ONE
HAYCRAFT DROPS FLANAGAN
BARNHART PUNTS ANOTHER BEAUTY
TB.
ALMQUIST
ALMQUIST
JOESTING IS INTERCEPTED
ALMQUIST
NYDAHL
IP
OFFSIDE ON PUNT
ILL. BLOCK
NAGURSKI RECOVERS FUMBLE
PHARMER KICKS P.A.T.
JOESTING JUMP PASS TO WAISH
TD.
MINN. 7
N.D. 7
KICKOFF
IP
BARNHART AVERAGED 51 YARDS PER PUNT ON AN INJURED LIMB.

George Gibson

THIS 1928 ALL-AMERICAN GUARD CAME NORTH FROM OKLAHOMA BECAUSE HE LIKED THE BIG TEN. HE PICKED MINNESOTA BECAUSE HIS FATHER, WHO WORKED FOR THE RAILROAD, COULD GET HIM FREE TICKETS HOME.

WHILE NOT CONSIDERED A FLASHY PLAYER HE WAS A LEADER WHO SHOWED HOW TO DO THE JOB. HE WAS A STOPPER ON DEFENSE AND ON OFFENSE COULD ALWAYS BE RELIED ON FOR OPENING GAPS.

GIBSON WAS A STRONG 195 POUNDS AND KNOWN TO OUT-WRESTLE HIS FRATERNITY ROOMMATE, BRONKO NAGURSKI.

HE SERVED AS GOPHER LINE COACH IN 1929 AND LATER AS HEAD COACH AT CARLETON. BETWEEN THESE JOBS HE PLAYED AND COACHED WITH THE MINNEAPOLIS RED JACKETS WHO WERE THE LOCAL ENTRY IN THE N.F.L.

AL PĀPAS Jr.

Fred Hovde

HOVDE PLAYED FOR THE GOPHERS IN 1927-28 AND WON FAME FOR HIS GREAT GENERALSHIP AT QUARTERBACK.

IN 1967 HE WON THE NATIONAL FOOTBALL FOUNDATION HALL OF FAME GOLD MEDAL AWARD. THIS AWARD'S PURPOSE WAS TO HONOR HIM FOR HIS COLLEGE FOOTBALL PLAY AND SUBSEQUENT LEADERSHIP IN AMERICAN BUSINESS AND EDUCATION. OTHER CONSIDERATIONS WERE HONESTY, INTEGRITY AND SERVICE TO THE WELFARE OF HIS COUNTRY AND CITIZENS THROUGHOUT A LIFETIME. HE WAS PRESIDENT OF PURDUE AS WELL AS DIRECTOR AND TRUSTEE OF SEVERAL COMPANIES SIMULTANEOUSLY.

THE GOLD MEDAL IS CONSIDERED THE HIGHEST AWARD TO BE GIVEN BY THE HALL OF FAME. HOVDE WAS THE ELEVENTH PERSON TO HAVE RECEIVED IT. HE JOINED THE RANKS OF SUCH NOTABLES AS PRESIDENTS HERBERT HOOVER, DWIGHT EISENHOWER AND JOHN KENNEDY AS WELL AS GENERAL DOUGLAS MACARTHUR, SUPREME COURT JUSTICE BYRON WHITE AND FOOTBALL LEGEND AMOS ALONZO STAGG.

AS AN OUTSTANDING STUDENT OFF THE FIELD HE WON A RHODES SCHOLARSHIP AT OXFORD. WHILE THERE HE BECAME A RUGBY PLAYER.

WHILE BEING RELATIVELY SMALL IN SIZE, THIS MINNEAPOLIS EAST PRODUCT WAS AN ALL-AMERICAN AT END IN 1928. HE SPECIALIZED IN SNATCHING LONG PASSES ON OR NEAR THE GOAL LINE. HE TEAMED UP IN THIS WAY WITH HERB JOESTING FOR MANY A TOUCH-DOWN. AFTER MINNESOTA HE PLAYED A LITTLE FOR THE PROS.

Bronko Nagurski

THE NAME BRONKO NAGURSKI IS SYNONYMOUS WITH FOOTBALL. WHEN ALL-TIME TEAMS ARE CHOSEN HIS NAME LEADS THE LISTS. COACH SPEARS SAID "HE CAN PLAY ANY ONE OF ELEVEN POSITIONS... AND BE BETTER THAN ANYONE ELSE" AT IT.

HE STARTED AS AN END BUT WIPED OUT SO MANY INTERFERERS HE WAS MOVED TO TACKLE. HE PLAYED TACKLE ONLY 120 MINUTES IN 1929 AND STILL MADE CONSENSUS ALL-AMERICAN AT THAT POSITION. HIS USUAL JOB WAS FULLBACK WHERE HE WAS ALSO ALL-AMERICAN. YOU MIGHT EVEN FIND HIM AT HALFBACK WHEN NEEDED.

IN HIS FIRST GAME AS A FULLBACK HE SCORED TWO TOUCHDOWNS AND KICKED THREE CONVERSIONS.

KNOWN AS A LINE PLUNGER, HE COULD PASS, TOO. ON RUNS HE WOULD TELEGRAPH HIS MOVES AND STILL BEAT THE DEFENSE. IT WAS SAID HE RAN HIS OWN INTERFERENCE. HE HAD TO BE GANG TACKLED.

IN OTHER SPORTS THIS INTERNATIONAL FALLS LEGEND PLAYED CENTER AND GUARD IN BASKETBALL. IN TRACK HE DID THE SHOT, DISCUS, HIGH JUMP AND RAN IN THE RELAY.

HE CAUSED THE FUMBLES IN THE BIG GAMES AGAINST NOTRE DAME (1927) AND WISCONSIN (1928) TO TURN THE TIDE IN FAVOR OF THE GOPHERS.

THE GREAT SPORTS AUTHORITY, GRANTLAND RICE, PICKED THE "BRONK" AS THE BEST ALL AROUND PLAYER OF ALL TIME.

HE SAID A TEAM OF "ELEVEN NAGURSKIS WOULD BE A MOP-UP. IT WOULD BE SOMETHING CLOSE TO MASSACRE."

IT MIGHT BE ADDED THIS MASSACRE WOULD BE BROUGHT ABOUT BY ONE CELEBRATED FOR HIS GENTLE TEMPERAMENT.

HE WAS A CHARTER MEMBER OF THE COLLEGE FOOTBALL HALL OF FAME AS A GOPHER AND A CHARTER MEMBER IN THE PRO HALL OF FAME FOR HIS PLAY AS A CHICAGO BEAR.

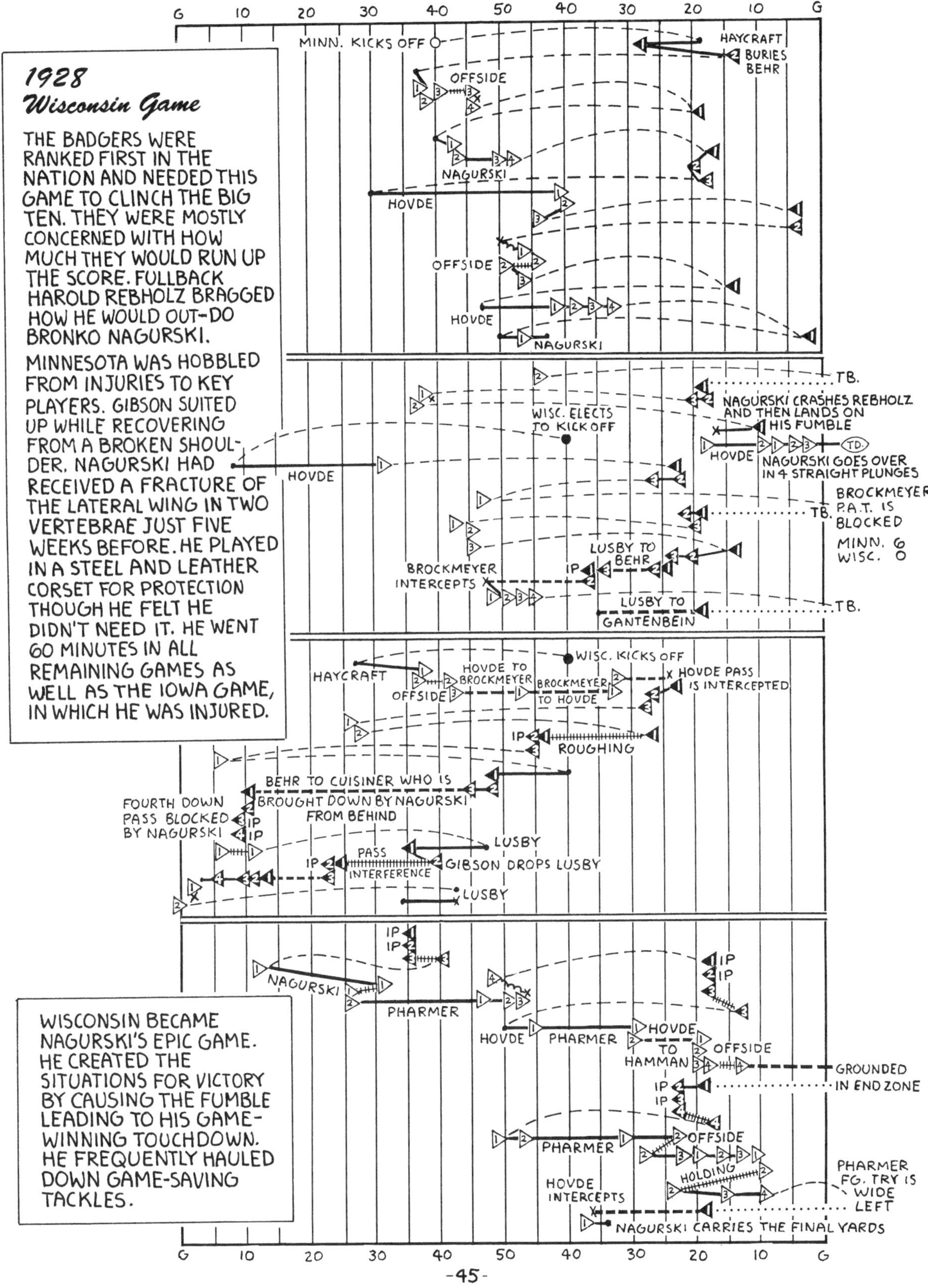

1928
Wisconsin Game
THE BADGERS WERE RANKED FIRST IN THE NATION AND NEEDED THIS GAME TO CLINCH THE BIG TEN. THEY WERE MOSTLY CONCERNED WITH HOW MUCH THEY WOULD RUN UP THE SCORE. FULLBACK HAROLD REBHOLZ BRAGGED HOW HE WOULD OUT-DO BRONKO NAGURSKI.
MINNESOTA WAS HOBBLED FROM INJURIES TO KEY PLAYERS. GIBSON SUITED UP WHILE RECOVERING FROM A BROKEN SHOULDER. NAGURSKI HAD RECEIVED A FRACTURE OF THE LATERAL WING IN TWO VERTEBRAE JUST FIVE WEEKS BEFORE. HE PLAYED IN A STEEL AND LEATHER CORSET FOR PROTECTION THOUGH HE FELT HE DIDN'T NEED IT. HE WENT 60 MINUTES IN ALL REMAINING GAMES AS WELL AS THE IOWA GAME, IN WHICH HE WAS INJURED.
G 10 20 30 40 50 40 30 20 10 G
MINN. KICKS OFF
HAYCRAFT
BURIES BEHR
OFFSIDE
NAGURSKI
HOVDE
OFFSIDE
HOVDE
NAGURSKI
TB.
NAGURSKI CRASHES REBHOLZ AND THEN LANDS ON HIS FUMBLE
WISC. ELECTS TO KICK OFF
TD.
HOVDE
HOVDE
NAGURSKI GOES OVER IN 4 STRAIGHT PLUNGES
BROCKMEYER P.A.T. IS BLOCKED
TB.
MINN. 6
WISC. 0
LUSBY TO BEHR
BROCKMEYER INTERCEPTS
IP
LUSBY TO GANTENBEIN
TB.
WISC. KICKS OFF
HAYCRAFT
HOVDE TO BROCKMEYER
BROCKMEYER TO HOVDE
HOVDE PASS IS INTERCEPTED
OFFSIDE
IP
ROUGHING
BEHR TO CUISINER WHO IS BROUGHT DOWN BY NAGURSKI FROM BEHIND
FOURTH DOWN PASS BLOCKED BY NAGURSKI
IP
IP
LUSBY
PASS INTERFERENCE
IP
GIBSON DROPS LUSBY
LUSBY
IP
IP
IP
IP
NAGURSKI
PHARMER
HOVDE
PHARMER
HOVDE TO HAMMAN
OFFSIDE
GROUNDED IN END ZONE
IP
IP
PHARMER
OFFSIDE
HOLDING
HOVDE INTERCEPTS
PHARMER FG. TRY IS WIDE LEFT
NAGURSKI CARRIES THE FINAL YARDS
WISCONSIN BECAME NAGURSKI'S EPIC GAME. HE CREATED THE SITUATIONS FOR VICTORY BY CAUSING THE FUMBLE LEADING TO HIS GAME-WINNING TOUCHDOWN. HE FREQUENTLY HAULED DOWN GAME-SAVING TACKLES.
G 10 20 30 40 50 40 30 20 10 G

Clarence "Biggie" Munn

"BIGGIE" WAS QUICK AND AGILE FOR HIS SIZE. HE STARTED AT FULLBACK AND THEN TACKLE BUT, UNFORTUNATELY FOR HIM, SO DID NAGURSKI. GUARD EVENTUALLY BECAME HIS CONSENSUS ALL-AMERICAN AND BIG TEN M.V.P. SPOT IN 1931.

HE WAS BORN IN ANOKA BUT WENT TO SCHOOL AT MINNEAPOLIS NORTH. AT MINNESOTA HE WAS CAPTAIN FOR BOTH FOOTBALL AND TRACK TEAMS.

MUNN KICKED OFF AND WOULD OFTEN COME BEHIND THE LINE TO RUN OR PASS. HE WAS THE BEST GOPHER PUNTER UP TO HIS TIME AND WOULD USE THE THREAT TO RUN FROM THE PUNT FORMATION. HE RECEIVED PUNTS, TOO.

COACHING WAS HIS NEXT POSITION. HE WAS COACH OF THE YEAR IN 1952 WHILE HIS MICHIGAN STATE TEAM WON THE NATIONAL CHAMPIONSHIP. THE FIRST YEAR THEY WERE ELIGIBLE IN THE BIG TEN HE TOOK THEM TO THE TITLE AND A ROSE BOWL VICTORY. ONLY RETIREMENT AS COACH TO BE ATHLETIC DIRECTOR ENDED HIS 28 GAME WIN STRING. HE ENTERED THE HALL OF FAME AS A COACH, FROM THERE.

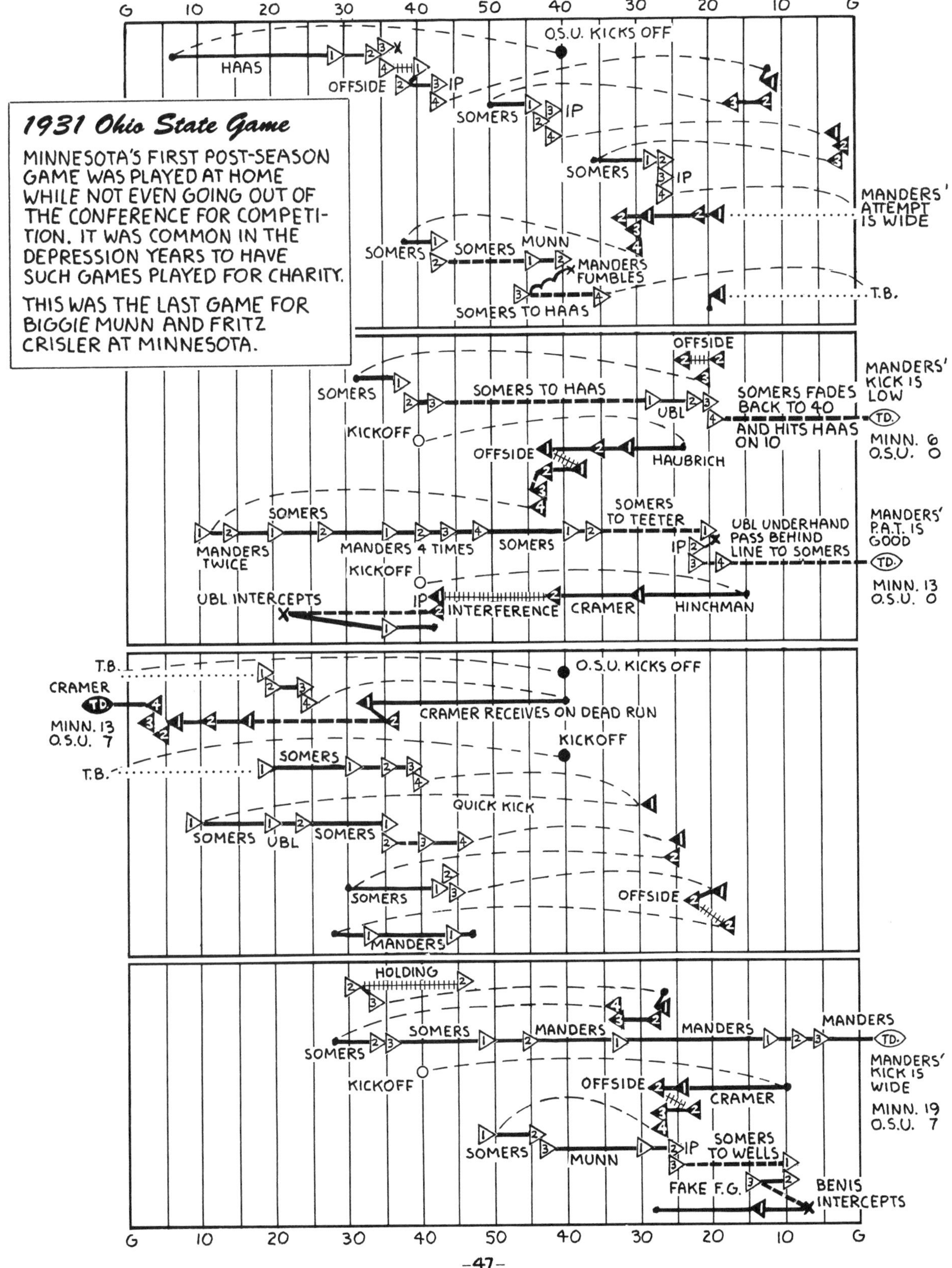

1931 Ohio State Game
MINNESOTA'S FIRST POST-SEASON GAME WAS PLAYED AT HOME WHILE NOT EVEN GOING OUT OF THE CONFERENCE FOR COMPETITION. IT WAS COMMON IN THE DEPRESSION YEARS TO HAVE SUCH GAMES PLAYED FOR CHARITY.
THIS WAS THE LAST GAME FOR BIGGIE MUNN AND FRITZ CRISLER AT MINNESOTA.
G 10 20 30 40 50 40 30 20 10 G
O.S.U. KICKS OFF
HAAS
OFFSIDE
IP
SOMERS
IP
SOMERS
IP
MANDERS' ATTEMPT IS WIDE
SOMERS
SOMERS
MUNN
MANDERS FUMBLES
SOMERS TO HAAS
T.B.
OFFSIDE
MANDERS' KICK IS LOW
SOMERS
SOMERS TO HAAS
UBL
SOMERS FADES BACK TO 40 AND HITS HAAS ON 10
TD.
KICKOFF
OFFSIDE
HAUBRICH
MINN. 6
O.S.U. 0
SOMERS
SOMERS TO TEETER
MANDERS' P.A.T. IS GOOD
MANDERS TWICE
MANDERS 4 TIMES
SOMERS
IP
UBL UNDERHAND PASS BEHIND LINE TO SOMERS
TD.
KICKOFF
MINN. 13
O.S.U. 0
UBL INTERCEPTS
IP
INTERFERENCE
CRAMER
HINCHMAN
T.B.
O.S.U. KICKS OFF
CRAMER
TD
CRAMER RECEIVES ON DEAD RUN
MINN. 13
O.S.U. 7
KICKOFF
SOMERS
T.B.
QUICK KICK
SOMERS
UBL
SOMERS
SOMERS
OFFSIDE
MANDERS
HOLDING
SOMERS
SOMERS
MANDERS
MANDERS
MANDERS
TD.
MANDERS' KICK IS WIDE
KICKOFF
OFFSIDE
CRAMER
MINN. 19
O.S.U. 7
SOMERS
MUNN
IP
SOMERS TO WELLS
FAKE F.G.
BENIS INTERCEPTS
G 10 20 30 40 50 40 30 20 10 G

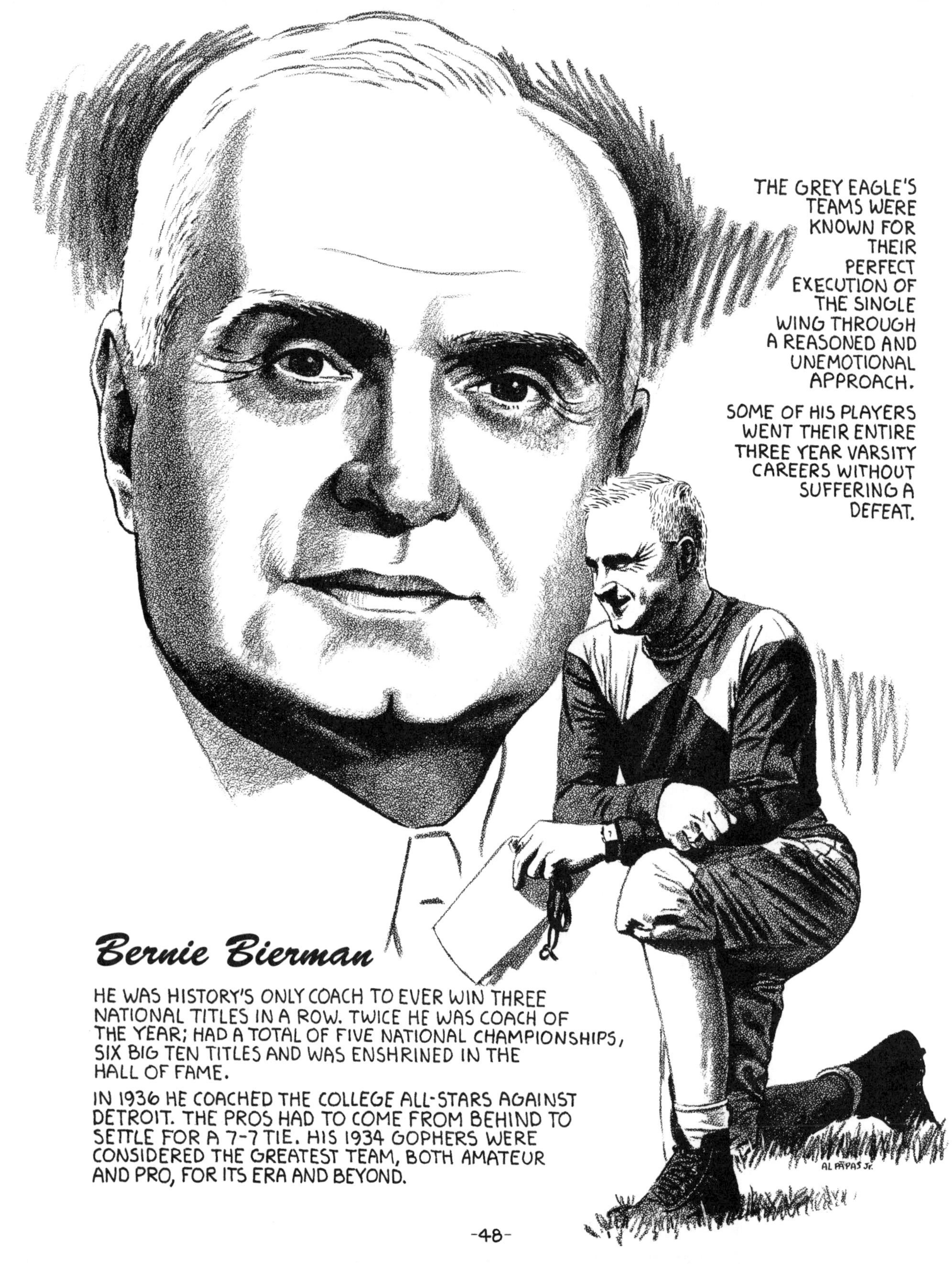

THE GREY EAGLE'S TEAMS WERE KNOWN FOR THEIR PERFECT EXECUTION OF THE SINGLE WING THROUGH A REASONED AND UNEMOTIONAL APPROACH.

SOME OF HIS PLAYERS WENT THEIR ENTIRE THREE YEAR VARSITY CAREERS WITHOUT SUFFERING A DEFEAT.

Bernie Bierman

HE WAS HISTORY'S ONLY COACH TO EVER WIN THREE NATIONAL TITLES IN A ROW. TWICE HE WAS COACH OF THE YEAR; HAD A TOTAL OF FIVE NATIONAL CHAMPIONSHIPS, SIX BIG TEN TITLES AND WAS ENSHRINED IN THE HALL OF FAME.

IN 1936 HE COACHED THE COLLEGE ALL-STARS AGAINST DETROIT. THE PROS HAD TO COME FROM BEHIND TO SETTLE FOR A 7-7 TIE. HIS 1934 GOPHERS WERE CONSIDERED THE GREATEST TEAM, BOTH AMATEUR AND PRO, FOR ITS ERA AND BEYOND.

Francis "Pug" Lund

AS A WALK-ON FROM RICE LAKE, WISCONSIN THEY SAID HE COULDN'T RUN OR PASS AND HAD TROUBLE HANDLING THE BALL DUE TO A STIFF FINGER INJURED IN A POLE VAULTING ACCIDENT. HE ANSWERED THEM BY BECOMING A TWO TIME ALL-AMERICAN, BIG TEN M.V.P., UNITED STATES M.V.P. AND INDUCTEE INTO THE HALL OF FAME.

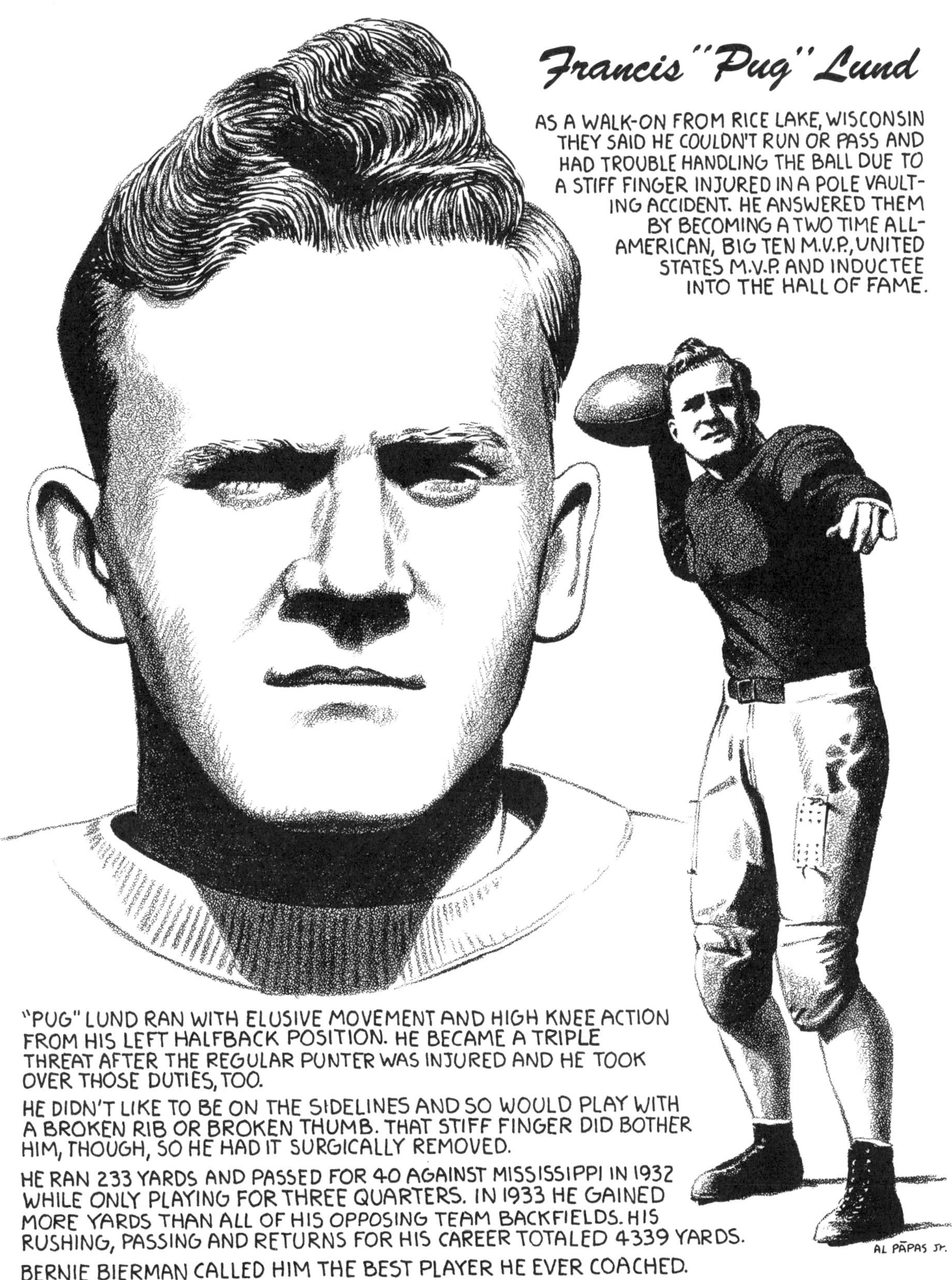

"PUG" LUND RAN WITH ELUSIVE MOVEMENT AND HIGH KNEE ACTION FROM HIS LEFT HALFBACK POSITION. HE BECAME A TRIPLE THREAT AFTER THE REGULAR PUNTER WAS INJURED AND HE TOOK OVER THOSE DUTIES, TOO.

HE DIDN'T LIKE TO BE ON THE SIDELINES AND SO WOULD PLAY WITH A BROKEN RIB OR BROKEN THUMB. THAT STIFF FINGER DID BOTHER HIM, THOUGH, SO HE HAD IT SURGICALLY REMOVED.

HE RAN 233 YARDS AND PASSED FOR 40 AGAINST MISSISSIPPI IN 1932 WHILE ONLY PLAYING FOR THREE QUARTERS. IN 1933 HE GAINED MORE YARDS THAN ALL OF HIS OPPOSING TEAM BACKFIELDS. HIS RUSHING, PASSING AND RETURNS FOR HIS CAREER TOTALED 4339 YARDS.

BERNIE BIERMAN CALLED HIM THE BEST PLAYER HE EVER COACHED.

Frank "Butch" Larson

IN THE OFF-SEASON "BUTCH" WAS A BUTCHER. ON THE GRIDIRON HE WOULD SLICE THROUGH OPPOSITION. NOT WAITING FOR A BALL CARRIER TO COME TO HIM, HE WOULD CUT AND LEAP THROUGH THE INTERFERENCE, SOMETIMES KNOCKING THEM DOWN, TO GET AT HIS TACKLE VICTIM.

TWO GAMES IN A ROW HE FACED HALFBACKS WITH REPUTATIONS AS BEING AMONG THE BEST IN THE COUNTRY. HE HELD THEM FOR A COMBINED TWO YARDS LOSS.

THE RIGHT END FROM DULUTH DENFELD WAS ALL-AMERICAN IN 1933 AND CONSENSUS ALL-AMERICAN IN 1934.

IN THE LATTER YEAR HIS OFF-FIELD HIGH JINKS BUDDY, BOB TENNER, COMPLIMENTED THE OTHER END SPOT BY ATTAINING ALL-AMERICAN STATUS, TOO.

HE WAS ALL ARMS AND LEGS STRUNG TOGETHER WITH COORDINATION. HE WOULD SEEM TO LOAF AND THEN TAKE OFF TO SNATCH PASSES HIGH IN THE AIR.

Bob Tenner

IN 1933 TENNER SCORED THE WINNING TOUCHDOWN AGAINST PITTSBURGH. THE FOLLOWING YEAR HE DID IT AGAIN ON A PASS FROM "PUG" LUND. THIS SECOND WIN CATAPULTED THE GOPHERS SOLIDLY INTO THE NATIONAL CHAMPIONSHIP.

TENNER WON ALL-AMERICAN HONORS AT LEFT END IN 1934. WITH HIS ELIGIBILITY ENDED THE FOLLOWING YEAR HE TOOK A VACATION FROM HIS STUDIES AND PLAYED A SEASON FOR GREEN BAY.

TENNER WAS THE ONLY PLAYER WHO COULD GET EXCUSED FROM PRACTICES, IN WHICH HE TOOK LITTLE INTEREST. HE DID, HOWEVER, EXCEL ON THE FIELD AND IN THE MEDICAL CLASSROOM. HE WON THE BIG TEN MEDAL FOR SCHOLARSHIP AND ATHLETIC ACHIEVEMENT.

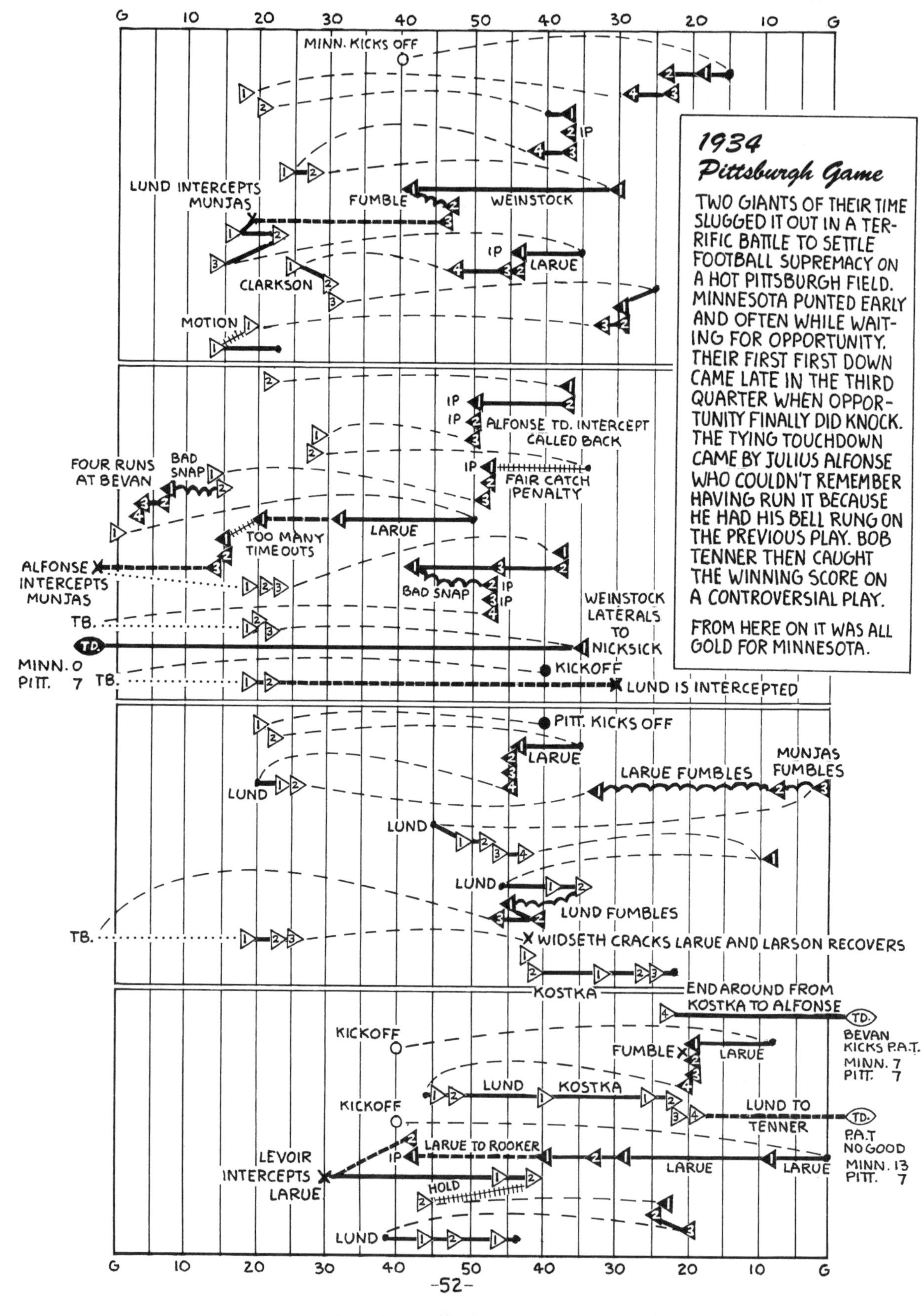

G 10 20 30 40 50 40 30 20 10 G
MINN. KICKS OFF
IP
LUND INTERCEPTS
MUNJAS
FUMBLE
WEINSTOCK
IP
LARUE
CLARKSON
MOTION
1934
Pittsburgh Game
TWO GIANTS OF THEIR TIME SLUGGED IT OUT IN A TERRIFIC BATTLE TO SETTLE FOOTBALL SUPREMACY ON A HOT PITTSBURGH FIELD. MINNESOTA PUNTED EARLY AND OFTEN WHILE WAITING FOR OPPORTUNITY. THEIR FIRST FIRST DOWN CAME LATE IN THE THIRD QUARTER WHEN OPPORTUNITY FINALLY DID KNOCK. THE TYING TOUCHDOWN CAME BY JULIUS ALFONSE WHO COULDN'T REMEMBER HAVING RUN IT BECAUSE HE HAD HIS BELL RUNG ON THE PREVIOUS PLAY. BOB TENNER THEN CAUGHT THE WINNING SCORE ON A CONTROVERSIAL PLAY.
FROM HERE ON IT WAS ALL GOLD FOR MINNESOTA.
IP
IP
ALFONSE TD. INTERCEPT
CALLED BACK
FOUR RUNS
AT BEVAN
BAD
SNAP
IP
FAIR CATCH
PENALTY
LARUE
TOO MANY
TIME OUTS
ALFONSE
INTERCEPTS
MUNJAS
BAD SNAP
IP
IP
WEINSTOCK
LATERALS
TO
NICKSICK
TB.
TD.
KICKOFF
MINN. 0
PITT. 7
TB.
LUND IS INTERCEPTED
PITT. KICKS OFF
LARUE
LUND
LARUE FUMBLES
MUNJAS
FUMBLES
LUND
LUND
LUND FUMBLES
TB.
WIDSETH CRACKS LARUE AND LARSON RECOVERS
KOSTKA
END AROUND FROM
KOSTKA TO ALFONSE
TD.
BEVAN
KICKS P.A.T.
MINN. 7
PITT. 7
KICKOFF
FUMBLE
LARUE
LUND
KOSTKA
KICKOFF
LUND TO
TENNER
TD.
P.A.T
NO GOOD
LARUE TO ROOKER
IP
LEVOIR
INTERCEPTS
LARUE
LARUE
LARUE
MINN. 13
PITT. 7
HOLD
LUND
G 10 20 30 40 50 40 30 20 10 G

Stan Kostka

THE "ATTILA OF THE WEST" WAS SIX FEET TALL AND 213 POUNDS BUT SEEMED MUCH BIGGER. HE PLAYED ON THE SECOND STRING, NO LESS, WHILE BEING AN ALL-AMERICAN IN HIS JUNIOR YEAR OF 1934. SUCH WAS THE DEPTH OF THAT GREAT SQUAD.

IOWA WAS LUCKY TO FIELD A TEAM AFTER HE AND HIS MATES GOT THROUGH WITH THEM: A BROKEN VERTEBRA, A BRUISE THAT DEVELOPED INTO A CLOT, TWO PLAYERS BEING KNOCKED OUT AND ADDITIONAL BUMPS.

HE WAS A POWERFUL FULLBACK WHO LOOKED LIKE A HALFBACK WHEN HE GOT PAST THE LINE. HE LED THE BIG TEN AND CAME IN SEVENTH IN THE NATION IN SCORING. AGAINST NORTH DAKOTA HE SCORED FOUR TOUCHDOWNS AND AVERAGED 9.3 YARDS PER CARRY IN 13 TRIES.

THE SOUTH ST. PAUL NATIVE HAD PLAYED INTERCOLLEGIATE BALL AS A FRESHMAN AT OREGON BEFORE TRANSFERRING TO MINNESOTA. THE BIG TEN DIDN'T ALLOW FRESHMEN TO PLAY, AND SO RULED HIM INELIGIBLE HIS SENIOR YEAR.

UNABLE TO COMPETE AS A GOPHER THE PROS SIGNED HIM FOR $5000 AND A $500 BONUS. THIS WAS THE RESULT OF A BIDDING WAR. FEAR OF SUCH FUTURE WARS RESULTED IN THE START OF THE COLLEGE DRAFT IN 1936.

Bill Bevan

PLACE-KICKING MADE HIM ONE OF THE HIGHEST-SCORING LINEMEN IN THE COUNTRY. HE ALSO DID THE KICKOFF AND WAS ONE OF THE BEST DROP-KICKERS OF HIS TIME.

ROUGH AND TOUGH WAS HIS GAME. HE SLASHED AND HIT HARD TO CLEAR OPENINGS FOR RUNNERS. BERNIE BIERMAN SAID "HE NEVER HIT HIS STRIDE UNTIL HE WAS KICKED IN THE FACE." THIS MAY HAVE HAPPENED OFTEN BECAUSE HE WAS THE LAST IN THE BIG TEN TO NOT WEAR HEADGEAR.

IN THE 1934 PITTSBURGH GAME THE GOPHERS FOUND THEMSELVES DEFENDING ON THE SIX WITH GOAL TO GO. IT WAS PITTS' BELIEF THAT THEY MUST WIN BY GOING THROUGH THE BEST OPPOSITION. THEY RAN FOUR STRAIGHT TIMES AT BEVAN AS HE SLAMMED THE DOOR ON THEM.

THE ST. PAUL CENTRAL GUARD WAS ONE OF FOUR CONSENSUS ALL-AMERICANS ON THE GREAT 1934 GOPHER TEAM.

BEVAN MISSED PLAYING IN 1935 DUE TO THE FRESHMAN ELIGIBILITY RULE. THIS DIDN'T PREVENT HIM FROM BEING ELECTED AS ALTERNATE CAPTAIN, THOUGH.

Sheldon Beise

BEISE PLAYED ON THE NATIONAL CHAMPIONSHIP TEAMS OF 1934 AND 35.

HE WAS KNOWN FOR HIS DEFENSIVE PLAY AND AS A STRONG BLOCKER. HE WAS, PERHAPS, THE BEST BLOCKING BACK IN THE COUNTRY. HE COULD ALSO SCORE, AS HE PILED UP 54 POINTS HIS FINAL YEAR.

HE WAS ALL-BIG TEN FOR THREE YEARS AND WAS ALL-AMERICAN IN 1935 TO CAP IT OFF.

BY A VOTE OF THE FANS THE MOUND NATIVE WAS SELECTED TO THE 1936 ALL-STAR TEAM.

HE LETTERED IN BASKETBALL AND TRACK, AS WELL. AFTER HIS PLAYING DAYS HE SERVED AS AN ASSISTANT GOPHER FOOTBALL COACH.

Floyd of Rosedale

MINNESOTA REPRESENTATIVE TO THE BIG TEN, JAMES PAGE, PUSHED THE CAUSE TO SUSPEND IOWA FOR SLUSH FUND VIOLATIONS OCCURING IN 1929. HE SUCCEEDED BUT IOWA WAS REINSTATED AFTER HUMBLING ITSELF AND AGREEING TO CHANGES. A CLEAN UP OF THE PROGRAM BROUGHT OSSIE SOLEM IN AS NEW HEAD COACH. HE HAD BEEN A GOPHER ON THE 1915 TEAM.

BECAUSE OF THIS SUSPENSION EPISODE A GRUDGE WAS BORN AND FESTERED. THE 1934 GAME AT IOWA RAISED THE HAWKEYE'S IRE EVEN MORE. THEIR STAR, OZZIE SIMMONS, WAS ALLEGEDLY GANGED UP ON AND HAD TO LEAVE THE GAME DUE TO INJURIES. MINNESOTA DENIED IT BECAUSE THEY DESTROYED EVERYONE CLEANLY WHO GOT IN THEIR WAY. THEY HAD NO REPUTATION FOR PLAYING DIRTY.

THE NEXT YEAR'S GAME WAS AGAIN AT IOWA AND THE FANS WERE STILL SIMMERING. IT REACHED FEVER PITCH WHEN IOWA GOVERNOR CLYDE HERRING SAID, "IF THE OFFICIALS STAND FOR ANY ROUGH TACTICS LIKE MINNESOTA USED LAST YEAR, I'M SURE THE CROWD WON'T." ALARMED, MINNESOTA GOVERNOR FLOYD OLSON TELEGRAPHED BACK, "MINNESOTA FOLKS EXCITED OVER YOUR STATEMENT ABOUT IOWA CROWD LYNCHING THE MINNESOTA FOOTBALL TEAM. I HAVE ASSURED THEM YOU ARE LAW-ABIDING GENTLEMAN AND ARE ONLY TRYING TO GET OUR GOAT... I WILL BET YOU A MINNESOTA PRIZE HOG AGAINST AN IOWA PRIZE HOG THAT MINNESOTA WINS." WITH THIS DIVERSION, THE FEVER BROKE.

MINNESOTA WON THE GAME AND THE FANS BEHAVED WITH RESTRAINT. THE IOWA HOG WAS PRESENTED TO OLSON IN GOOD HUMOR. CHARLES BRIOSCHI, OF ST. PAUL, DESIGNED A STATUE OF THE PIG TO BE A GAME TROPHY. IT WAS NAMED "FLOYD OF ROSEDALE" AFTER THE GOVERNOR AND THE TOWN IN WHICH HE LIVED.

BACK IN IOWA SOMEONE TRIED TO HAVE GOVERNOR HERRING ARRESTED FOR GAMBLING.

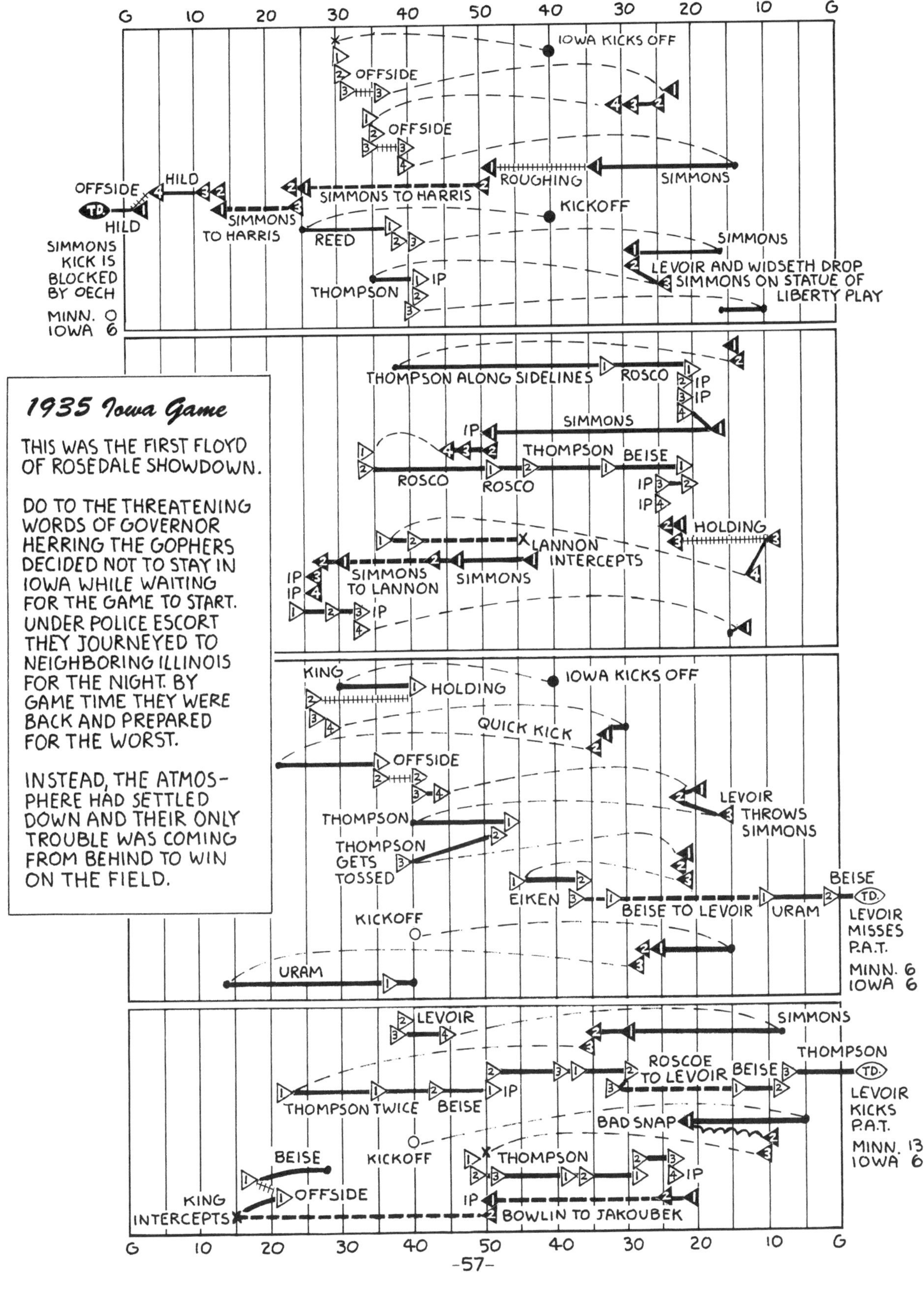
1935 Iowa Game
THIS WAS THE FIRST FLOYD OF ROSEDALE SHOWDOWN.
DO TO THE THREATENING WORDS OF GOVERNOR HERRING THE GOPHERS DECIDED NOT TO STAY IN IOWA WHILE WAITING FOR THE GAME TO START. UNDER POLICE ESCORT THEY JOURNEYED TO NEIGHBORING ILLINOIS FOR THE NIGHT. BY GAME TIME THEY WERE BACK AND PREPARED FOR THE WORST.
INSTEAD, THE ATMOSPHERE HAD SETTLED DOWN AND THEIR ONLY TROUBLE WAS COMING FROM BEHIND TO WIN ON THE FIELD.
G 10 20 30 40 50 40 30 20 10 G
IOWA KICKS OFF
OFFSIDE
OFFSIDE
ROUGHING
SIMMONS
OFFSIDE
HILD
SIMMONS TO HARRIS
TD.
HILD
SIMMONS TO HARRIS
KICKOFF
REED
SIMMONS
SIMMONS KICK IS BLOCKED BY OECH
LEVOIR AND WIDSETH DROP SIMMONS ON STATUE OF LIBERTY PLAY
THOMPSON
IP
MINN. 0
IOWA 6
THOMPSON ALONG SIDELINES
ROSCO
IP
IP
SIMMONS
IP
THOMPSON
BEISE
ROSCO
ROSCO
IP
IP
HOLDING
LANNON INTERCEPTS
SIMMONS TO LANNON
SIMMONS
IP
IP
IP
KING
IOWA KICKS OFF
HOLDING
QUICK KICK
OFFSIDE
LEVOIR THROWS SIMMONS
THOMPSON
THOMPSON GETS TOSSED
EIKEN
BEISE TO LEVOIR
URAM
BEISE
TD.
LEVOIR MISSES P.A.T.
KICKOFF
URAM
MINN. 6
IOWA 6
LEVOIR
SIMMONS
THOMPSON
ROSCOE TO LEVOIR
BEISE
TD.
THOMPSON TWICE
BEISE
IP
LEVOIR KICKS P.A.T.
BAD SNAP
MINN. 13
IOWA 6
BEISE
KICKOFF
THOMPSON
IP
OFFSIDE
KING INTERCEPTS
IP
BOWLIN TO JAKOUBEK
G 10 20 30 40 50 40 30 20 10 G

Dick Smith

HE WAS FAST FOR A BIG GUY. OPPONENTS WOULD FIND HIM IN THEIR BACKFIELDS BEFORE THEY COULD GET OUT.

HE COVERED PUNTS LIKE AN END AND WAS EVEN PUT IN THE END POSITION FOR THE 1934 WISCONSIN GAME. FROM THERE HE WAS ABLE TO SCORE A TOUCHDOWN.

FANS VOTED HIM TO PLAY IN THE 1936 ALL-STAR GAME.

SMITH CAME FROM ROCKFORD, ILLINOIS TO PLAY HOCKEY. AS A FRESHMAN HE INJURED HIS KNEE AND THEN DROPPED THE SPORT AT BERNIE BIERMAN'S REQUEST.

STILL WANTING SOMETHING TO DO IN THE WINTER, HE WENT OUT FOR BASKETBALL.

ON THE FOOTBALL FIELD SMITH WON THE ALL-AMERICAN SPOT AT TACKLE IN 1935.

Charles "Bud" Wilkinson

IN 1935 THIS ALL-AMERICAN GUARD, FROM SOUTH MINNEAPOLIS AND SHATTUCK MILITARY ACADEMY, PROVED TO BE A GREAT DOWN-FIELD BLOCKER. HE COULD ALSO PUT POINTS ON THE BOARD BY KICKING CONVERSIONS.

THE GOPHERS NEEDED A QUARTERBACK IN 1936, AND SO HE WAS MOVED TO THAT POSITION. HE PROCEEDED TO WIN HONORABLE MENTION ALL-AMERICAN AT HIS NEW SPOT.

WILKINSON SERVED AS CAPTAIN OF THE 1935 HOCKEY TEAM, WHERE HE WAS AN ALL-AMERICAN GOALIE.

AS 18 YEAR HEAD COACH FOR OKLAHOMA HE FASHIONED AN INCREDIBLE RECORD: COACH OF THE YEAR FOR 1949; 14 CONFERENCE TITLES; 5 UNBEATEN TEAMS; 3 NATIONAL TITLES; 139-27-4 RECORD WITH AN .829 WINNING PERCENTAGE, THE LONGEST WINNING STRING IN COLLEGIATE HISTORY AT 47 GAMES, AND INDUCTION INTO THE HALL OF FAME.

Ed Widseth

ED WAS FROM CROOKSTON AND BECAME ALL-AMERICAN IN 1934 AND UNANIMOUS ALL-AMERICAN IN 1935 AND 36 AT TACKLE. THE U.P.I. NAMED HIM BIG-TEN M.V.P. HE WAS A BIG CHUNK IN THE "SEVEN BLOCKS OF GRANITE" AS THE GOPHER LINE WAS KNOWN.

HE HAD POWER, SIZE AND QUICK HANDS. GRANTLAND RICE CALLED HIM THE "FIFTH MAN IN THE OPPONENT'S BACKFIELD."

HIS BLOCKING OPENED BIG HOLES AND HE WAS THE FIRST ONE DOWN UNDER PUNTS. A SPECIAL TACKLE-ELIGIBLE PLAY WAS DEVISED TO UTILIZE HIS SPEED SO THIS HALL OF FAMER COULD RECEIVE PASSES.

WIDSETH WENT ON TO PLAY FIVE YEARS FOR THE NEW YORK GIANTS, WHERE HE MADE ALL-PRO THREE TIMES AND WAS N.F.L. PLAYER OF THE YEAR IN 1938.

Julius Alfonse

"JULIE" CAME IN BEHIND ONLY BRUCE SMITH, "PUG" LUND AND GEORGE FRANCK IN TOTAL POINTS SCORED DURING MINNESOTA'S GOLDEN ERA.

HE SCORED THE FIRST TOUCHDOWN AGAINST PITTSBURGH IN THE 1934 CLASSIC STRUGGLE. DURING THAT DAY HE ALSO INTERCEPTED A PITT AERIAL IN THE END ZONE. HE HAD ANOTHER INTERCEPTION FOR A 50 YARD SCORE THAT WAS CALLED BACK.

IN THE SAME SEASON HE RETURNED INTERCEPTIONS THAT COUNTED AGAINST MICHIGAN (77 YARDS) AND IOWA (76 YARDS). THE IOWA GAME WAS HIS BEST FOR RUSHING WITH 144 YARDS.

HE LED THE GOPHERS IN AVERAGE YARDS PER CARRY IN 1933 AND 1934. HE MISSED PLAYING IN 1935 BUT RETURNED IN 1936 TO MAKE ALL-AMERICAN DISTINCTION AT RIGHT HALFBACK.

TO START OFF THE GOPHERS' THIRD STRAIGHT NATIONAL CHAMPIONSHIP YEAR, IN 1936, HE GRABBED TWO BACK-TO-THE-WALL INTERCEPTS AGAINST WASHINGTON AND ONE IN THE END ZONE AGAINST NEBRASKA TO KEEP VICTORY OUT OF THEIR GRASP. BOTH THOSE POWERFUL TEAMS FINISHED FIRST IN THEIR RESPECTIVE CONFERENCES.

ALFONSE WENT ON TO PLAY WITH THE PROS FOR CLEVELAND.

George Roscoe

INTO THE DAYLIGHT FROM "PUG" LUND'S SHADOW EMERGED GEORGE ROSCOE. HE WAS A TRIPLE THREAT FROM MINNEAPOLIS CENTRAL. IN 1935 HE AVERAGED BETTER THAN FIVE YARDS PER CARRY WHILE LEADING THE TEAM WITH 1348 YARDS. HE COMPILED 36 POINTS.

AS THE SEASON BEGAN HE SEEMED WELL ON HIS WAY TO ALL-AMERICAN RECOGNITION.

IN THE BIG NEBRASKA GAME HE RETURNED THE OPENING KICKOFF 74 YARDS. HE SCORED BOTH MINNESOTA TOUCHDOWNS TO WIN THE GAME.

TROUBLE FINALLY HIT THE GOPHERS IN THE NORTHWESTERN GAME. THEY TRAILED AT HALF TIME DUE TO LACK OF BLOCKING POWER FROM THE RIGHT HALFBACK POSITION. IN BIERMAN'S SINGLE WING THE LEFT HALFBACK WAS THE CHIEF BALL CARRIER AND STANDOUT POSITION. RIGHT HALF WAS MORE UNHERALDED. IT WAS AT THE BREAK THAT ROSCOE VOLUNTEERED TO SWITCH HIS POSITION FOR THE SAKE OF THE TEAM. THE SWITCH WORKED AND HE WAS ABLE TO BLOCK FOR THE NEW BALL CARRIER, WHO RECORDED A SENSATIONAL DAY WITH A VICTORY.

MINNESOTA WAS THEN ABLE TO GO ON TO ITS SECOND NATIONAL TITLE IN A ROW. THE UNSELFISH ACT BY ROSCOE TO PLAY IN A LESS VISIBLE POSITION COST HIM ALL-AMERICAN LAURELS. IT DOES, HOWEVER, EARN HIM ALL-AMERICAN ADMIRATION AND RESPECT FROM TEAM AND FANS WHO LOVE THE GAME AND THE CHARACTER HE EXHIBITED.

Vernal "Babe" Le Voir

"BABE" PLAYED ALL POSITIONS IN THE BACKFIELD IN 1935. BEING A JACK OF ALL TRADES AND MASTER OF ALL EARNED HIM A SPECIAL DISTINCTION AS AN ALL-AMERICAN UTILITY PLAYER.

IN 1936 HE BECAME THE FIRST ALL-STAR TO EVER SCORE A POINT AGAINST A PRO TEAM.

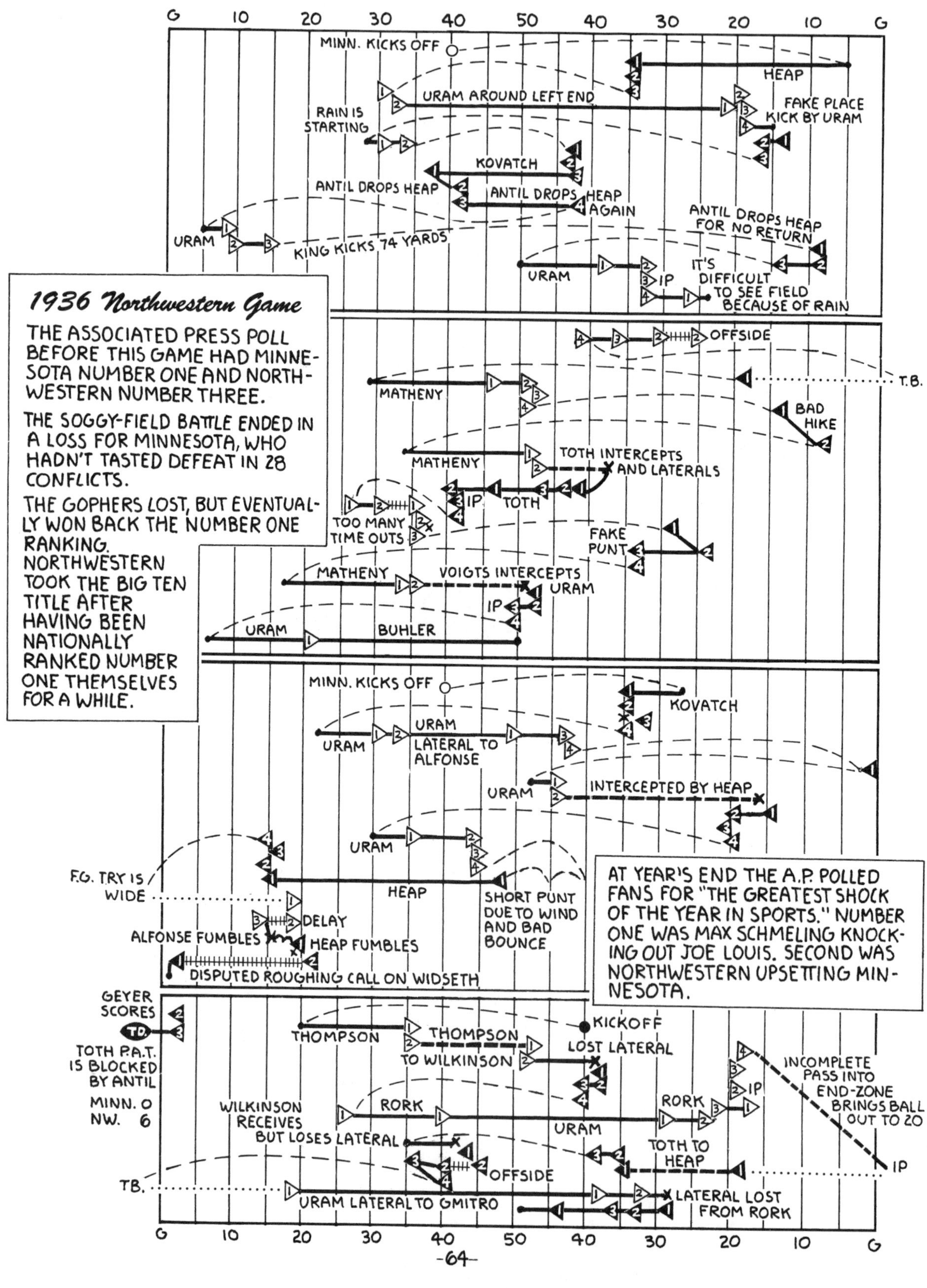
1936 Northwestern Game
THE ASSOCIATED PRESS POLL BEFORE THIS GAME HAD MINNESOTA NUMBER ONE AND NORTHWESTERN NUMBER THREE.
THE SOGGY-FIELD BATTLE ENDED IN A LOSS FOR MINNESOTA, WHO HADN'T TASTED DEFEAT IN 28 CONFLICTS.
THE GOPHERS LOST, BUT EVENTUALLY WON BACK THE NUMBER ONE RANKING. NORTHWESTERN TOOK THE BIG TEN TITLE AFTER HAVING BEEN NATIONALLY RANKED NUMBER ONE THEMSELVES FOR A WHILE.
AT YEAR'S END THE A.P. POLLED FANS FOR "THE GREATEST SHOCK OF THE YEAR IN SPORTS." NUMBER ONE WAS MAX SCHMELING KNOCKING OUT JOE LOUIS. SECOND WAS NORTHWESTERN UPSETTING MINNESOTA.
G 10 20 30 40 50 40 30 20 10 G
MINN. KICKS OFF
HEAP
URAM AROUND LEFT END
FAKE PLACE KICK BY URAM
RAIN IS STARTING
KOVATCH
ANTIL DROPS HEAP
ANTIL DROPS HEAP AGAIN
ANTIL DROPS HEAP FOR NO RETURN
URAM
KING KICKS 74 YARDS
URAM
IP
IT'S DIFFICULT TO SEE FIELD BECAUSE OF RAIN
OFFSIDE
T.B.
MATHENY
BAD HIKE
MATHENY
TOTH INTERCEPTS AND LATERALS
IP
TOTH
TOO MANY TIME OUTS
FAKE PUNT
MATHENY
VOIGTS INTERCEPTS
URAM
IP
URAM
BUHLER
MINN. KICKS OFF
KOVATCH
URAM
URAM
LATERAL TO ALFONSE
URAM
INTERCEPTED BY HEAP
URAM
F.G. TRY IS WIDE
HEAP
SHORT PUNT DUE TO WIND AND BAD BOUNCE
DELAY
ALFONSE FUMBLES
HEAP FUMBLES
DISPUTED ROUGHING CALL ON WIDSETH
GEYER SCORES
TD
TOTH P.A.T. IS BLOCKED BY ANTIL
MINN. 0
NW. 6
THOMPSON
THOMPSON TO WILKINSON
KICKOFF
LOST LATERAL
INCOMPLETE PASS INTO END-ZONE BRINGS BALL OUT TO 20
IP
WILKINSON RECEIVES BUT LOSES LATERAL
RORK
RORK
URAM
TOTH TO HEAP
IP
OFFSIDE
TB.
URAM LATERAL TO GMITRO
LATERAL LOST FROM RORK
G 10 20 30 40 50 40 30 20 10 G

Andy Uram

MINNEAPOLIS MARSHALL GAVE ANDY URAM TO MINNESOTA. HE WAS A TRIPLE THREAT WITH A FAST AND A LONG LOPING STRIDE. HE WAS ALL-AMERICAN FULLBACK IN 1936 BUT BROKE HIS WRIST EARLY IN 1937 TO END HIS COLLEGE CAREER.

HE HAD HIS SHARE OF LONG, EXCITING PLAYS. IN 1935, AGAINST MICHIGAN, HE REPLACED INJURED TUFFY THOMPSON AND RAN TOUCHDOWNS OF 58 AND 73 YARDS. ALTOGETHER HE DASHED 187 YARDS ON 11 CARRIES THAT DAY.

AGAINST WISCONSIN HE TOOK A LATERAL ON A KICKOFF AND SCAMPERED FOR AN 83-YARD TOUCHDOWN.

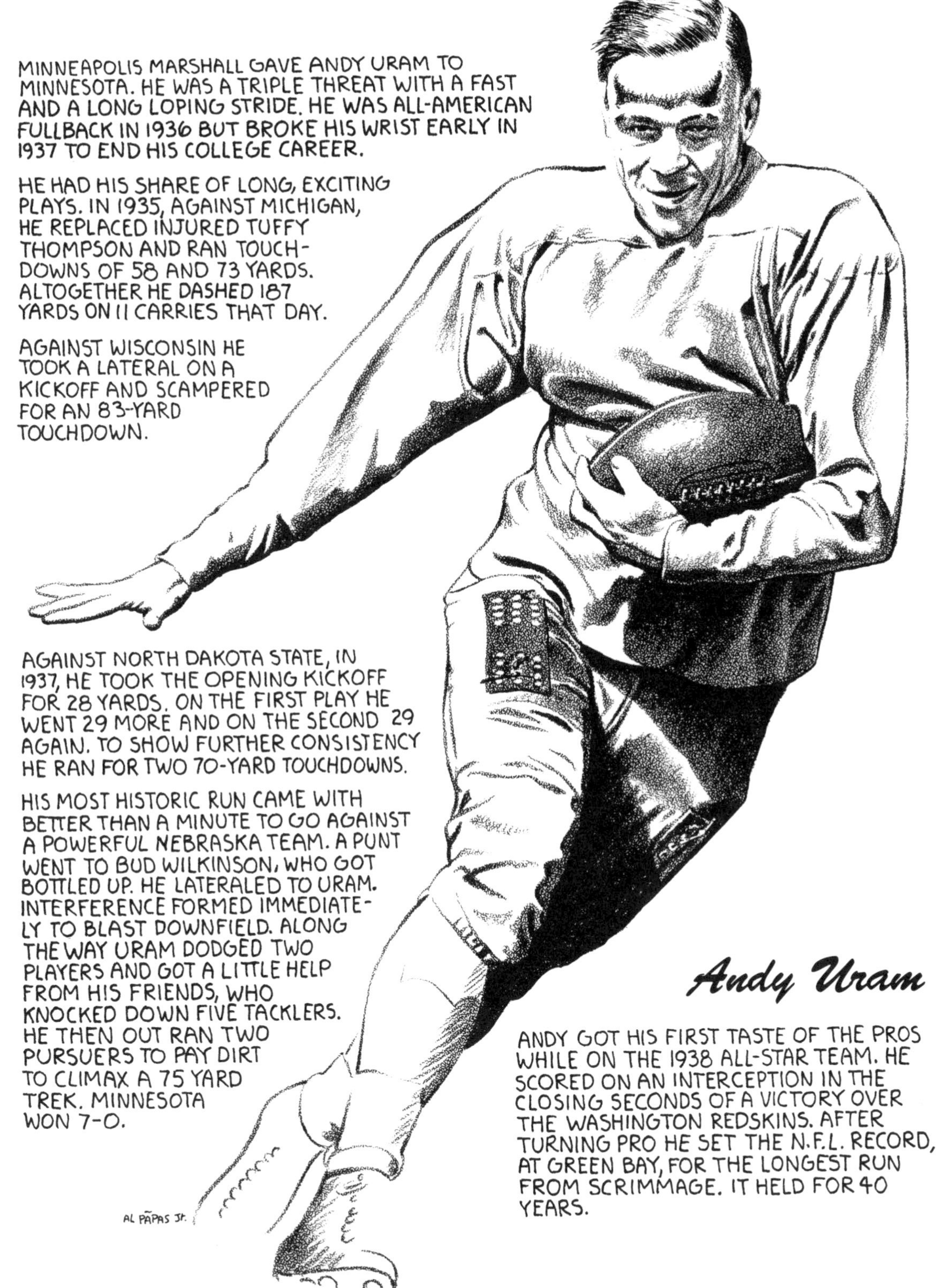

AGAINST NORTH DAKOTA STATE, IN 1937, HE TOOK THE OPENING KICKOFF FOR 28 YARDS. ON THE FIRST PLAY HE WENT 29 MORE AND ON THE SECOND 29 AGAIN. TO SHOW FURTHER CONSISTENCY HE RAN FOR TWO 70-YARD TOUCHDOWNS.

HIS MOST HISTORIC RUN CAME WITH BETTER THAN A MINUTE TO GO AGAINST A POWERFUL NEBRASKA TEAM. A PUNT WENT TO BUD WILKINSON, WHO GOT BOTTLED UP. HE LATERALED TO URAM. INTERFERENCE FORMED IMMEDIATELY TO BLAST DOWNFIELD. ALONG THE WAY URAM DODGED TWO PLAYERS AND GOT A LITTLE HELP FROM HIS FRIENDS, WHO KNOCKED DOWN FIVE TACKLERS. HE THEN OUT RAN TWO PURSUERS TO PAY DIRT TO CLIMAX A 75 YARD TREK. MINNESOTA WON 7-0.

ANDY GOT HIS FIRST TASTE OF THE PROS WHILE ON THE 1938 ALL-STAR TEAM. HE SCORED ON AN INTERCEPTION IN THE CLOSING SECONDS OF A VICTORY OVER THE WASHINGTON REDSKINS. AFTER TURNING PRO HE SET THE N.F.L. RECORD, AT GREEN BAY, FOR THE LONGEST RUN FROM SCRIMMAGE. IT HELD FOR 40 YEARS.

Ray King

THOUGH BORN IN ST. PAUL, RAY KING ATTENDED DULUTH DENFELD WHERE HE WAS A STAR HURDLER.

ON THE GRIDIRON HE WAS ONE OF THE NATION'S FASTEST ENDS. IN 1937 HE SCAMPERED BACK A NORTHWESTERN INTERCEPTION 57 YARDS.

HE WAS A TERRIFIC PUNTER, TOO. ON ONE SOGGY FIELD HE LET ONE FLOAT FOR 74 YARDS.

HE WAS ALL-AMERICAN IN 1936 AND 37 AND WAS CAPTAIN OF THE 1937 ALL-AMERICAN TEAM.

Harold Van Every

SPORTS ILLUSTRATED NAMED VAN EVERY A SILVER ANNIVERSARY ALL-AMERICAN.

AS A SOPHOMORE IN 1937, HE LED THE TEAM IN ALL CATEGORIES: PASSING, RUNNING, AND KICKOFF AND PUNT RETURNS FOR A TOTAL 1314 YARDS. HE PUNTED AN AVERAGE 34.9 YARDS AND SCORED SEVEN TOUCHDOWNS.

HIS LONGEST RUN WAS AGAINST NORTH DAKOTA STATE. HE WENT 76 YARDS WHILE FINISHING THAT DAY WITH 147 YARDS IN FIVE ATTEMPTS.

AN INJURY IN HIS NEXT SEASON CUT HIS PLAYING TIME SHORT. IN 1939 HE LED THE NATION IN INTERCEPTIONS WITH EIGHT.

AFTER RECEIVING THE BIG TEN SCHOLASTIC AND ATHLETIC ACHIEVEMENT AWARD, HE WAS DRAFTED BY GREEN BAY IN THE FIRST ROUND.

Butch Nash

THOUGH HE HAS MEANT SO MUCH TO FOOTBALL, BUTCH NASH ORIGINALLY PREFERRED BASKETBALL, WHERE HE WON THREE LETTERS PLAYING AT GUARD AND FORWARD. HE CONTRIBUTED TO A BIG TEN CHAMPIONSHIP TEAM.

IN FOOTBALL THIS MINNEAPOLIS EDISON GRAD STARRED AT END WHERE HE RECEIVED ALL-AMERICAN HONORS IN 1938. HIS GREATEST FAME CAME LATER ON THE SIDE LINES.

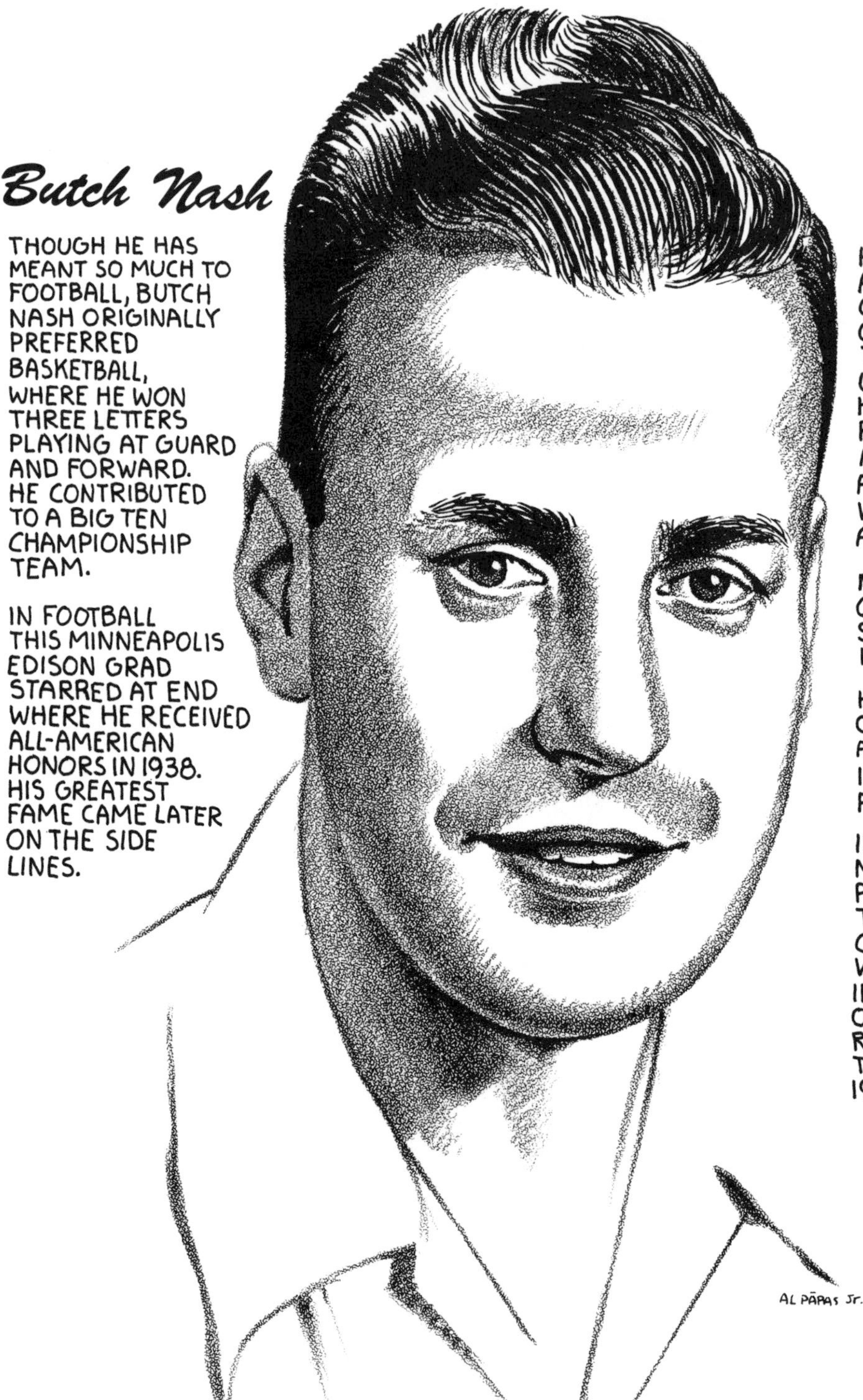

HE HAD EARLY SUCCESS AS A HIGH SCHOOL COACH BEFORE COMING HOME TO THE 'U' AS END COACH UNDER BERNIE BIERMAN. HE REMAINED AS A PERMANENT FIXTURE AFTER BIERMAN LEFT AND SERVED FESLER, WARMATH, STOLL AND SALEM.

NASH TAUGHT MANY GREAT GOPHER ENDS, SOME OF WHOM WENT INTO THE PRO RANKS.

HOLTZ CALLED HIM OUT OF RETIREMENT AND HE HAS ALSO PUT IN PROFITABLE TIME FOR GUTEKUNST.

IN PREPARATION FOR MICHIGAN GAMES, HIS PEP TALKS REPLACED THOSE OF SIG HARRIS OF OLD. THESE TALKS WERE CREDITED FOR INSPIRING VICTORIES OVER NATIONALLY RANKED WOLVERINE TEAMS IN 1977 AND 1986.

Francis Twedell

TWEDELL CAME FROM AUSTIN, MINNESOTA TO LEAD THE GOPHERS AS CAPTAIN IN 1938.

SOME THOUGHT THE GOPHERS' DAYS WERE NUMBERED AS THEY "SLIPPED" TO TENTH IN THE NATION THAT YEAR. THEY STILL WON THE BIG TEN, HOWEVER. THOUGH THERE WAS CONCERN FOR THE BACKFIELD, THERE WAS NOTHING WRONG IN THE MIDDLE OF THE LINE, WHERE TWEDELL HELD THINGS DOWN AS AN ALL-AMERICAN GUARD.

AFTER MINNESOTA HE PLAYED PRO FOR GREEN BAY.

Urban Odson

URBAN ODSON WAS A CONSENSUS ALL-AMERICAN TACKLE IN 1940. HE STOPPED MICHIGAN WITHIN THE FIVE THAT YEAR, AND THEN RECOVERED THEIR FUMBLE. HE ALSO LED THE BLOCKING IN THE FAMOUS TALKING PLAY THE FOLLOWING YEAR.

HE WAS BIG AND WORE THE LARGEST PAIR OF SHOULDER PADS IN THE NATION.

ON THE FIRST DAY OF PRACTICE IN 1941 HE SPRAINED HIS KNEE. IT HAMPERED HIM FROM REPEATING AS ALL-AMERICAN. HE WENT THROUGH THE YEAR WEARING A METAL BRACE AND PLAYING IN PAIN.

George "Sonny" Franck

"SONNY" FRANCK WAS A WORLD CLASS SPRINTER FROM DAVENPORT, IOWA. HE WAS CAPTAIN OF THE GOPHER TRACK TEAM AND USED HIS SPEED AS AN EXCITING WEAPON ON THE GRIDIRON.

HE RETURNED TWO KICK-OFFS FOR TOUCHDOWNS IN HIS 1940 CONSENSUS ALL-AMERICAN YEAR. AMONG OTHER THINGS, HE RECEIVED TWO SCORING PASSES IN A FOUR-TOUCHDOWN DAY AGAINST IOWA. IN A THREE WEEK PERIOD HE THREW ONLY THREE PASSES... ALL GOOD FOR TOUCHDOWNS. AGAINST WISCONSIN HE WAS THE GAME DIFFERENCE THROUGH HIS SCORING AND PREVENTING A BADGER TALLY BY MAKING A CRITICAL PASS INTERCEPTION.

HE WAS ALSO WELL-KNOWN FOR HIS KICKING, BLOCKING AND TACKLING. HE BASHED INTO OPPOSITION WITH NO REGARD FOR HIS OWN BODILY STRUCTURE. IN ONE SUCH INSTANCE HE WAS THE LAST OBSTACLE OF A WASHINGTON BALL CARRIER. FRANCK RAMMED HIM SO HARD HE KNOCKED HIMSELF OUT. IT WAS A GAME-SAVING STOPPER THAT PROTECTED HIS EARLIER 98 YARD KICKOFF-RETURN SCORE.

THE A.P. COACHES' POLL RATED THIS HALFBACK, WHO CAME IN THIRD FOR THE HEISMAN TROPHY, HIGHER THAN THE ACTUAL HEISMAN WINNER.

HE WAS M.V.P. IN THE ALL-STAR GAME BEFORE JOINING THE N.Y. GIANTS.

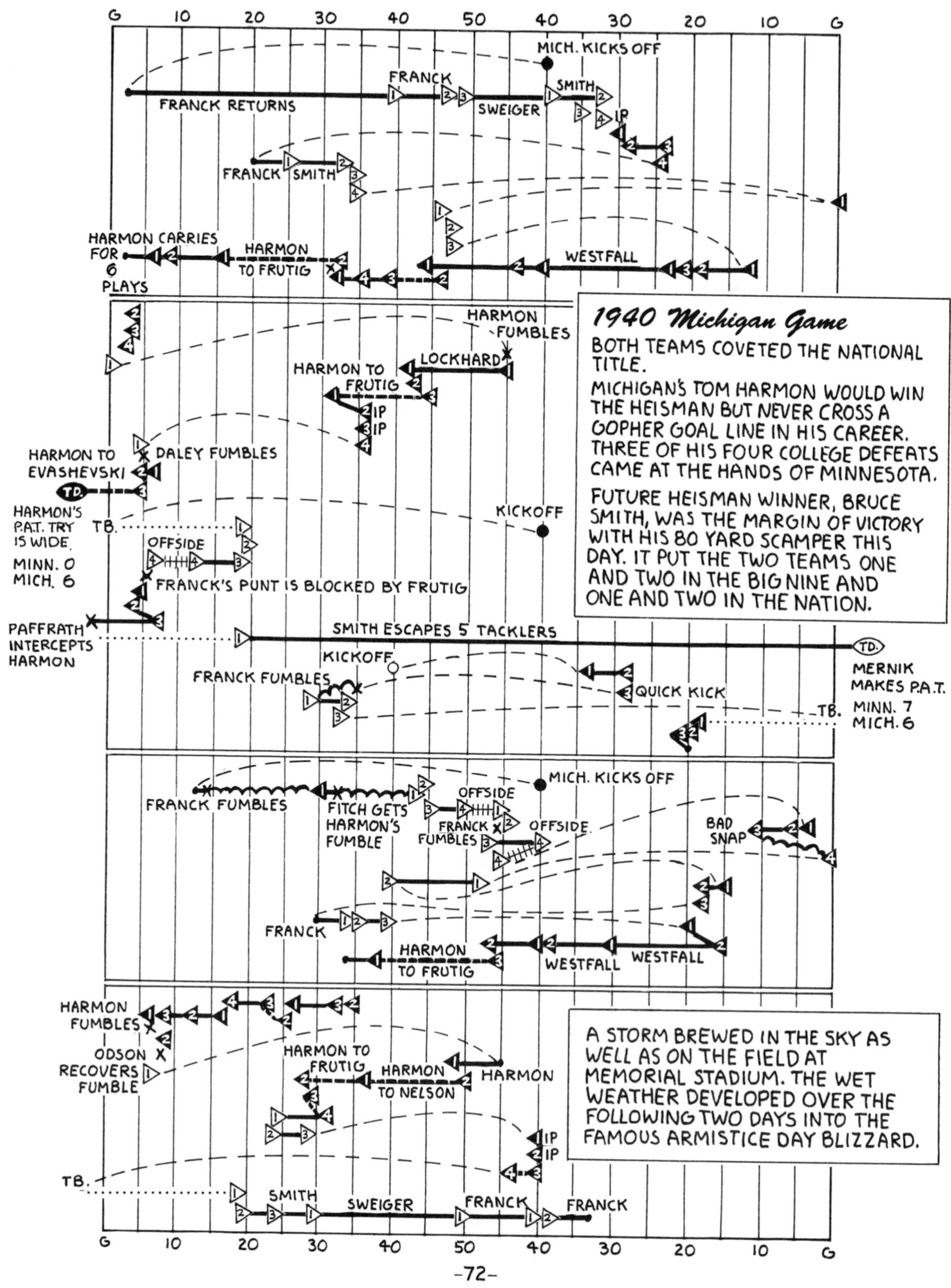
1940 Michigan Game
BOTH TEAMS COVETED THE NATIONAL TITLE.
MICHIGAN'S TOM HARMON WOULD WIN THE HEISMAN BUT NEVER CROSS A GOPHER GOAL LINE IN HIS CAREER. THREE OF HIS FOUR COLLEGE DEFEATS CAME AT THE HANDS OF MINNESOTA.
FUTURE HEISMAN WINNER, BRUCE SMITH, WAS THE MARGIN OF VICTORY WITH HIS 80 YARD SCAMPER THIS DAY. IT PUT THE TWO TEAMS ONE AND TWO IN THE BIG NINE AND ONE AND TWO IN THE NATION.
A STORM BREWED IN THE SKY AS WELL AS ON THE FIELD AT MEMORIAL STADIUM. THE WET WEATHER DEVELOPED OVER THE FOLLOWING TWO DAYS INTO THE FAMOUS ARMISTICE DAY BLIZZARD.
MICH. KICKS OFF
FRANCK RETURNS
FRANCK
SWEIGER
SMITH
IP
FRANCK
SMITH
HARMON CARRIES FOR 6 PLAYS
HARMON TO FRUTIG
WESTFALL
HARMON FUMBLES
LOCKHARD
HARMON TO FRUTIG
IP
IP
DALEY FUMBLES
HARMON TO EVASHEVSKI
TD.
HARMON'S P.A.T. TRY IS WIDE
TB.
KICKOFF
OFFSIDE
MINN. 0
MICH. 6
FRANCK'S PUNT IS BLOCKED BY FRUTIG
PAFFRATH INTERCEPTS HARMON
SMITH ESCAPES 5 TACKLERS
TD.
MERNIK MAKES P.A.T.
MINN. 7
MICH. 6
KICKOFF
FRANCK FUMBLES
QUICK KICK
TB.
MICH. KICKS OFF
FRANCK FUMBLES
FITCH GETS HARMON'S FUMBLE
OFFSIDE
FRANCK FUMBLES
OFFSIDE
BAD SNAP
FRANCK
HARMON TO FRUTIG
WESTFALL
WESTFALL
HARMON FUMBLES
ODSON RECOVERS FUMBLE
HARMON TO FRUTIG
HARMON TO NELSON
HARMON
IP
IP
TB.
SMITH
SWEIGER
FRANCK
FRANCK

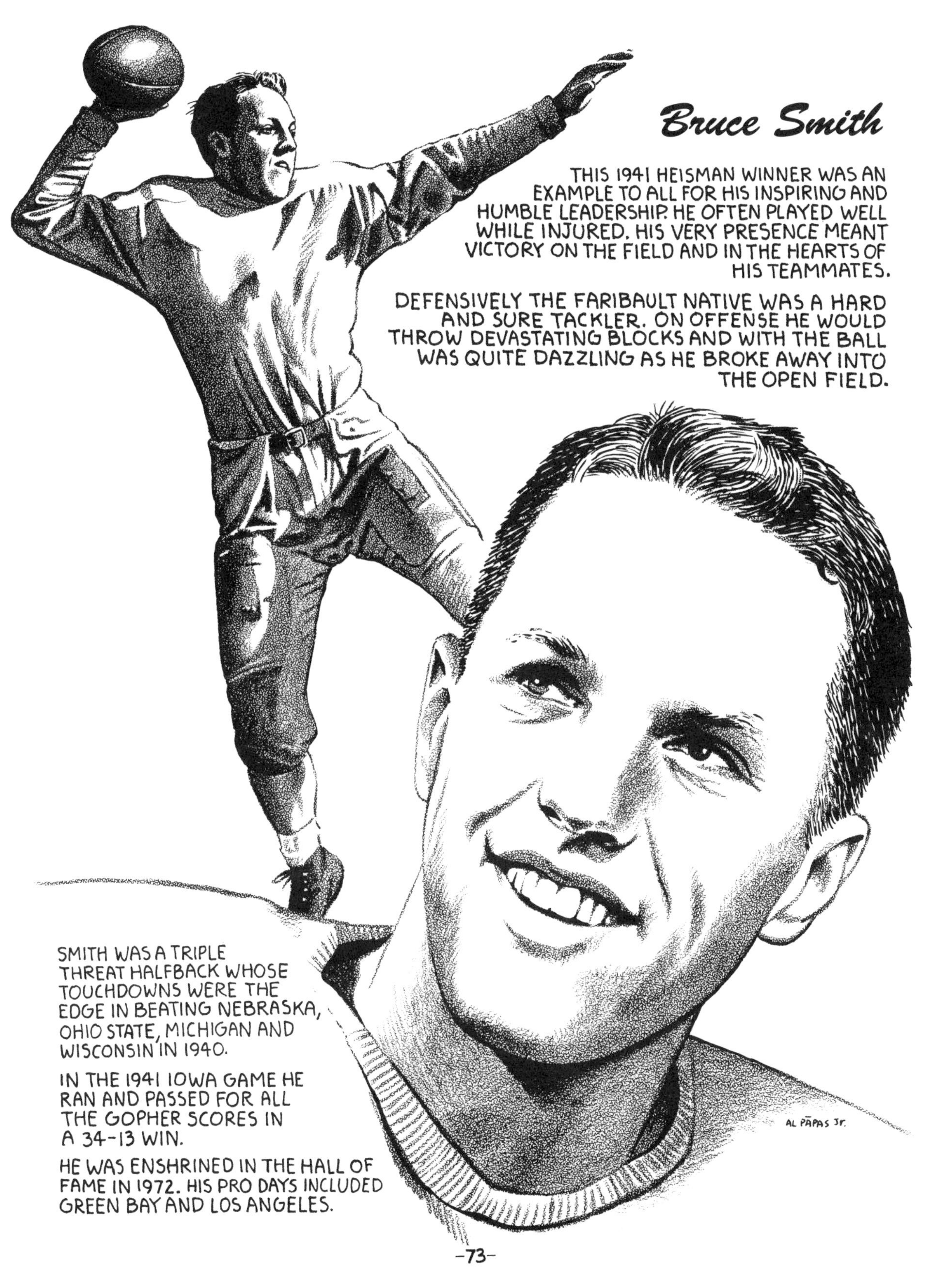

Bruce Smith

THIS 1941 HEISMAN WINNER WAS AN EXAMPLE TO ALL FOR HIS INSPIRING AND HUMBLE LEADERSHIP. HE OFTEN PLAYED WELL WHILE INJURED. HIS VERY PRESENCE MEANT VICTORY ON THE FIELD AND IN THE HEARTS OF HIS TEAMMATES.

DEFENSIVELY THE FARIBAULT NATIVE WAS A HARD AND SURE TACKLER. ON OFFENSE HE WOULD THROW DEVASTATING BLOCKS AND WITH THE BALL WAS QUITE DAZZLING AS HE BROKE AWAY INTO THE OPEN FIELD.

SMITH WAS A TRIPLE THREAT HALFBACK WHOSE TOUCHDOWNS WERE THE EDGE IN BEATING NEBRASKA, OHIO STATE, MICHIGAN AND WISCONSIN IN 1940.

IN THE 1941 IOWA GAME HE RAN AND PASSED FOR ALL THE GOPHER SCORES IN A 34-13 WIN.

HE WAS ENSHRINED IN THE HALL OF FAME IN 1972. HIS PRO DAYS INCLUDED GREEN BAY AND LOS ANGELES.

The Talking Play

MINNESOTA WAS ON ITS WAY TO THE NATIONAL TITLE IN 1941 WHEN IT MET UP WITH NORTHWESTERN. THE WILDCATS WERE PRIMED TO UPSET THE GOPHERS AS THEY HAD DONE IN 1936. THEY MADE A HABIT OF UPSETTING BIERMAN-COACHED TEAMS. WHEN BIERMAN WAS AT TULANE THEY ENDED A LONG WINNING STRING OF HIS THERE, TOO.

IN THIS GAME MINNESOTA OPENED THE SCORING WITH A SAFETY IN THE FIRST QUARTER. TOWARD THE END OF THE HALF THE GREAT PASSER, OTTO GRAHAM, TOSSED ONE TO THE END ZONE TO PUT NORTHWESTERN UP 7-2. BRUCE SMITH HAD BEEN TAKEN FROM THE GAME WITH A LEG INJURY, TO MAKE MATTERS WORSE.

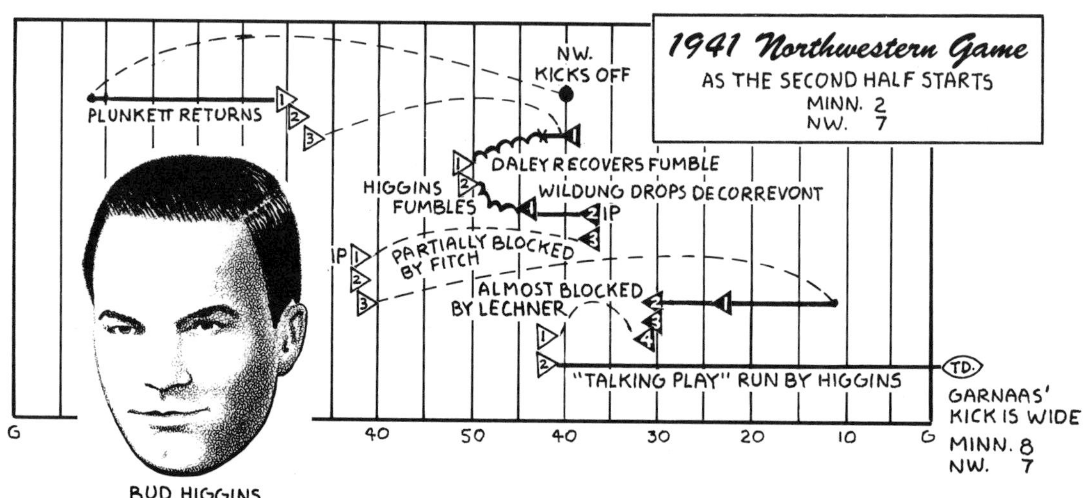

BUD HIGGINS

MINNESOTA WAS PLAYING THE BETTER GAME BUT SIMPLY COULDN'T SCORE. FINALLY IN THE THIRD QUARTER A WILDCAT PUNT WAS PARTIALLY BLOCKED. MINNESOTA LOOKED READY TO GET SOMETHING STARTED.

FIRST DOWN GOT NOWHERE. THEN WITH PLAYERS STANDING AROUND ENGAGED IN TALK, THE CENTER PICKED UP THE BALL AND FLIPPED IT UNDERHAND TO BUD HIGGINS. HE WAS THE SMALLEST GUY ON THE TEAM. SUDDENLY HE WAS DASHING AROUND RIGHT END FOR PAY DIRT. HE WAS LED BY URBAN ODSON, THE BIGGEST PLAYER IN THE COUNTRY.

NO ONE NOTICED THE PLAY BEGIN BUT IT WAS GAINING ATTENTION NOW. ODSON DOWNED ONE AWAKENING DEFENDER AND THEN ANOTHER AS HIGGINS DODGED HIS WAY DOWN THE FIELD. TWO WILDCATS HAD A CHANCE FOR HIM AT THE GOAL LINE BUT HE BULLDOZED HIS 155 POUNDS OVER FOR THE SCORE.

IT WASN'T THE FIRST TIME IN HISTORY SUCH A PLAY HAD BEEN USED. TO MAKE SURE IT WOULD COUNT THE GOPHERS EXPLAINED IT TO THE OFFICIALS BEFORE THE GAME AND WARNED THEM AS TO WHEN IT WOULD BEGIN. THE OFFICIALS PAID STRICT ATTENTION FOR ANYTHING WRONG.

THE IDEA WAS TO DISTRACT NORTWESTERN WITH TALK WHILE THE LINEMEN STOOD STILL TO THE RIGHT OF THE BALL. THE BACKS ALSO STOOD MOTIONLESS. THE BALL WAS PUT IN PLAY AS IN TOUCH FOOTBALL STYLE. IT TURNED OUT TO BE THE EDGE TO WIN. SINCE NO ONE BUT THE GOPHERS AND OFFICIALS KNEW THE PLAY WAS COMING, NO CAMERAMEN CAUGHT THE START ON FILM.

NORTHWESTERN OBJECTED, BUT TO NO AVAIL. CONTROVERSY CONTINUED IN THE NATIONAL NEWS.

PEARL HARBOR WAS ATTACKED A MONTH AFTER THE GAME. IT BROUGHT THIS COMMENT AS REPORTED IN THE MINNEAPOLIS TIMES: SEC. TAYLOR..."BERNIE BIERMAN'S EFFORTS TO CONCEAL THE FINE POINTS OF THAT FAST PLAY HIS TEAM PULLED TO DEFEAT NORTHWESTERN—THE PLAY NOBODY SAW—WERE IN VAIN. THE JAPANESE GOT THE IDEA ALL RIGHT. THEY ENGAGED US IN CONVERSATION AND SNAPPED THE BALL WHILE WE WEREN'T LOOKING."

Dick Wildung
DICK WILDUNG WAS A CONSENSUS ALL-AMERICAN IN BOTH 1941 AND 42. BERNIE BIERMAN CALLED HIM HIS BEST TACKLE.
HE WAS BORN IN ST. PAUL BUT CAME TO THE GOPHERS BY WAY OF LUVERNE HIGH SCHOOL.
THOUGH NOT BIG BY TODAY'S STANDARDS, JUST OVER 200 POUNDS, HE HAD SAVVY WHICH WAS PUT IN ACTION BY HIS AGILITY. HE SCORED FOUR TOUCHDOWNS AGAINST PITTSBURGH IN 1942. HE WAS NAMED TO THE HALL OF FAME.
WILDUNG SPENT HIS LONG PROFESSIONAL CAREER WITH GREEN BAY.
AL PĀPAS Jr.

Bill Garnaas

GARNAAS CAME FROM NORTHFIELD BY WAY OF MINNEAPOLIS MARSHALL.

HE PLAYED QUARTERBACK AND DID THE PUNTING. AGAINST PITTSBURGH, IN HIS ALL-AMERICAN SOPHOMORE YEAR OF 1941, HE LET ONE FLY 75 YARDS WITH NO RETURN.

HE WAS THE LEADING GOPHER PASS RECEIVER AND MANAGED TO PICK OFF A COUPLE FROM MICHIGAN, TOO.

HE DID EXTRA DUTY BY SWITCHING FROM HIS REGULAR POSITION TO FILL IN FOR BRUCE SMITH AND HERMAN FRICKEY WHEN THEY WERE INJURED.

IN HIS JUNIOR YEAR GARNAAS WAS UNABLE TO REPEAT AS ALL-AMERICAN DUE TO MISSING TOO MANY GAMES BECAUSE OF INJURY. AGAIN IN HIS LAST YEAR HE MISSED BECAUSE HE WAS CALLED INTO THE MILITARY AT MID-SEASON.

AFTER WORLD WAR II HE PLAYED PRO FOR PITTSBURGH.

IN THE 1942 OPENER GARNAAS GOT A TORN KNEE LIGAMENT. IT PUT HIM OUT OF THE LINE-UP FOR THREE GAMES. HE CAME BACK IN TIME FOR MICHIGAN TO KICK THE LAST EVER DROP-KICK SCORED IN THE BIG TEN. IT CAME DURING THE HURRY OF THE CLOCK RUNNING OUT IN THE FIRST HALF. IT PROVED TO BE THE GAME WINNER.

Charles W. Schultz

THIS TACKLE, FROM ST. PAUL, PLAYED FOR THE GOPHERS FROM 1935-37.

AFTER LEAVING MINNESOTA HE WENT ON TO PLAY FOR GREEN BAY.

WHEN WAR BROKE OUT HE ENLISTED AND WAS "ASSIGNED" TO PLAY FOOTBALL FOR IOWA PRE-FLIGHT AND HIS FORMER COACH, BERNIE BIERMAN.

PROFESSIONAL AND COLLEGE PLAYERS LINED UP TOGETHER ON THIS TEAM. THEY COULDN'T BE AWAY FROM CAMP MORE THAN 48 HOURS SO THEY PLAYED AGAINST COLLEGE TEAMS NEARBY. IT WAS UNDER THIS CIRCUMSTANCE HE WAS NAMED BY LOOK MAGAZINE TO THE ALL-SERVICE TEAM IN 1942.

George Svendsen
SVENDSEN WAS A CENTER HAILING FROM MINNEAPOLIS MARSHALL.
IN 1935 HE WAS ANOTHER VICTIM OF THE FRESHMAN ELIGIBILITY RULE AND WAS FORCED TO MISS HIS SENIOR YEAR.
HE BECAME THE FIRST IN A LONG STRING OF GOPHERS TO PLAY FOR GREEN BAY.
UPON PLAYING FOR IOWA PREFLIGHT IN 1942, HE WON ACCLAIM BY COLLIERS AND LOOK MAGAZINES ON THEIR ALL-SERVICE TEAM. THIS SOMEWHAT MADE UP FOR THE ALL-AMERICAN RECOGNITION HE SURELY WOULD HAVE MADE IN 1935.
AFTER THE WAR HE CAME HOME TO COACH THE GOPHER LINE FROM 1945-50.
AL PAPAS Jr.

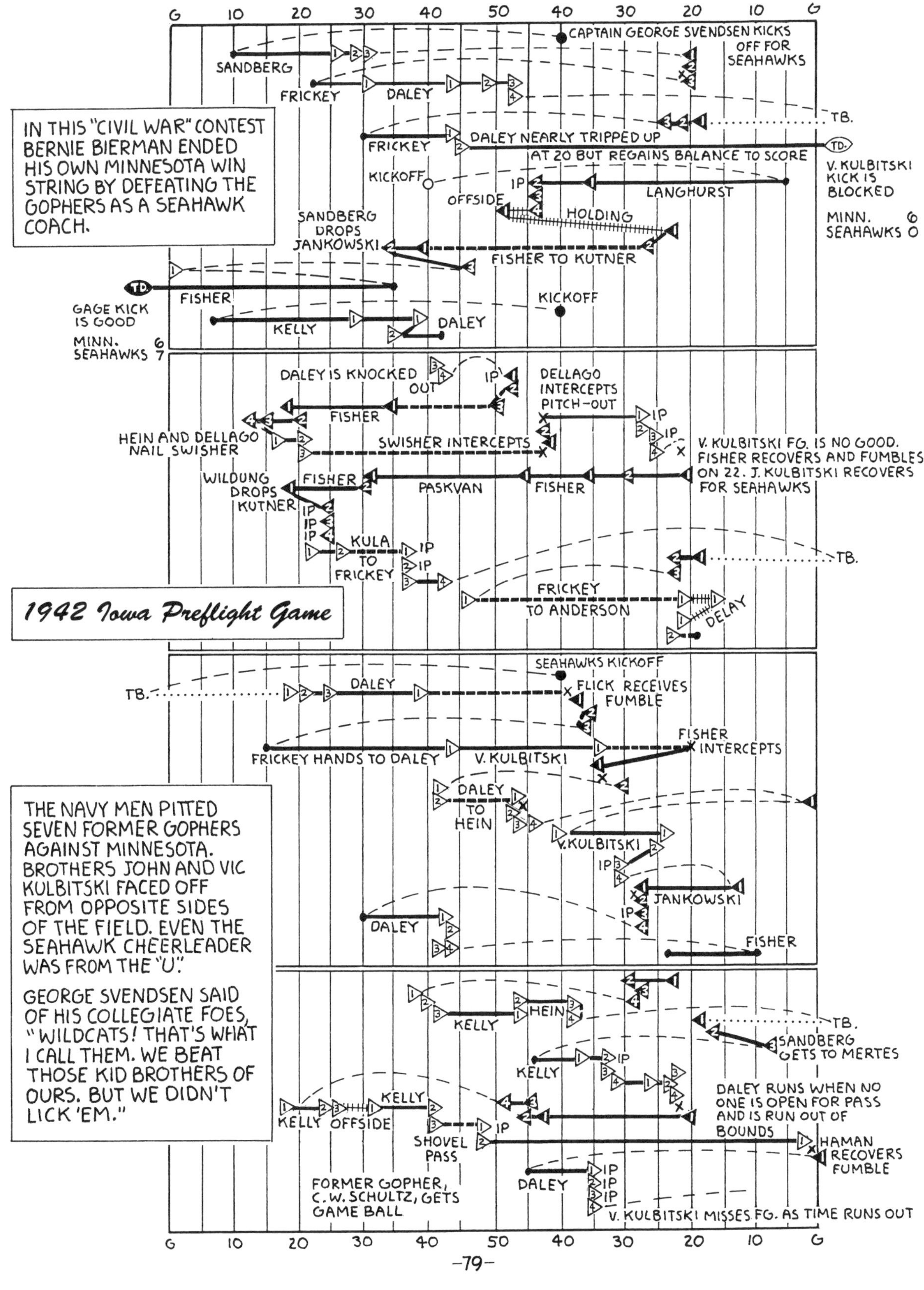
1942 Iowa Preflight Game
IN THIS "CIVIL WAR" CONTEST BERNIE BIERMAN ENDED HIS OWN MINNESOTA WIN STRING BY DEFEATING THE GOPHERS AS A SEAHAWK COACH.
THE NAVY MEN PITTED SEVEN FORMER GOPHERS AGAINST MINNESOTA. BROTHERS JOHN AND VIC KULBITSKI FACED OFF FROM OPPOSITE SIDES OF THE FIELD. EVEN THE SEAHAWK CHEERLEADER WAS FROM THE "U".
GEORGE SVENDSEN SAID OF HIS COLLEGIATE FOES, "WILDCATS! THAT'S WHAT I CALL THEM. WE BEAT THOSE KID BROTHERS OF OURS. BUT WE DIDN'T LICK 'EM."
G 10 20 30 40 50 40 30 20 10 G
CAPTAIN GEORGE SVENDSEN KICKS OFF FOR SEAHAWKS
SANDBERG
FRICKEY
DALEY
TB.
FRICKEY
DALEY NEARLY TRIPPED UP AT 20 BUT REGAINS BALANCE TO SCORE
TD.
V. KULBITSKI KICK IS BLOCKED
KICKOFF
IP
LANGHURST
OFFSIDE
HOLDING
MINN. 6
SEAHAWKS 0
SANDBERG DROPS JANKOWSKI
FISHER TO KUTNER
TD.
FISHER
GAGE KICK IS GOOD
KICKOFF
KELLY
DALEY
MINN. 6
SEAHAWKS 7
DALEY IS KNOCKED OUT
IP
DELLAGO INTERCEPTS PITCH-OUT
FISHER
IP
IP
HEIN AND DELLAGO NAIL SWISHER
SWISHER INTERCEPTS
V. KULBITSKI FG. IS NO GOOD. FISHER RECOVERS AND FUMBLES ON 22. J. KULBITSKI RECOVERS FOR SEAHAWKS
WILDUNG DROPS KUTNER
FISHER
PASKVAN
FISHER
IP
IP
IP
KULA TO FRICKEY
IP
IP
TB.
FRICKEY TO ANDERSON
DELAY
SEAHAWKS KICKOFF
TB.
DALEY
FLICK RECEIVES FUMBLE
FISHER INTERCEPTS
FRICKEY HANDS TO DALEY
V. KULBITSKI
DALEY TO HEIN
V. KULBITSKI
IP
JANKOWSKI
IP
DALEY
FISHER
KELLY
HEIN
TB.
SANDBERG GETS TO MERTES
IP
KELLY
DALEY RUNS WHEN NO ONE IS OPEN FOR PASS AND IS RUN OUT OF BOUNDS
KELLY
KELLY OFFSIDE
IP
SHOVEL PASS
HAMAN RECOVERS FUMBLE
IP
IP
IP
DALEY
FORMER GOPHER, C.W. SCHULTZ, GETS GAME BALL
V. KULBITSKI MISSES FG. AS TIME RUNS OUT
G 10 20 30 40 50 40 30 20 10 G

Bill Daley

DALEY WAS A THREE YEAR IRON MAN FROM MELROSE WHO PLAYED FOR TWO GOPHER NATIONAL CHAMPIONSHIP TEAMS.

AFTER COLLEGE HE PLAYED PROFESSIONALLY FOR BROOKLYN, MIAMI AND CHICAGO.

WITH THE OUTBREAK OF WORLD WAR II HE HAD TO TRANSFER TO MICHIGAN WHERE THERE WAS A MILITARY UNIT. THIS WAS SO HE COULD FINISH HIS SCHOOLING BEFORE GOING INTO THE SERVICE. HE REPORTED TO MINNESOTA IN 1943 BUT ENDED UP AT MICHIGAN WHERE, AS A BACK, HE EARNED CONSENSUS ALL-AMERICAN HONORS. BOTH SCHOOLS CLAIM HIM AS THEIR OWN.

IN 1941, AGAINST MICHIGAN, DALEY MADE TWO INTERCEPTIONS. ONE WAS IN THE END ZONE AND THE OTHER ON HIS OWN 12 TO HALT THE WOLVERINES AT THE END. MINNESOTA WON 7-0.

AS ONE OF THE FASTEST MEN ON THE SQUAD HE RAN A 73 YARD OPEN FIELD SCORE AGAINST ILLINOIS WITH BRUCE SMITH DOING THE BLOCKING. BY THE END OF THE SEASON HE ACTUALLY RUSHED MORE YARDS IN MORE TRIES WITH A HIGHER YARDS PER CARRY AVERAGE THAN HIS HEISMAN TEAMMATE.

UNDER THE SAME CIRCUMSTANCES AS DALEY, HERB HEIN WON HIS ALL-AMERICAN HONORS WHILE AWAY FROM MINNESOTA.
Herb Hein
HE WAS ALL-AMERICAN END FOR NORTH-WESTERN IN 1943.
MINNESOTA
AS A WILDCAT, HEIN SCORED FROM A PASS FOR THE FIRST TOUCHDOWN AGAINST HIS MINNESOTA TEAMMATES. 36 OF NORTHWESTERN'S 42 POINTS, THAT DAY, WERE SCORED BY GOPHERS IN MILITARY UNITS.
HEIN RETURNED TO MINNESOTA AFTER THE WAR TO PLAY OUT HIS SENIOR YEAR. INJURIES PREVENTED HIS REPEATING AS ALL-AMERICAN.
AL PĀPAS Jr.

Wayne "Red" Williams

"RED" WILLIAMS HAD A BIG DAY AGAINST IOWA IN 1943 BY SCORING FOUR TOUCHDOWNS. HE THEN HAD A BIG YEAR AGAINST EVERYBODY IN 1944. HE LED THE NATION IN TOTAL YARDS GAINED THROUGH RUSHING, PUNT AND KICK RETURNS. HE MADE 1467 YARDS WHILE AVERAGING 163 YARDS PER GAME.

AFTER A BACK INJURY HE CONTINUED PLAY WHILE WEARING A HARNESS.

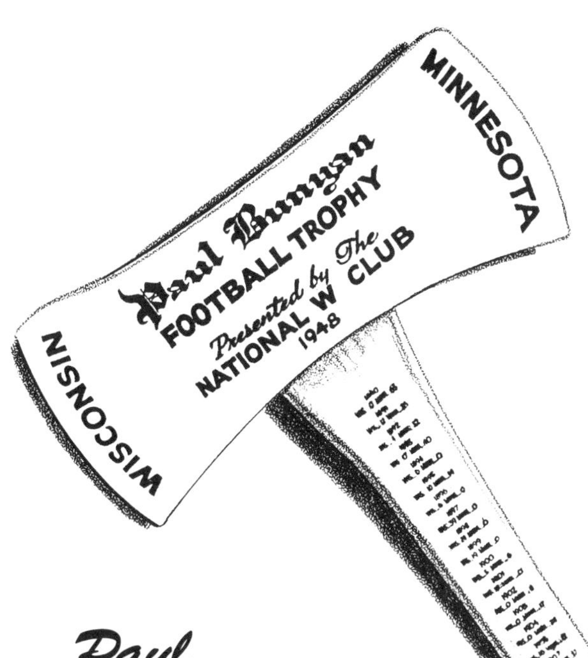

Paul Bunyan Ax

ORIGINALLY IT WAS THE SLAB OF BACON TROPHY THAT WENT TO THE WINNER OF THE MINNESOTA-WISCONSIN GAME. IT WAS CREATED IN 1930 BY DR. R.B. FOUCH OF MINNEAPOLIS. IT HAD A BACON SLAB DONE IN BLACK WALNUT WITH A FOOTBALL ON TOP. DEPENDING ON HOW IT WAS DISPLAYED IT SHOWED AN "M" OR "W" ON THE BALL. HALF THE BALL WAS GOLD AND HALF WAS RED.

IN 1948 THE WISCONSIN "W" CLUB INTRODUCED THE PAUL BUNYAN AX WHICH IS THE PRESENT-DAY TROPHY. THE GAME SCORES FROM 1890 TO THE PRESENT ARE RECORDED ON THE LONG HANDLE.

THE SERIES BETWEEN THESE TWO TEAMS IS THE LONGEST IN DIVISION I-A FOOTBALL. IT IS THE THIRD LONGEST CONTINUOUS SERIES. ITS ONLY INTERRUPTION CAME IN 1906. THE REASON WAS DUE TO PRESIDENT THEODORE ROOSEVELT'S DESIRE TO COOL OFF HOT RIVALRIES. THERE HAD FLARED UP A RASH OF GRID INJURIES IN THE LAND AND THIS WAS ONE ACTION THOUGHT TO HELP END THEM.

THE MINNESOTA-WISCONSIN SERIES HAS BASICALLY BEEN PLAYED UNDER GOOD FEELINGS, THOUGH IT DIDN'T START OUT THAT WAY. IN 1890 AN OVERCONFIDENT TEAM FROM MADISON CAME TO TOWN. THEY REFUSED TO SET FOOT ON THE MINNESOTA CAMPUS. THIS RILED THE GOPHERS WHO PROMISED ONE ANOTHER TO GIVE A GOOD SHOWING. THEY DID JUST THAT TO THE TUNE OF 63-0. GENE PATTERSON CHALKED UP SEVEN TOUCHDOWNS.

THOUGH MINNESOTA HAS WON MOST OF THE GAMES, WISCONSIN CAN BE A PAIN IN THE FOOT. THE FOOT OF PAT O'DAY, THE KICKER FROM AUSTRALIA, THAT IS.

IN 1897 O'DAY MADE AN ALL-TIME RECORD PUNT OF 110 YARDS AGAINST THE GOPHERS. A COUPLE OF YEARS LATER, DURING A TIGHT GAME, MINNESOTA PUNTED TO HIM. HE RECEIVED AND DROP-KICKED IT RIGHT BACK FOR A 50 YARD FIELD GOAL WHILE ON THE RUN. THE ACT DEVASTATED MINNESOTA. WISCONSIN ROMPED 19-0.

WISCONSIN WON AGAIN IN 1908 WITH AN END LYING ON THE GROUND BY THE SIDELINE AND THEN DASHING FOR AN UNEXPECTED PASS. MINNESOTA MUST HAVE LEARNED FROM IT BECAUSE THEY USED THE SAME PLAY THE FOLLOWING WEEK TO BEAT CARLISLE.

MINNESOTA'S FIRST HOMECOMING GAME WAS PLAYED AGAINST THE BADGERS IN 1914. THE BADGERS' FIRST HOMECOMING WAS AGAINST THE GOPHERS IN 1919. MINNESOTA WON BOTH CONTESTS.

TIES HAVE SEEMED TO COME IN BUNCHES BETWEEN THESE TWO TEAMS. THE SEASONS OF 1923-24-25 WERE ALL TIES AS WELL AS 1952 & 53. THE LATTER TWO GAMES WERE BY IDENTICAL SCORES 21-21. MINNESOTA HAS TIED WITH WISCONSIN MORE THAN ANY OTHER TEAM.

FROM 1933-82 THEY SAVED ONE ANOTHER FOR PLAYING LAST ON THEIR SCHEDULES. MANY A TIME THE UNDERDOG WOULD WIN TO END THE TITLE HOPES FOR THE OTHER.

AL PĀPAS Jr.

Leo Nomellini

LEO "THE LION" NOMELLINI CAME FROM CHICAGO, THOUGH BORN IN ITALY. HE REPORTED AS A FULL-BACK BUT WENT ON TO BE A CONSENSUS ALL-AMERICAN TACKLE IN 1948 AND 49.

A STARTER BROKE HIS LEG ON THE FIRST PLAY OF THE 1946 SEASON AND THE FRESHMAN NOMELLINI WENT IN TO REPLACE HIM. IT WAS THE FIRST GAME HE HAD EVER PLAYED IN HIS LIFE. HE WAS A REGULAR BY THE FOLLOWING YEAR AT GUARD. AT 6'2" AND 250 POUNDS HE WAS ONE OF THE FASTEST LINEMEN ON THE SQUAD AS HE DEVELOPED INTO ALL-TIME ALL-BIG TEN CALIBER.

"GIUSEPPE" WAS A FIRST ROUND DRAFT PICK IN THE N.F.L. AND WAS ALL-PRO HIS FIRST YEAR. HE MADE THE HALL OF FAME AS A GOPHER AND AS A PRO.

"TWO-TON TONNY" WAS A UNANIMOUS ALL-AMERICAN AT CENTER IN 1949 WHO BECAME A MEMBER OF THE HALL OF FAME.

SOME COLLEGE SCOUTS SOUGHT THE MINNEAPOLIS EDISON ATHLETE TO PLAY BASKETBALL AND NOT FOOTBALL.

Clayton Tonnemaker

NATIONAL CHAMPION MICHIGAN COULD GAIN ONLY 22 YARDS RUSHING AGAINST TONNEMAKER AND NOMELLINI IN 1948. THE FOLLOWING WEEK THIS DUO HELD INDIANA TO MINUS 23 YARDS RUSHING AND 73 YARDS OVER-ALL.

IN THE EAST-WEST GAME TONNEMAKER INTERCEPTED A PASS AND RETURNED 67 YARDS FOR A SCORE.

HE WAS DRAFTED BY GREEN BAY IN THE FIRST ROUND AND PLAYED IN THE PRO BOWL HIS FIRST SEASON.

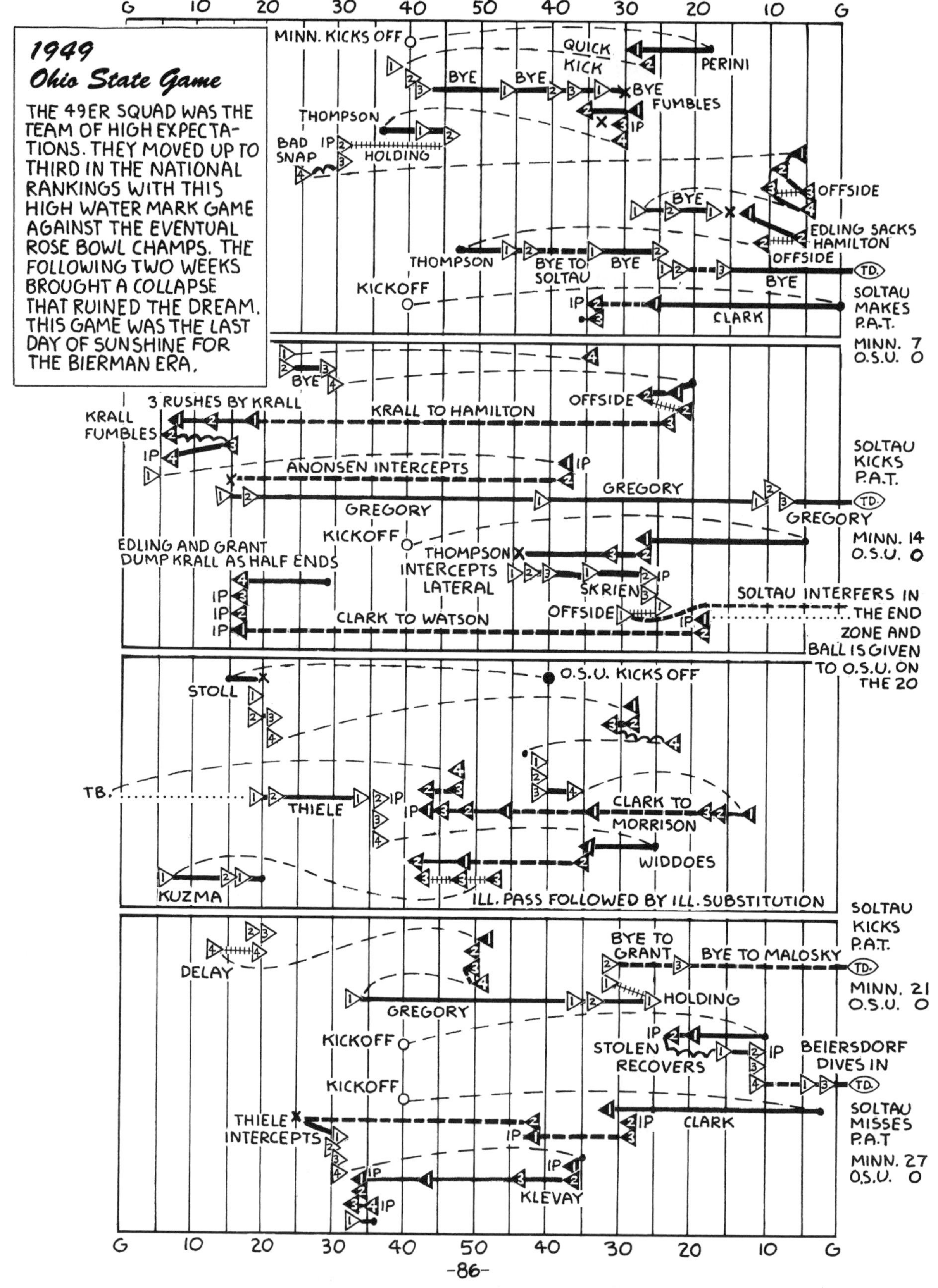

1949
Ohio State Game
THE 49ER SQUAD WAS THE TEAM OF HIGH EXPECTATIONS. THEY MOVED UP TO THIRD IN THE NATIONAL RANKINGS WITH THIS HIGH WATER MARK GAME AGAINST THE EVENTUAL ROSE BOWL CHAMPS. THE FOLLOWING TWO WEEKS BROUGHT A COLLAPSE THAT RUINED THE DREAM. THIS GAME WAS THE LAST DAY OF SUNSHINE FOR THE BIERMAN ERA.
MINN. KICKS OFF
QUICK KICK
PERINI
BYE
BYE
BYE FUMBLES
THOMPSON
IP
BAD SNAP
IP
HOLDING
OFFSIDE
BYE
EDLING SACKS HAMILTON
OFFSIDE
THOMPSON
BYE TO SOLTAU
BYE
BYE
TD.
KICKOFF
IP
CLARK
SOLTAU MAKES P.A.T.
MINN. 7
O.S.U. 0
BYE
OFFSIDE
3 RUSHES BY KRALL
KRALL FUMBLES
KRALL TO HAMILTON
IP
ANONSEN INTERCEPTS
IP
SOLTAU KICKS P.A.T.
GREGORY
GREGORY
TD.
GREGORY
KICKOFF
MINN. 14
O.S.U. 0
EDLING AND GRANT DUMP KRALL AS HALF ENDS
THOMPSON INTERCEPTS LATERAL
SKRIEN
IP
IP
IP
IP
CLARK TO WATSON
OFFSIDE
IP
SOLTAU INTERFERS IN THE END ZONE AND BALL IS GIVEN TO O.S.U. ON THE 20
O.S.U. KICKS OFF
STOLL
TB.
THIELE
IP
IP
CLARK TO MORRISON
WIDDOES
KUZMA
ILL. PASS FOLLOWED BY ILL. SUBSTITUTION
SOLTAU KICKS P.A.T.
DELAY
BYE TO GRANT
BYE TO MALOSKY
TD.
MINN. 21
O.S.U. 0
GREGORY
HOLDING
KICKOFF
IP
STOLEN RECOVERS
IP
BEIERSDORF DIVES IN
TD.
KICKOFF
THIELE INTERCEPTS
IP
IP
CLARK
SOLTAU MISSES P.A.T
MINN. 27
O.S.U. 0
IP
IP
IP
KLEVAY
G 10 20 30 40 50 40 30 20 10 G

"Bud" Grant

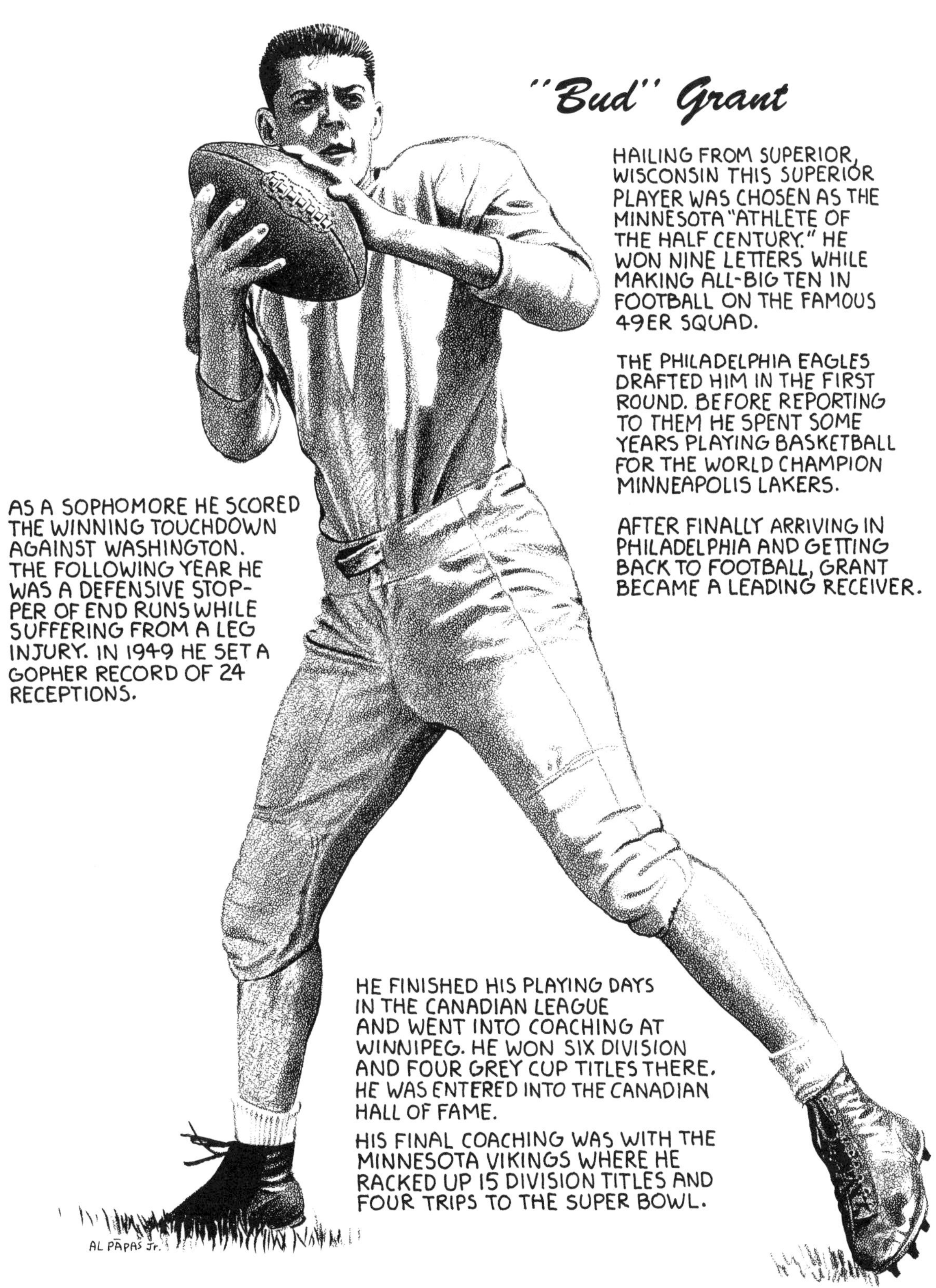

HAILING FROM SUPERIOR, WISCONSIN THIS SUPERIOR PLAYER WAS CHOSEN AS THE MINNESOTA "ATHLETE OF THE HALF CENTURY." HE WON NINE LETTERS WHILE MAKING ALL-BIG TEN IN FOOTBALL ON THE FAMOUS 49ER SQUAD.

THE PHILADELPHIA EAGLES DRAFTED HIM IN THE FIRST ROUND. BEFORE REPORTING TO THEM HE SPENT SOME YEARS PLAYING BASKETBALL FOR THE WORLD CHAMPION MINNEAPOLIS LAKERS.

AFTER FINALLY ARRIVING IN PHILADELPHIA AND GETTING BACK TO FOOTBALL, GRANT BECAME A LEADING RECEIVER.

AS A SOPHOMORE HE SCORED THE WINNING TOUCHDOWN AGAINST WASHINGTON. THE FOLLOWING YEAR HE WAS A DEFENSIVE STOPPER OF END RUNS WHILE SUFFERING FROM A LEG INJURY. IN 1949 HE SET A GOPHER RECORD OF 24 RECEPTIONS.

HE FINISHED HIS PLAYING DAYS IN THE CANADIAN LEAGUE AND WENT INTO COACHING AT WINNIPEG. HE WON SIX DIVISION AND FOUR GREY CUP TITLES THERE. HE WAS ENTERED INTO THE CANADIAN HALL OF FAME.

HIS FINAL COACHING WAS WITH THE MINNESOTA VIKINGS WHERE HE RACKED UP 15 DIVISION TITLES AND FOUR TRIPS TO THE SUPER BOWL.

GIEL WAS AN ALL-AMERICAN BASEBALL PITCHER. IN HIS JUNIOR YEAR HE TURNED DOWN A PRO OFFER SO HE COULD FINISH HIS FOOTBALL CAREER.

Paul Giel

THE WINONA GREAT DID IT ALL: CALL PLAYS, PASS, CATCH, RUSH, KICK, BLOCK, HOLD FOR CONVERSIONS AND BE A "TEAM" MAN. HE MADE ALL-AMERICAN HALFBACK IN 1952 AND WAS UNANIMOUS IN 1953. BOTH YEARS HE WAS BIG TEN M.V.P.

HE SCORED 212 OF HIS TEAM'S 443 POINTS IN THREE YEARS. HE NARROWLY MISSED THE HEISMAN BUT WAS STILL VOTED PLAYER OF THE YEAR AND BACK OF THE YEAR.

GIEL WAS INDUCTED INTO THE HALL OF FAME AND SERVED MINNESOTA AS ATHLETIC DIRECTOR LONGER THAN ANY OTHER.

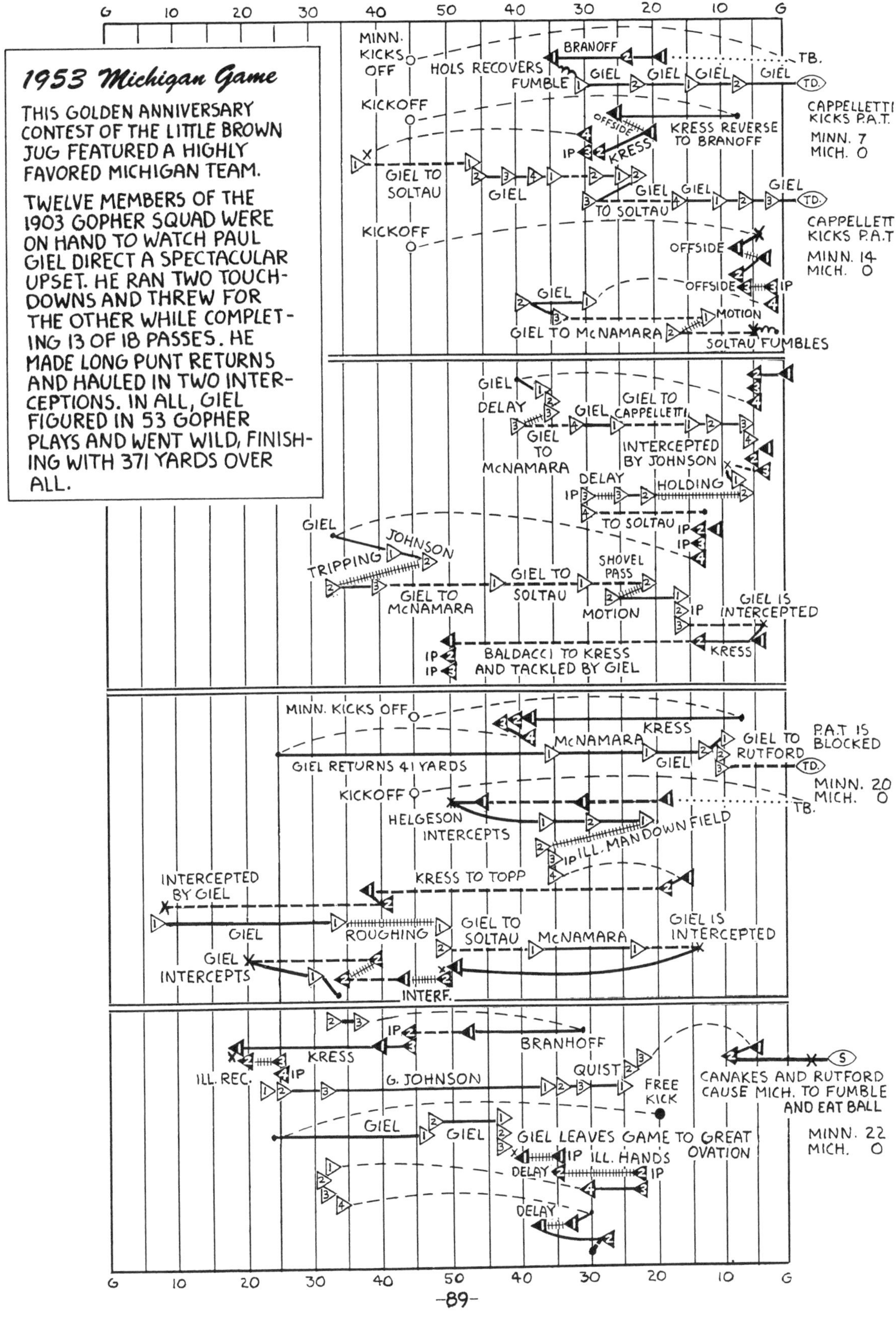

1953 Michigan Game
THIS GOLDEN ANNIVERSARY CONTEST OF THE LITTLE BROWN JUG FEATURED A HIGHLY FAVORED MICHIGAN TEAM.
TWELVE MEMBERS OF THE 1903 GOPHER SQUAD WERE ON HAND TO WATCH PAUL GIEL DIRECT A SPECTACULAR UPSET. HE RAN TWO TOUCHDOWNS AND THREW FOR THE OTHER WHILE COMPLETING 13 OF 18 PASSES. HE MADE LONG PUNT RETURNS AND HAULED IN TWO INTERCEPTIONS. IN ALL, GIEL FIGURED IN 53 GOPHER PLAYS AND WENT WILD, FINISHING WITH 371 YARDS OVER ALL.
G 10 20 30 40 50 40 30 20 10 G
MINN. KICKS OFF
BRANOFF
TB.
HOLS RECOVERS FUMBLE
GIEL
GIEL
GIEL
GIEL
TD.
KICKOFF
CAPPELLETTI KICKS P.A.T.
MINN. 7
MICH. 0
OFFSIDE
KRESS REVERSE TO BRANOFF
KRESS
IP
GIEL TO SOLTAU
GIEL
GIEL TO SOLTAU
GIEL
GIEL
TD.
KICKOFF
CAPPELLETTI KICKS P.A.T
MINN. 14
MICH. 0
OFFSIDE
OFFSIDE
IP
GIEL
MOTION
GIEL TO McNAMARA
SOLTAU FUMBLES
GIEL
DELAY
GIEL
GIEL TO CAPPELLETTI
GIEL TO McNAMARA
INTERCEPTED BY JOHNSON
DELAY
HOLDING
IP
TO SOLTAU
IP
IP
GIEL
JOHNSON
TRIPPING
GIEL TO SOLTAU
SHOVEL PASS
GIEL TO McNAMARA
MOTION
IP
GIEL IS INTERCEPTED
BALDACCI TO KRESS AND TACKLED BY GIEL
KRESS
IP
IP
MINN. KICKS OFF
KRESS
McNAMARA
GIEL TO RUTFORD
P.A.T IS BLOCKED
GIEL
GIEL RETURNS 41 YARDS
TD.
MINN. 20
MICH. 0
KICKOFF
TB.
HELGESON INTERCEPTS
IP ILL. MAN DOWN FIELD
INTERCEPTED BY GIEL
KRESS TO TOPP
GIEL
ROUGHING
GIEL TO SOLTAU
McNAMARA
GIEL IS INTERCEPTED
GIEL INTERCEPTS
INTERF.
IP
BRANHOFF
KRESS
ILL. REC.
IP
G. JOHNSON
QUIST
CANAKES AND RUTFORD CAUSE MICH. TO FUMBLE AND EAT BALL
S
FREE KICK
GIEL
GIEL
GIEL LEAVES GAME TO GREAT OVATION
IP
ILL. HANDS
DELAY
IP
MINN. 22
MICH. 0
DELAY
G 10 20 30 40 50 40 30 20 10 G

Dr. George Hauser

THE FORMER MINNESOTA ALL-AMERICAN SERVED AS LINE COACH FROM THE EARLY 1930'S. WITH THE OUTBREAK OF WORLD WAR II THE TEAM WAS BROKEN UP FOR MILITARY EXPEDIENCY. 17 PLAYERS WERE LOST. EVEN BIERMAN WAS SENT OFF. HAUSER TOOK OVER FOR THE DURATION. ABOUT 350 OTHER COLLEGES SUSPENDED FOOTBALL ALTOGETHER DURING THIS TIME.

ALTHOUGH BEING VICTORIOUS OVER WISCONSIN, HAUSER TOLD THE BADGERS TO HOLD THE "SLAB OF BACON" GAME TROPHY UNTIL COMPLETION OF THE WAR.

AL PĀPAS Jr.

Wes Fesler

AFTER SUCCESS AS AN OHIO STATE ALL-AMERICAN AND COACH, WES FESLER DECIDED TO RETIRE FROM THE PRESSURE OF THE GAME. MINNESOTA TALKED HIM INTO GIVING COACHING ANOTHER TRY.

HIS SECOND YEAR WAS HIS MOST SUCCESSFUL AS A GOPHER. HIS RATHER AVERAGE TEAM HEADED BY AN OUTSTANDING LEADER, PAUL GIEL, ALMOST SNATCHED THE BIG TEN TITLE.

HIS HIGHLIGHT, HOWEVER, WAS THE STUNNING UPSET OF MICHIGAN IN HIS FINAL SEASON OF 1953.

WARMATH HAD BEEN AN END AT TENNESSEE IN THE 1930'S. HE HELD SEVERAL COACH-ING POSITIONS BEFORE COMING TO MINNESOTA IN 1954.
Murray Warmath
WHILE BEING A DRIVING PERFECTIONIST HE KEPT HIS PLAYERS LOOSE WITH HIS HUMOR AND WARM SMILE.
HE BELIEVED IN DEFENSE TO WIN GAMES BY CAPITAL-IZING WHEN OPPO-NENTS MADE MISTAKES.
AL PAPAS Jr.
WARMATH RECEIVED SEVERE TESTING IN 1958 AND 59. HE HELD HIS COURSE, WITH FAITH IN HIS PLAYERS AND HIMSELF, TO GO FROM LAST IN THE BIG TEN TO FIRST IN THE NATION. IN THIS RAGS TO RICHES ERA HE RECEIVED COACH OF THE YEAR RECOGNITION AND TOOK THE GOPHERS TO THE ROSE BOWL. OVER HIS CAREER HE DEVELOPED MANY PLAYERS WHO WENT ON INTO THE PROS.
AT DIFFERENT TIMES HE COACHED BOTH SIDES IN THE BLUE AND GREY GAME.

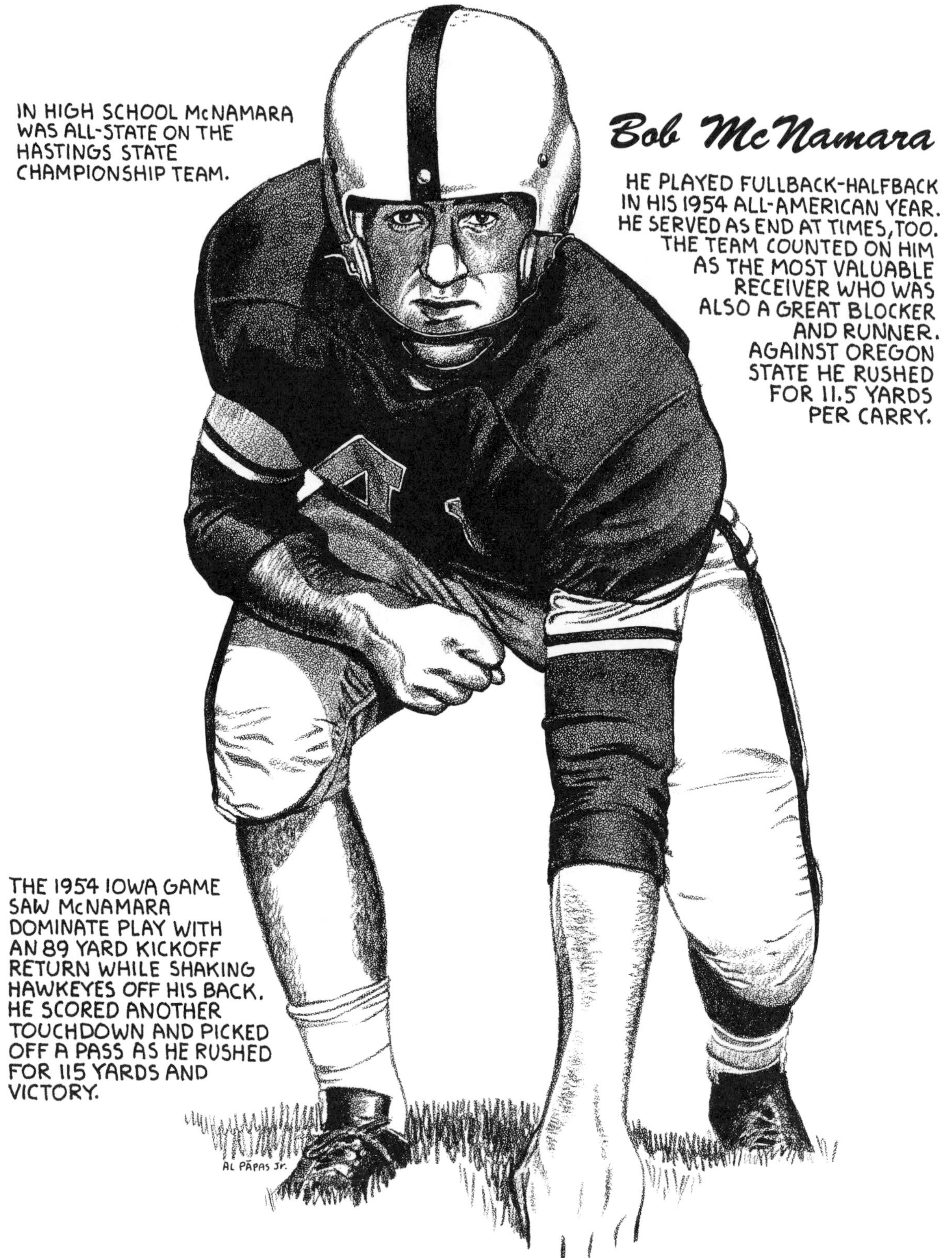
IN HIGH SCHOOL McNAMARA WAS ALL-STATE ON THE HASTINGS STATE CHAMPIONSHIP TEAM.
Bob McNamara
HE PLAYED FULLBACK-HALFBACK IN HIS 1954 ALL-AMERICAN YEAR. HE SERVED AS END AT TIMES, TOO. THE TEAM COUNTED ON HIM AS THE MOST VALUABLE RECEIVER WHO WAS ALSO A GREAT BLOCKER AND RUNNER. AGAINST OREGON STATE HE RUSHED FOR 11.5 YARDS PER CARRY.
THE 1954 IOWA GAME SAW McNAMARA DOMINATE PLAY WITH AN 89 YARD KICKOFF RETURN WHILE SHAKING HAWKEYES OFF HIS BACK. HE SCORED ANOTHER TOUCHDOWN AND PICKED OFF A PASS AS HE RUSHED FOR 115 YARDS AND VICTORY.
AL PĀPAS Jr.

Bob Hobert

BOB HOBERT, A TWIN, CAME FROM CHARLES CITY, IOWA. HE MADE ALL-AMERICAN IN 1956 AS A TACKLE AFTER HAVING STARTED EVERY GAME FROM HIS SOPHOMORE YEAR ON.

HE ALSO MADE THE ALL-ACADEMIC ALL-AMERICA TEAM AND BECAME THE FIRST GOPHER GRIDDER TO EARN PHI BETA KAPPA.

Tom Brown

COACH WARMATH CALLED "BROWNIE" A "ONE MAN INTERIOR LINE."

HE CAME IN SECOND FOR THE HEISMAN TROPHY, BUT TOOK ALL OTHER POSSIBLE HONORS: BIG TEN M.V.P., UNANIMOUS ALL-AMERICAN, OUTLAND AWARD AND LEADER OF THE GOPHERS TO THE 1960 NATIONAL CHAMPIONSHIP.

A KNEE INJURY HOBBLED THE GUARD FROM MINNEAPOLIS CENTRAL IN 1959, BUT THE FOLLOWING YEAR HE SETTLED IN AS THE "HUMAN ROCK OF GIBRALTAR."

IN THE KEY GAME OF 1960 HE TRASHED THE IOWA LINE. THE HAWKEYE CENTER, EVER MINDFUL OF BROWN THROWING HIM AROUND, HIKED THE BALL SIX FEET OVER HIS PUNTER'S HEAD TO SET UP THE GOPHERS' FIRST SCORE. A LITTLE LATER BROWN BOWLED AN IOWA LINEMAN INTO THE BACKFIELD, TOPPLING THE INTERFERENCE BLOCKER AND BALL CARRIER IN ONE MOTION. HE DOMINATED THE GAME WITHOUT TOUCHING THE BALL.

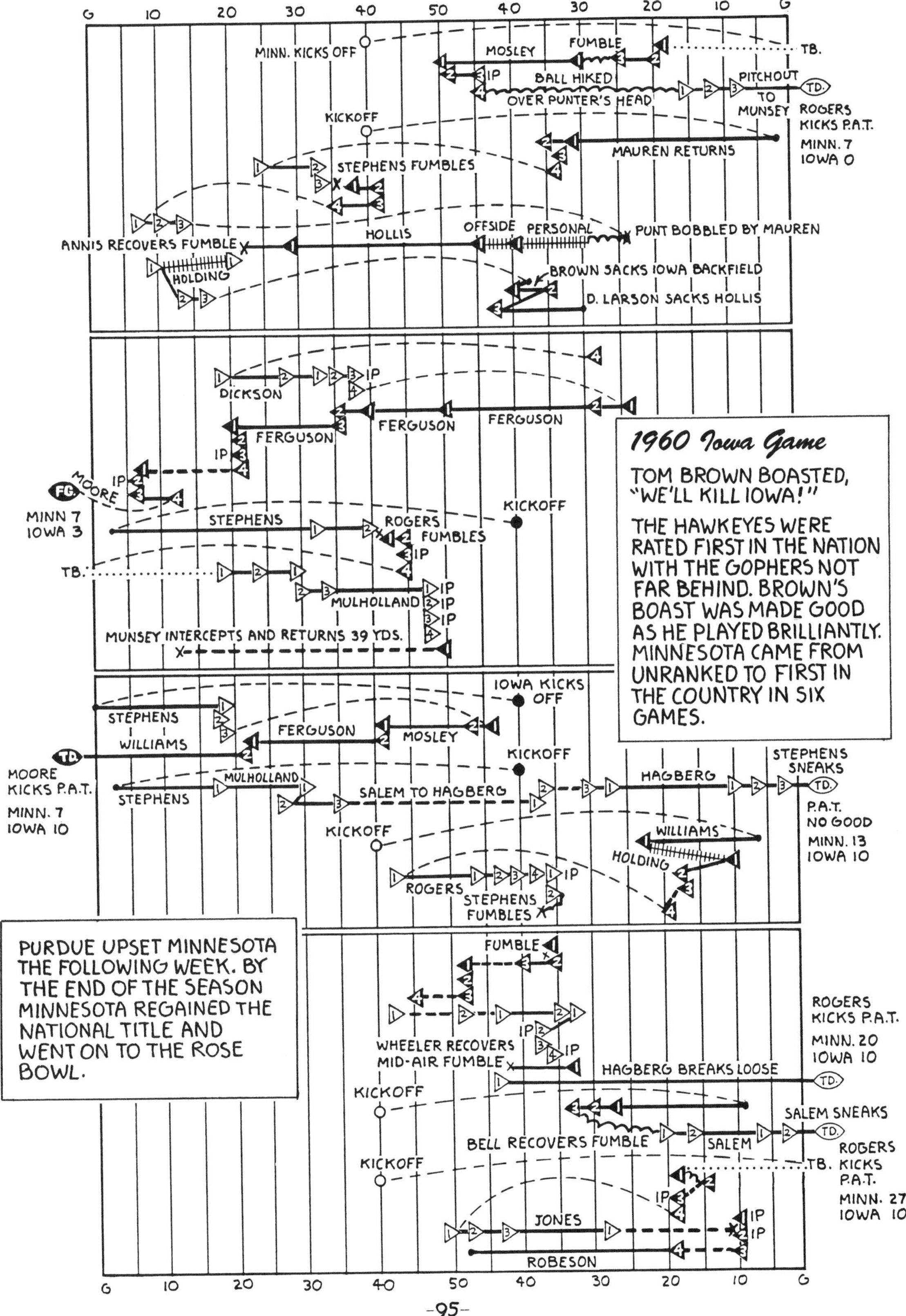

1960 Iowa Game
TOM BROWN BOASTED, "WE'LL KILL IOWA!"
THE HAWKEYES WERE RATED FIRST IN THE NATION WITH THE GOPHERS NOT FAR BEHIND. BROWN'S BOAST WAS MADE GOOD AS HE PLAYED BRILLIANTLY. MINNESOTA CAME FROM UNRANKED TO FIRST IN THE COUNTRY IN SIX GAMES.
PURDUE UPSET MINNESOTA THE FOLLOWING WEEK. BY THE END OF THE SEASON MINNESOTA REGAINED THE NATIONAL TITLE AND WENT ON TO THE ROSE BOWL.
G 10 20 30 40 50 40 30 20 10 G
MINN. KICKS OFF
MOSLEY
FUMBLE
TB.
IP
BALL HIKED OVER PUNTER'S HEAD
PITCHOUT TO MUNSEY
TD.
ROGERS KICKS P.A.T.
MINN. 7 IOWA 0
KICKOFF
MAUREN RETURNS
STEPHENS FUMBLES
OFFSIDE
PERSONAL
PUNT BOBBLED BY MAUREN
ANNIS RECOVERS FUMBLE
HOLLIS
HOLDING
BROWN SACKS IOWA BACKFIELD
D. LARSON SACKS HOLLIS
DICKSON
IP
FERGUSON
FERGUSON
FERGUSON
IP
IP
FG
MOORE
MINN 7 IOWA 3
KICKOFF
STEPHENS
ROGERS
FUMBLES
IP
TB.
MULHOLLAND
IP
IP
IP
MUNSEY INTERCEPTS AND RETURNS 39 YDS.
IOWA KICKS OFF
STEPHENS
FERGUSON
MOSLEY
WILLIAMS
TD.
MOORE KICKS P.A.T.
MINN. 7 IOWA 10
KICKOFF
MULHOLLAND
STEPHENS
SALEM TO HAGBERG
HAGBERG
STEPHENS SNEAKS
TD.
P.A.T. NO GOOD
MINN. 13 IOWA 10
KICKOFF
WILLIAMS
HOLDING
ROGERS
IP
STEPHENS FUMBLES
FUMBLE
IP
IP
WHEELER RECOVERS MID-AIR FUMBLE
HAGBERG BREAKS LOOSE
TD.
ROGERS KICKS P.A.T.
MINN. 20 IOWA 10
KICKOFF
SALEM SNEAKS
TD.
BELL RECOVERS FUMBLE
SALEM
KICKOFF
TB.
ROGERS KICKS P.A.T.
MINN. 27 IOWA 10
IP
JONES
IP
IP
ROBESON
G 10 20 30 40 50 40 30 20 10 G

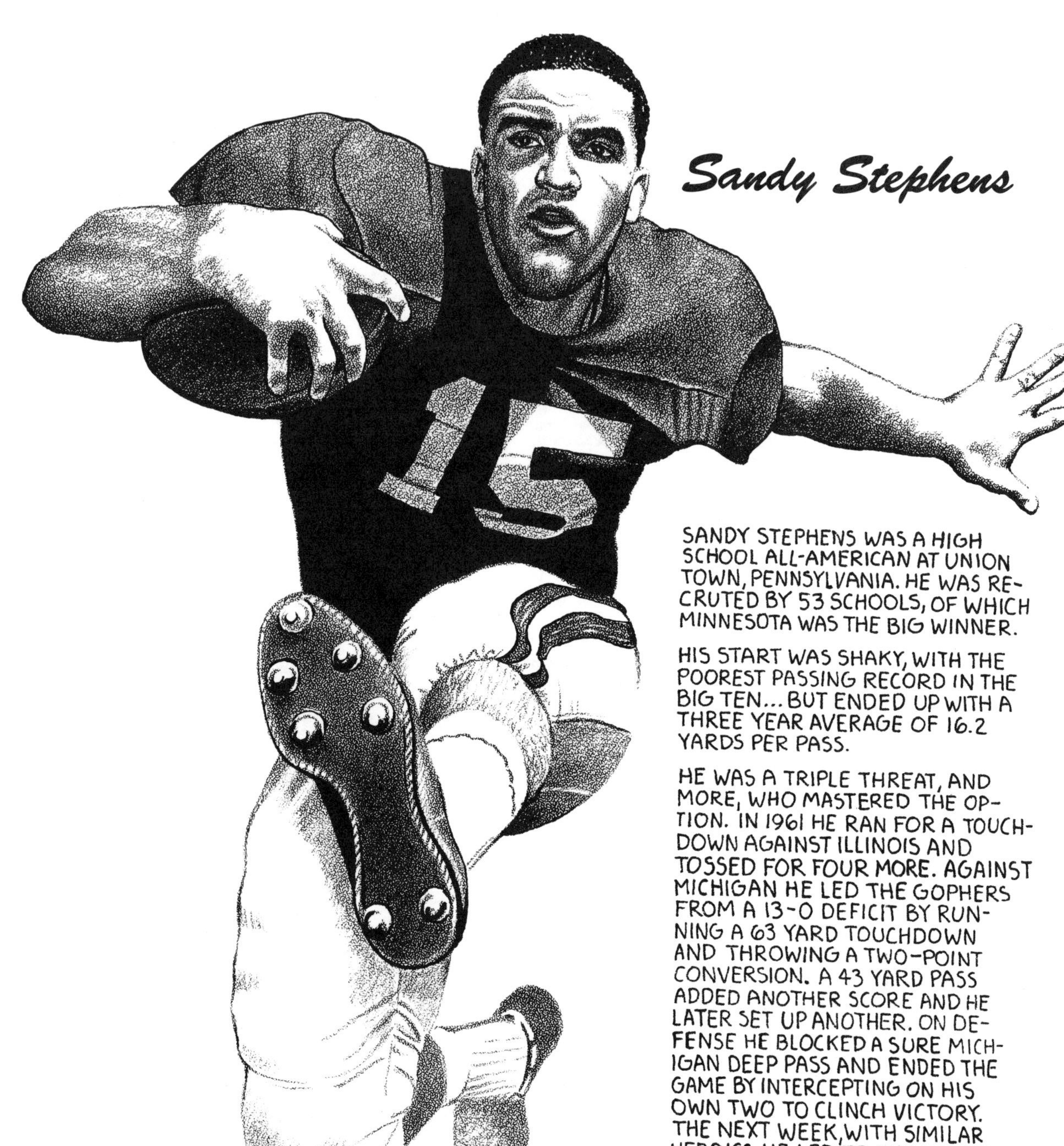

Sandy Stephens

SANDY STEPHENS WAS A HIGH SCHOOL ALL-AMERICAN AT UNION TOWN, PENNSYLVANIA. HE WAS RECRUTED BY 53 SCHOOLS, OF WHICH MINNESOTA WAS THE BIG WINNER.

HIS START WAS SHAKY, WITH THE POOREST PASSING RECORD IN THE BIG TEN... BUT ENDED UP WITH A THREE YEAR AVERAGE OF 16.2 YARDS PER PASS.

HE WAS A TRIPLE THREAT, AND MORE, WHO MASTERED THE OPTION. IN 1961 HE RAN FOR A TOUCHDOWN AGAINST ILLINOIS AND TOSSED FOR FOUR MORE. AGAINST MICHIGAN HE LED THE GOPHERS FROM A 13-0 DEFICIT BY RUNNING A 63 YARD TOUCHDOWN AND THROWING A TWO-POINT CONVERSION. A 43 YARD PASS ADDED ANOTHER SCORE AND HE LATER SET UP ANOTHER. ON DEFENSE HE BLOCKED A SURE MICHIGAN DEEP PASS AND ENDED THE GAME BY INTERCEPTING ON HIS OWN TWO TO CLINCH VICTORY. THE NEXT WEEK, WITH SIMILAR HEROICS, HE LED TO THE DEFEAT OF MICHIGAN STATE AS SHOWN IN THE GAME CHART ON THE NEXT PAGE.

STEPHENS CAPPED OFF HIS CAREER WITH A ROSE BOWL WIN, CONSENSUS ALL-AMERICAN HONORS AT QUARTERBACK AND BIG TEN M.V.P. RECOGNITION FOR 1961.

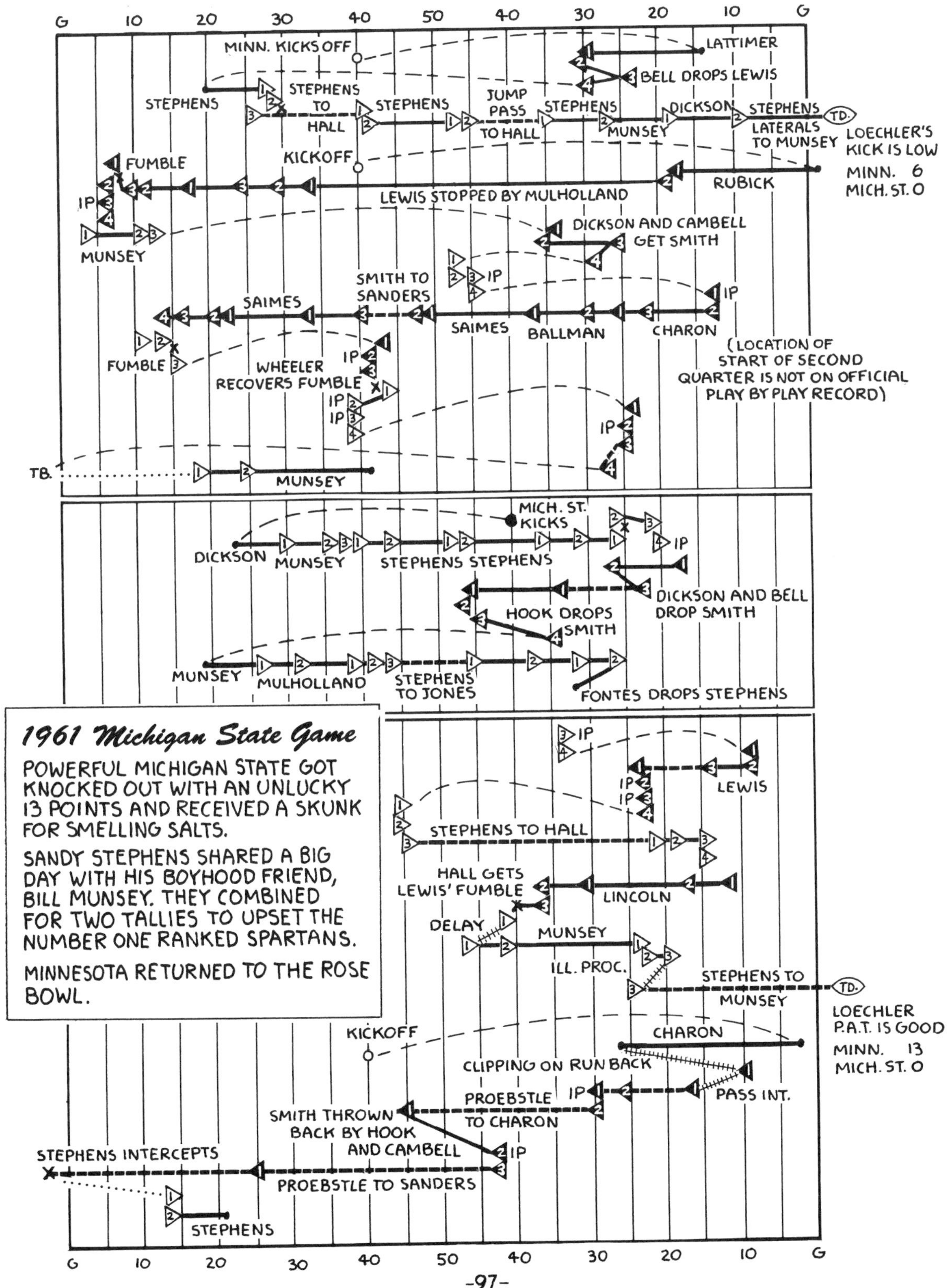

G 10 20 30 40 50 40 30 20 10 G
MINN. KICKS OFF
LATTIMER
BELL DROPS LEWIS
STEPHENS
STEPHENS TO HALL
STEPHENS
JUMP PASS TO HALL
STEPHENS
MUNSEY
DICKSON
STEPHENS LATERALS TO MUNSEY
TD.
LOECHLER'S KICK IS LOW
MINN. 6
MICH. ST. 0
KICKOFF
FUMBLE
IP
LEWIS STOPPED BY MULHOLLAND
RUBICK
MUNSEY
DICKSON AND CAMBELL GET SMITH
SMITH TO SANDERS
IP
SAIMES
SAIMES
BALLMAN
CHARON
IP
(LOCATION OF START OF SECOND QUARTER IS NOT ON OFFICIAL PLAY BY PLAY RECORD)
FUMBLE
WHEELER RECOVERS FUMBLE
IP
IP
IP
IP
TB.
MUNSEY
MICH. ST. KICKS
DICKSON
MUNSEY
STEPHENS STEPHENS
IP
DICKSON AND BELL DROP SMITH
HOOK DROPS SMITH
MUNSEY
MULHOLLAND
STEPHENS TO JONES
FONTES DROPS STEPHENS
1961 Michigan State Game
POWERFUL MICHIGAN STATE GOT KNOCKED OUT WITH AN UNLUCKY 13 POINTS AND RECEIVED A SKUNK FOR SMELLING SALTS.
SANDY STEPHENS SHARED A BIG DAY WITH HIS BOYHOOD FRIEND, BILL MUNSEY. THEY COMBINED FOR TWO TALLIES TO UPSET THE NUMBER ONE RANKED SPARTANS.
MINNESOTA RETURNED TO THE ROSE BOWL.
IP
LEWIS
IP
IP
STEPHENS TO HALL
HALL GETS LEWIS' FUMBLE
LINCOLN
DELAY
MUNSEY
ILL. PROC.
STEPHENS TO MUNSEY
TD.
LOECHLER P.A.T. IS GOOD
MINN. 13
MICH. ST. 0
KICKOFF
CHARON
CLIPPING ON RUN BACK
PROEBSTLE TO CHARON
IP
PASS INT.
SMITH THROWN BACK BY HOOK AND CAMBELL
IP
STEPHENS INTERCEPTS
PROEBSTLE TO SANDERS
STEPHENS
G 10 20 30 40 50 40 30 20 10 G

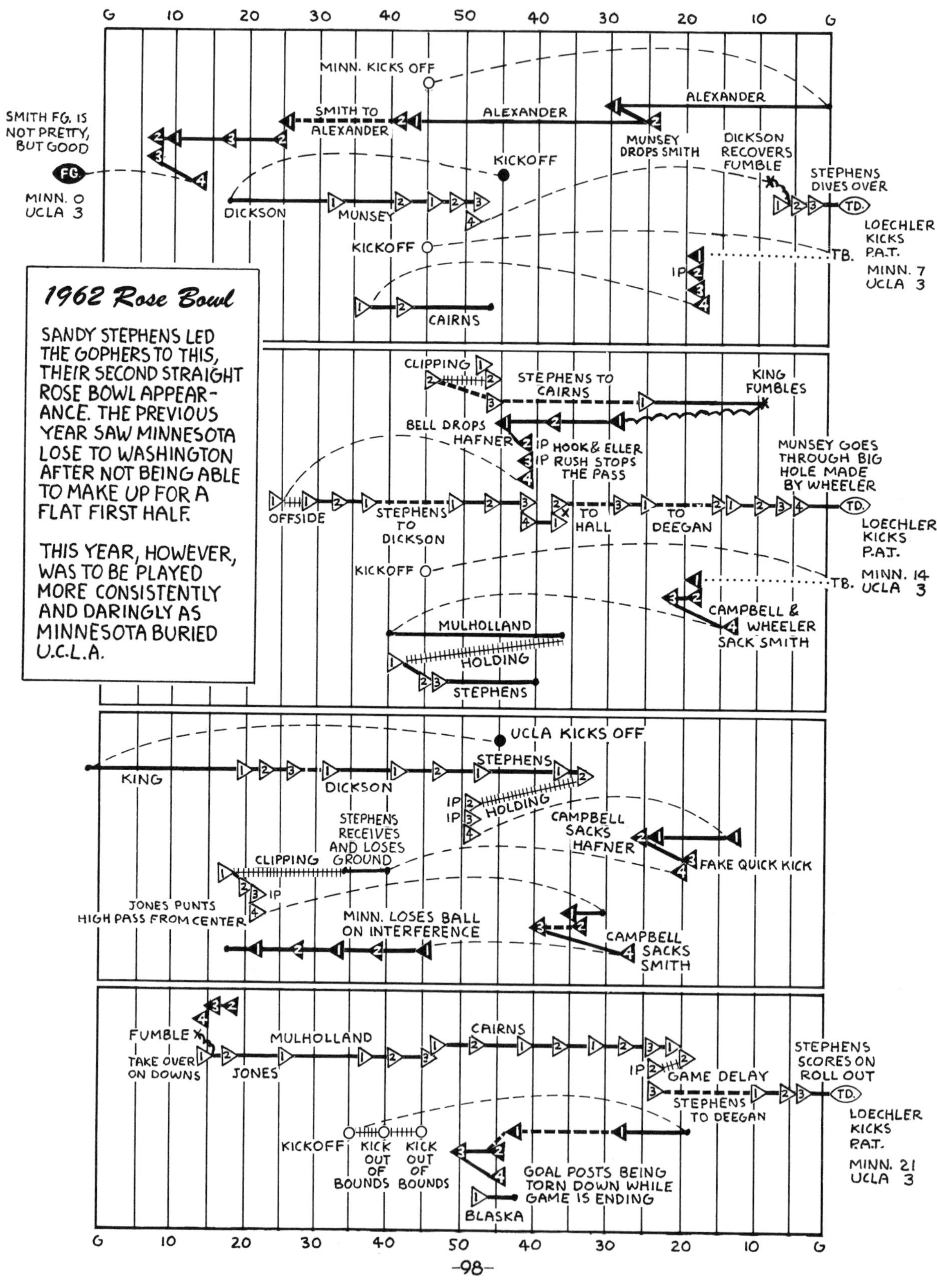
G 10 20 30 40 50 40 30 20 10 G
MINN. KICKS OFF
ALEXANDER
SMITH TO ALEXANDER
ALEXANDER
SMITH FG. IS NOT PRETTY, BUT GOOD
MUNSEY DROPS SMITH
DICKSON RECOVERS FUMBLE
KICKOFF
STEPHENS DIVES OVER
FG.
MINN. 0
UCLA 3
DICKSON
MUNSEY
TD.
LOECHLER KICKS P.A.T.
KICKOFF
TB.
IP
MINN. 7
UCLA 3
CAIRNS
1962 Rose Bowl
SANDY STEPHENS LED THE GOPHERS TO THIS, THEIR SECOND STRAIGHT ROSE BOWL APPEARANCE. THE PREVIOUS YEAR SAW MINNESOTA LOSE TO WASHINGTON AFTER NOT BEING ABLE TO MAKE UP FOR A FLAT FIRST HALF.
THIS YEAR, HOWEVER, WAS TO BE PLAYED MORE CONSISTENTLY AND DARINGLY AS MINNESOTA BURIED U.C.L.A.
CLIPPING
STEPHENS TO CAIRNS
KING FUMBLES
BELL DROPS HAFNER
IP HOOK & ELLER
IP RUSH STOPS THE PASS
MUNSEY GOES THROUGH BIG HOLE MADE BY WHEELER
OFFSIDE
STEPHENS TO DICKSON
TO HALL
TO DEEGAN
TD.
LOECHLER KICKS P.A.T.
KICKOFF
TB.
MINN. 14
UCLA 3
CAMPBELL & WHEELER SACK SMITH
MULHOLLAND
HOLDING
STEPHENS
UCLA KICKS OFF
STEPHENS
KING
DICKSON
IP
IP
HOLDING
CAMPBELL SACKS HAFNER
STEPHENS RECEIVES AND LOSES GROUND
CLIPPING
FAKE QUICK KICK
IP
JONES PUNTS HIGH PASS FROM CENTER
MINN. LOSES BALL ON INTERFERENCE
CAMPBELL SACKS SMITH
CAIRNS
FUMBLE
MULHOLLAND
TAKE OVER ON DOWNS
JONES
IP
GAME DELAY
STEPHENS SCORES ON ROLL OUT
STEPHENS TO DEEGAN
TD.
LOECHLER KICKS P.A.T.
KICKOFF
KICK OUT OF BOUNDS
KICK OUT OF BOUNDS
GOAL POSTS BEING TORN DOWN WHILE GAME IS ENDING
MINN. 21
UCLA 3
BLASKA
G 10 20 30 40 50 40 30 20 10 G

Bobby Bell

BELL CAME TO MINNESOTA FROM SHELBY, NORTH CAROLINA TO BE A QUARTERBACK. IT TURNED OUT HE WAS GREAT AT WHATEVER HE DID AND WAS NEEDED AT TACKLE MORE. HE COULDN'T BELIEVE THEY WOULD REALLY PUT HIM THERE, BUT HE DID ALL RIGHT. HE MADE ALL-AMERICAN IN 1961 AND UNANIMOUS ALL-AMERICAN IN 1962. IN ADDITION HE RECEIVED THE OUTLAND AWARD, SIGNIFYING THE NATION'S BEST INTERIOR LINEMAN. HE WON THE OUTSTANDING LINEMAN AWARD FOR THE ALL-AMERICAN BOWL GAME, TOO.

TO HIS TEAMMATES BELL WAS POPULAR, WITH A GREAT SENSE OF HUMOR. TO OPPONENTS HE WAS UNPOPULAR FOR USING HIS GREAT MIXTURE OF STRENGTH, AGILITY, SAVVY AND DESIRE AGAINST THEM. ALTHOUGH DOUBLE-TEAMED BY BIGGER PLAYERS, HE WOULD ESCAPE THEM TO MAKE HIS TACKLE. HE WAS ALSO ONE OF THE FASTEST GOPHERS ON THE SQUAD. AT 6'4", WITH LONG ARMS AND BIG HANDS, BELL WAS THE MAJOR REASON MINNESOTA HAD ONE OF THE BEST PASS DEFENSES IN THE COUNTRY. THOSE BIG HANDS HELPED HIM AS THE TEAM CENTER ON PUNTS AND KICKS, TOO.

IN THE 1961 WISCONSIN GAME HE GOT TWO RIBS CRACKED IN THE FIRST HALF. WITH A LITTLE TAPE AND BANDAGING, HE PLAYED A GREAT SECOND HALF AND LATER WENT ON TO WIN IN THE ROSE BOWL.

BELL BECAME AN ALL-PRO FOR KANSAS CITY AND EARNED A SUPER BOWL RING BY DEFEATING THE MINNESOTA VIKINGS.

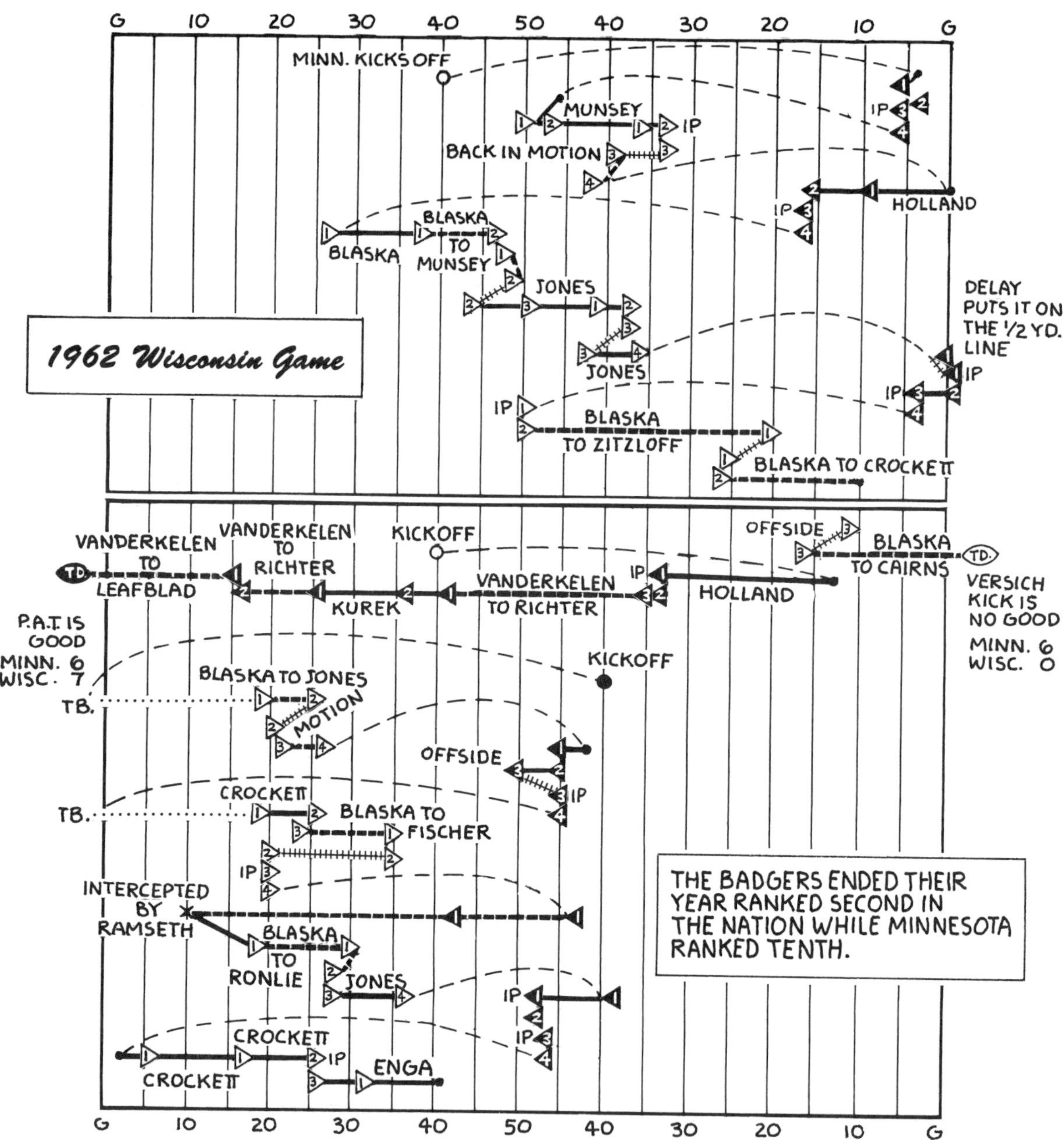

THE BIG TEN CHAMPIONSHIP AND A THIRD TRIP IN A ROW TO THE ROSE BOWL WERE AT STAKE. IT WAS NOT TO BE, THOUGH. THE HIGH STAKES AND HEATED MANNER IN WHICH THIS GAME WAS LOST IS WHAT MADE IT SO MEMORABLE. PLAYERS ON BOTH SIDES WERE SUBJECTED TO ERRATIC OFFICIATING. AFTER SNATCHING GAME-WINNING PLAYS AWAY FROM MINNESOTA IT APPEARED THE REFS TRIED TO REPENT AND GIVE THEM BACK AGAIN DURING A LATE GOPHER MARCH. WISCONSIN HUNG TOUGH AND WENT ON TO THE ROSE BOWL.

THE HEARTBREAKING PLAYS STARTED (A) WHEN BILL MUNSEY CLAIMED TO HAVE BARELY GOTTEN OVER FOR A SCORE. HE WAS DRIVEN BACK BUT THERE WAS NO WHISTLE. DUANE BLASKA, THE PASSER ON THE PLAY, CAME DOWN FIELD AND PUSHED MUNSEY OVER AGAIN. THE PENALTY FOR AIDING A BALL CARRIER IN THIS MANNER PUT A TOUCHDOWN OUT OF REACH AT THE 15. THE

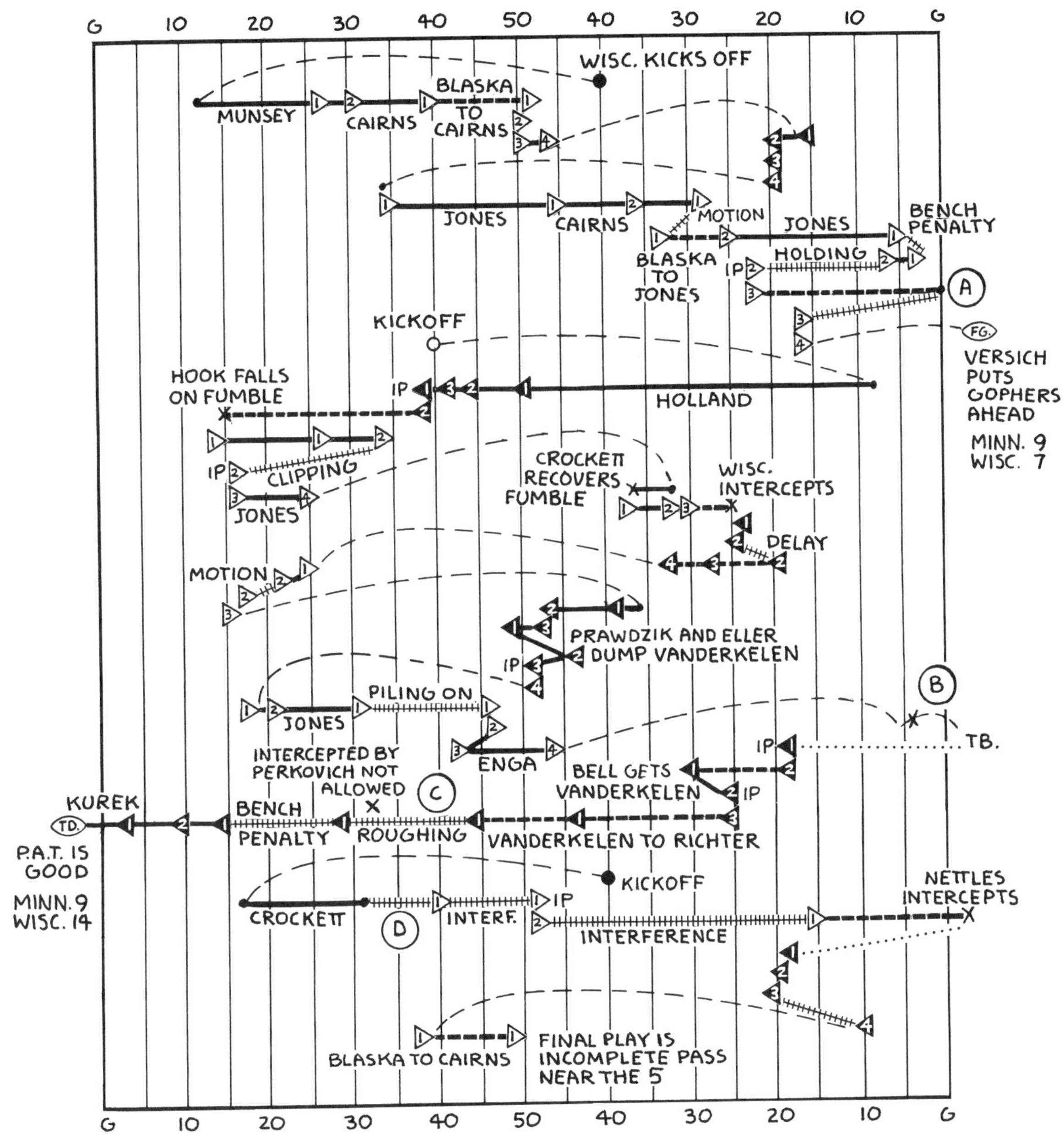

GOPHERS HAD TO SETTLE FOR A FIELD GOAL.

LATER A PUNT BOUNCED OFF A BADGER RECEIVER'S LEG INTO THE END ZONE Ⓑ. IT WAS JUMPED ON BY THE GOPHERS FOR WHAT SEEMED TO BE A TOUCHDOWN BUT POSSESSION WAS GIVEN TO WISCONSIN AT THE 20 INSTEAD.

TEMPERS BOILED OVER AFTER BOBBY BELL MADE HIS MOST TIMELY AND BRILLIANT PLAY Ⓒ OF THE GAME. WHILE COMING DOWN ON THE PASSER HE DEFLECTED THE BALL INTO THE ARMS OF TEAMMATE JOHN PERKOVICH. THE GAME SEEMED ON ICE, BUT INSTEAD, BELL WAS MIRACULOUSLY CALLED FOR ROUGHING. WITH THE ADDITION OF A BENCH PENALTY, WISCONSIN WAS PUT DEEP IN MINNESOTA TERRITORY WHERE IT MADE THE DECISIVE SCORE. LATE INTERFERENCE CALLS Ⓓ TO MINNESOTA'S ADVANTAGE COULDN'T CHANGE THE FINAL TALLY.

Carl Eller

HAILING FROM SALEM, NORTH CAROLINA, THE "GENTLEMANLY GIANT" HAD A FONDNESS FOR ANCIENT GREEK DRAMA. ON THE FIELD HE WAS DRAMATIC TRAGEDY TO OPPONENTS.

EVEN WITH HIS LARGE SIZE, ELLER WAS QUICK TO RUSH ENEMY BACKFIELDS AND STOP PLAY WITH A CRACKLING TACKLE. IN 1962 HE LED MINNESOTA IN THROWING NAVY FOR A MINUS 31 YARDS RUSHING.

ON OFFENSE HE WAS AN OUTSTANDING BLOCKER AND EVEN RECEIVED ON A TACKLE ELIGIBLE PASS PLAY.

HE MADE CONSENSUS ALL-AMERICAN IN 1963 AND WAS DRAFTED NUMBER ONE BY THE MINNESOTA VIKINGS.

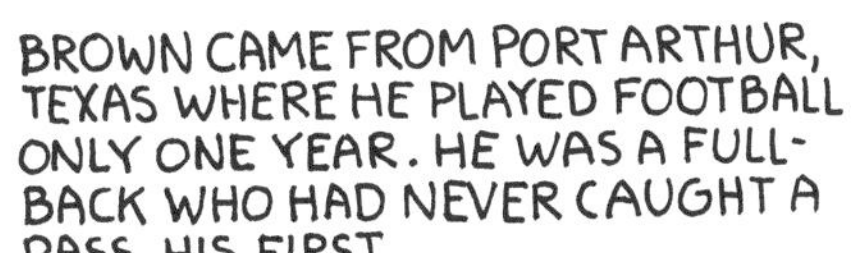

BROWN CAME FROM PORT ARTHUR, TEXAS WHERE HE PLAYED FOOTBALL ONLY ONE YEAR. HE WAS A FULL-BACK WHO HAD NEVER CAUGHT A PASS. HIS FIRST SPORT WAS BASKETBALL.

Aaron Brown

AFTER COMING TO MINNESOTA HE WAS MADE INTO AN END, WHERE HE PLAYED BOTH WAYS.

TWO-PLATOON FOOTBALL CREATED TEAM SPECIALISTS IN OFFENSE AND DEFENSE, AND SO ALL-AMERICAN ROSTERS CHANGED TO SHOW THIS IN 1965. IT WAS AT THIS TIME BROWN BECAME CONSENSUS ALL-AMERICAN AT DEFENSIVE END.

HE PREFERRED DEFENSE MOST FOR ITS HITTING, FREEDOM AND INITIATIVE.

ON OFFENSE HE WAS NO SLOUCH EITHER. HE HAULED IN 27 PASSES, TO SET A SCHOOL RECORD IN 1964.

IN THE SECOND GAME OF 1965 HE SUFFERED A BROKEN JAW AFTER BEING CLOTHSLINED. HE CONTINUED PLAY WHILE OCCASIONALLY GOING TO THE SIDELINE TO SPIT BLOOD. HE FINISHED THE SEASON WITH HIS MOUTH WIRED SHUT. DEFENSE WAS HIS MAIN DUTY AFTER THE INJURY, BUT HE MANAGED TO PULL DOWN 24 PASSES ON OFFENSE ANYWAY.

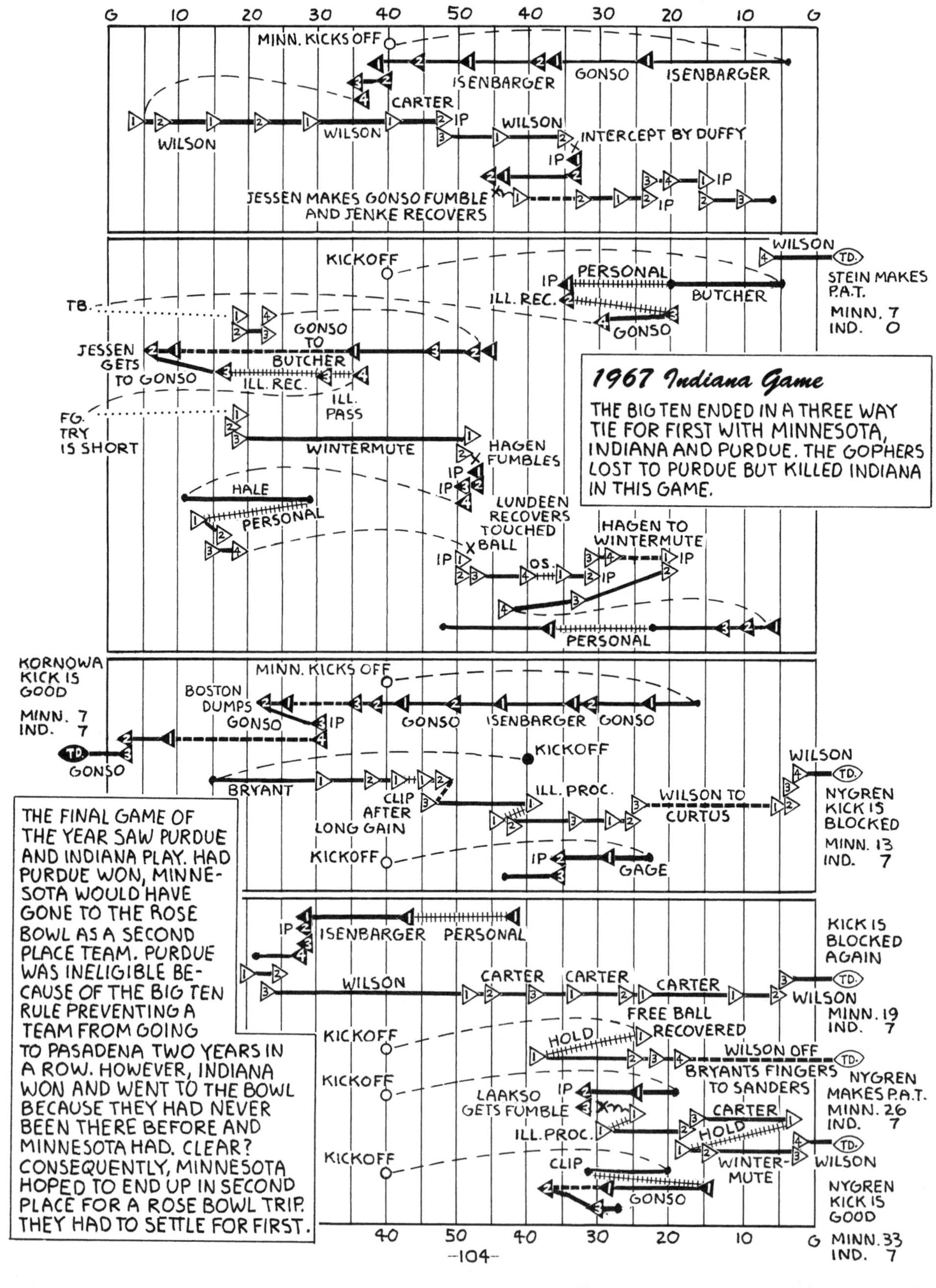

1967 Indiana Game

THE BIG TEN ENDED IN A THREE WAY TIE FOR FIRST WITH MINNESOTA, INDIANA AND PURDUE. THE GOPHERS LOST TO PURDUE BUT KILLED INDIANA IN THIS GAME.

THE FINAL GAME OF THE YEAR SAW PURDUE AND INDIANA PLAY. HAD PURDUE WON, MINNESOTA WOULD HAVE GONE TO THE ROSE BOWL AS A SECOND PLACE TEAM. PURDUE WAS INELIGIBLE BECAUSE OF THE BIG TEN RULE PREVENTING A TEAM FROM GOING TO PASADENA TWO YEARS IN A ROW. HOWEVER, INDIANA WON AND WENT TO THE BOWL BECAUSE THEY HAD NEVER BEEN THERE BEFORE AND MINNESOTA HAD. CLEAR? CONSEQUENTLY, MINNESOTA HOPED TO END UP IN SECOND PLACE FOR A ROSE BOWL TRIP. THEY HAD TO SETTLE FOR FIRST.

Bob Stein

BOB STEIN, FROM ST. LOUIS PARK, WAS ALL-AMERICAN AT DEFENSIVE END IN 1967 AND 68.

AMONG HIS BEST ABILITES WAS HIS RUSH ON THE PASSER AS WELL AS BEING A LEADING FIELD GOAL KICKER.

IN HIS SOPHOMORE YEAR HE WAS INJURED AFTER ONLY TWO GAMES. UP TO THAT POINT HE WAS LEADING THE BIG TEN IN THROWING THE MOST NUMBER OF OPPONENTS FOR A LOSS, WITH EIGHT. THOUGH HE WAS OUT FOR THE REST OF THE SEASON, HE STILL TIED FOR THIRD IN THAT DEPARTMENT FOR THE YEAR.

HE MADE THE ALL-AMERICAN SCHOLASTIC TEAM IN 1968 AND POST GRADUATE TEAM IN 1969.

HE WENT ON TO PLAY FOR THE KANSAS CITY CHIEFS AND BECOME PRESIDENT OF THE MINNESOTA TIMBERWOLVES BASKETBALL TEAM OF THE N.B.A.

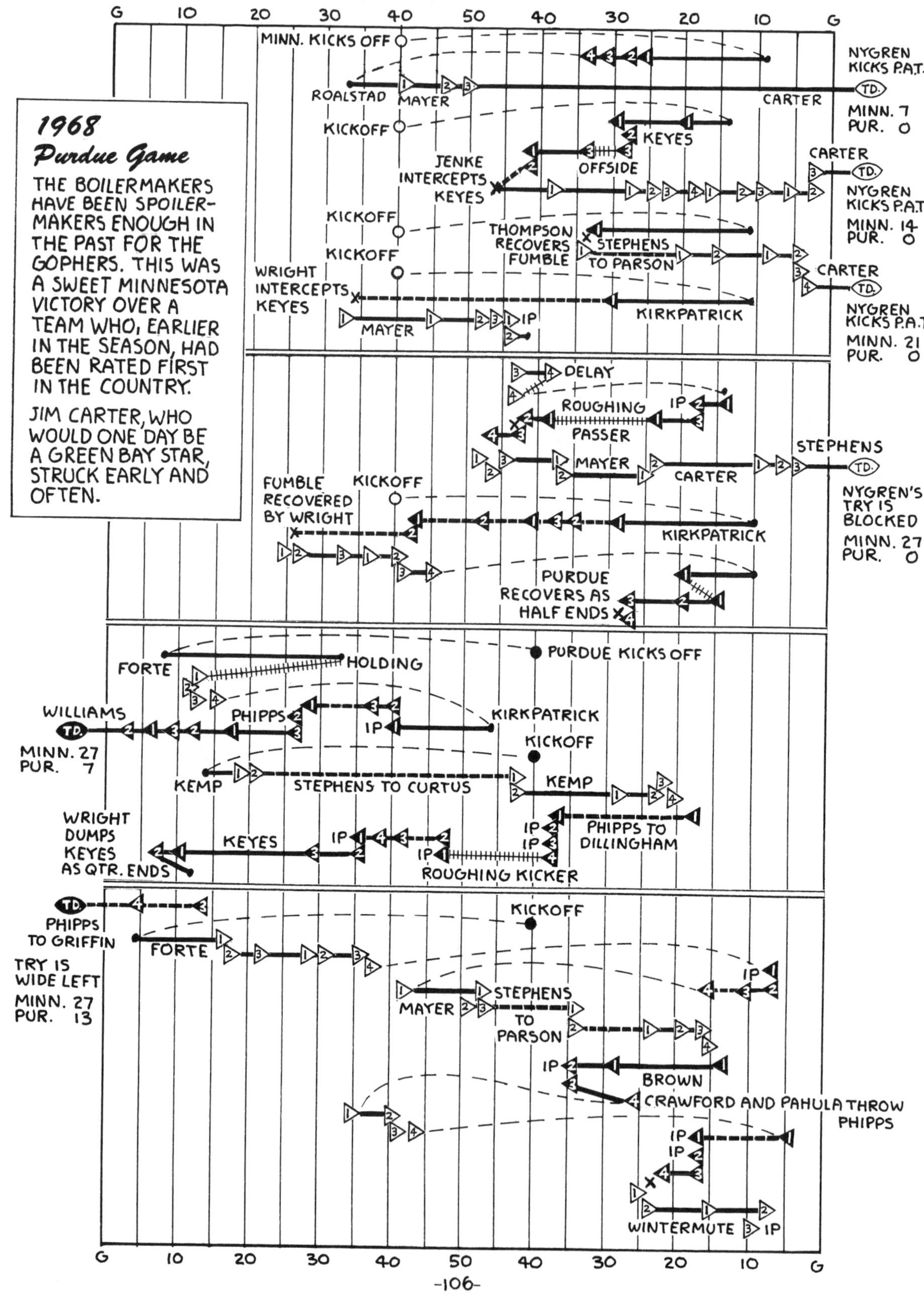
1968
Purdue Game
THE BOILERMAKERS HAVE BEEN SPOILERMAKERS ENOUGH IN THE PAST FOR THE GOPHERS. THIS WAS A SWEET MINNESOTA VICTORY OVER A TEAM WHO, EARLIER IN THE SEASON, HAD BEEN RATED FIRST IN THE COUNTRY.
JIM CARTER, WHO WOULD ONE DAY BE A GREEN BAY STAR, STRUCK EARLY AND OFTEN.
G 10 20 30 40 50 40 30 20 10 G
MINN. KICKS OFF
ROALSTAD
MAYER
CARTER
TD.
NYGREN KICKS P.A.T.
MINN. 7
PUR. 0
KICKOFF
KEYES
JENKE INTERCEPTS KEYES
OFFSIDE
CARTER
NYGREN KICKS P.A.T.
MINN. 14
PUR. 0
KICKOFF
THOMPSON RECOVERS FUMBLE
STEPHENS TO PARSON
KICKOFF
WRIGHT INTERCEPTS KEYES
CARTER
KIRKPATRICK
MAYER
IP
NYGREN KICKS P.A.T.
MINN. 21
PUR. 0
DELAY
ROUGHING PASSER
IP
MAYER
CARTER
STEPHENS
NYGREN'S TRY IS BLOCKED
MINN. 27
PUR. 0
FUMBLE RECOVERED BY WRIGHT
KICKOFF
KIRKPATRICK
PURDUE RECOVERS AS HALF ENDS
FORTE
HOLDING
PURDUE KICKS OFF
WILLIAMS
PHIPPS
KIRKPATRICK
IP
MINN. 27
PUR. 7
KICKOFF
KEMP
STEPHENS TO CURTUS
KEMP
WRIGHT DUMPS KEYES AS QTR. ENDS
KEYES
IP
IP
IP
IP
PHIPPS TO DILLINGHAM
ROUGHING KICKER
PHIPPS TO GRIFFIN
KICKOFF
FORTE
TRY IS WIDE LEFT
MINN. 27
PUR. 13
IP
STEPHENS
MAYER
TO PARSON
IP
BROWN
CRAWFORD AND PAHULA THROW PHIPPS
IP
IP
WINTERMUTE
IP
G 10 20 30 40 50 40 30 20 10 G

Doug Kingsriter

AT RICHFIELD, KINGSRITER WAS PREP ATHLETE OF THE YEAR. AT MINNESOTA HE USED HIS ABILITY TO PITCH ON THE BASEBALL TEAM AS WELL AS CATCH ON THE FOOTBALL TEAM.

QUARTERBACK IS WHERE HE EXPECTED TO PLAY, BUT WAS SOON MOVED TO CENTER AND FINALLY TIGHT END, WHERE HE EARNED ALL-AMERICAN STATUS IN 1971.

AS A FRESHMAN HE BROKE HIS WRIST AND HAD TO SIT OUT A YEAR. WHEN HE GOT HIS CHANCE IN THE MIDDLE OF THE FOLLOWING YEAR, ON HIS FIRST PLAY HE GRABBED A 20 YARD PASS. IN ALL, HE GOT SIX RECEPTIONS THAT DAY AND WENT ON TO LEAD THE TEAM FOR THE SEASON WITH 26.

THOUGH HE WAS A GOOD RUNNER WITH THE BALL, HE WAS A MASTER AT THE ONE-HANDED GRAB.

Cal Stoll

CAL STOLL'S FIRST STINT WITH MINNESOTA WAS AS A DEFENSIVE END ON THE TALENTED 1949 TEAM. HE RETURNED AS HEAD COACH IN 1972. IN BETWEEN HE SERVED AS END COACH AT MICHIGAN STATE IN THE CHAMPIONSHIP YEARS OF DUFFY DAUGHERTY. HE HAD HEAD COACHING SUCCESS HIMSELF, AT WAKE FOREST.

1977 WAS HIS BIG YEAR WITH GOPHER WINS OVER BOTH ROSE BOWL PARTICIPANTS, WASHINGTON AND MICHIGAN. MICHIGAN HAD BEEN RATED FIRST IN THE COUNTRY AS STOLL'S BOYS SHUT THEM DOWN TO THE TUNE OF 16-0. IT WAS THE FIRST SKUNK MICHIGAN HAD RECEIVED IN 113 GAMES. MINNESOTA WENT ON TO PLAY IN THE HALL OF FAME BOWL.

Joe Salem

ANOTHER FORMER GOPHER TO RETURN AS COACH WAS JOE SALEM. HE WAS CALLED "SMOKEY" JOE BY MURRAY WARMATH. IT HAD TO DO WITH THE EXCITING WAY HE WOULD COME INTO THE GAME AS A RESERVE QUARTERBACK IN THE NATIONAL CHAMPIONSHIP YEAR OF 1960.

SALEM WAS A SUCCESSFUL COACH AT SOUTH DAKOTA AND NORTHERN ARIZONA BUT RAN INTO HARD TIMES AT HIS ALMA MATER.

Lou Holtz

LOU HOLTZ PICKED UP A SAGGING FOOTBALL PROGRAM WITH HIS OPTIMISM AND DRIVE. AT HIS PRODDING THE NEW INDOOR FACILITIES WERE BUILT AND NICKNAMED THE TAJ-MA-HOLTZ.

RECRUITING IMPROVED AND HIS 1984 BUILDING YEAR WAS CLIMAXED WITH AN UPSET OVER IOWA. IN 1985 HIS SQUAD ALMOST TIPPED THE SCALE AGAINST NATIONAL CHAMPION OKLAHOMA BY GOING DOWN TO THE FINAL PLAY OF THE GAME.

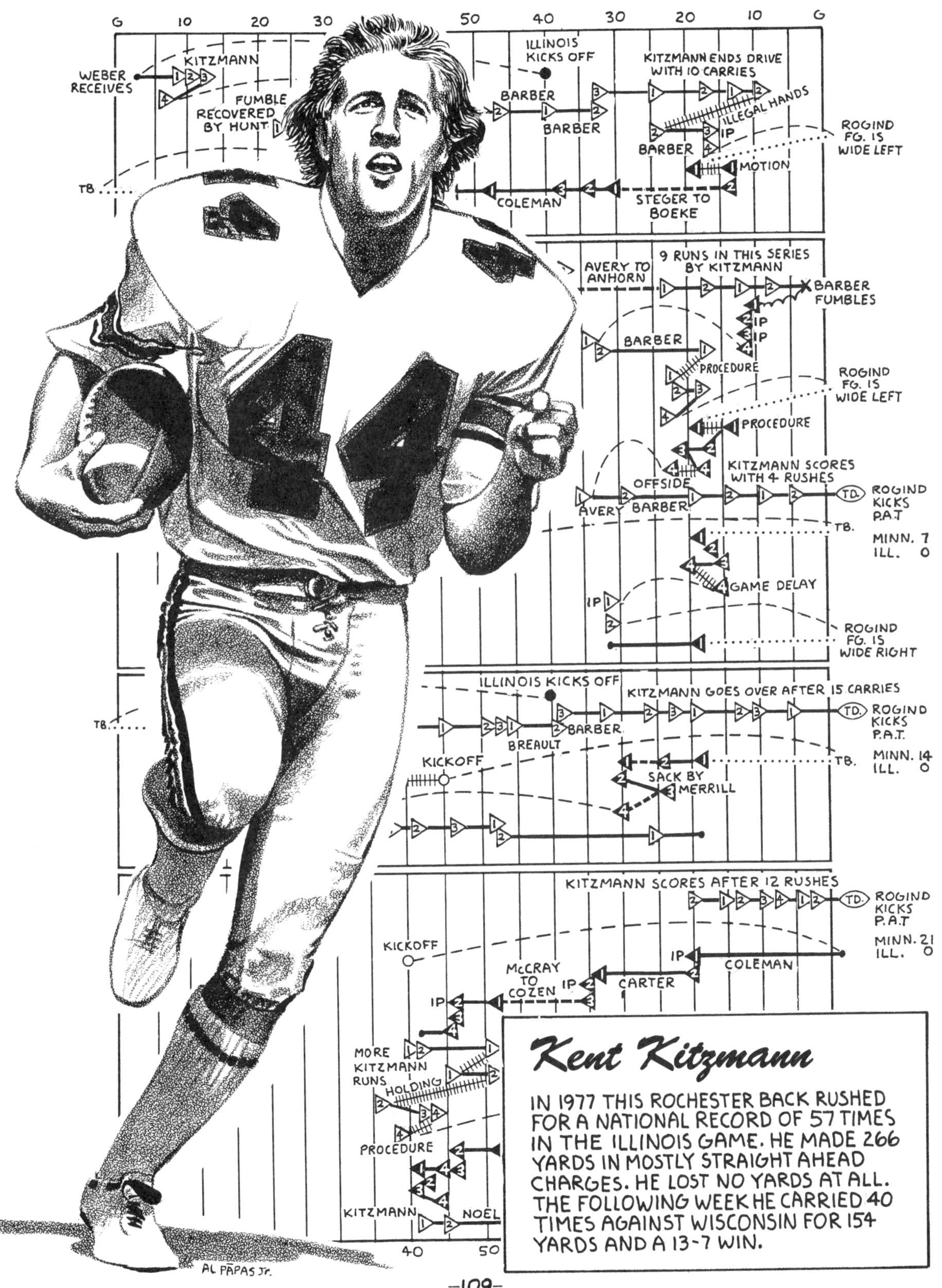

Kent Kitzmann

IN 1977 THIS ROCHESTER BACK RUSHED FOR A NATIONAL RECORD OF 57 TIMES IN THE ILLINOIS GAME. HE MADE 266 YARDS IN MOSTLY STRAIGHT AHEAD CHARGES. HE LOST NO YARDS AT ALL. THE FOLLOWING WEEK HE CARRIED 40 TIMES AGAINST WISCONSIN FOR 154 YARDS AND A 13-7 WIN.

Lloyd Stein
CENTERS WERE KNOWN AS "SNAPPERS" IN CANADA WHERE LLOYD STEIN PLAYED SOME EARLY FOOTBALL. HE BECAME KNOWN AS "SNAPPER" THE REST OF HIS LIFE. THE TWO HARBORS NATIVE WAS STARTING GOPHER CENTER IN THE LATE 1920'S. HE WAS ONCE KNOWN TO OUT-PLAY AN ALL-AMERICAN ON THE OTHER SIDE OF THE BALL FROM HIM.
AFTER HIS PLAYING DAYS HE SERVED AS TEAM TRAINER FOR 42 YEARS. HE GUESSED HE HAD TAPED AROUND 700,000 ANKLES IN HIS TIME.
"SNAPPER'S" CONTRIBUTIONS IN METHODS, THEORIES AND TECHNIQUES TO HIS ART EARNED HIM ENTRY INTO THE HALL OF FAME AS A TRAINER.
AL PĀPAS Jr.

MANY PLAYERS HOLD THE NATIONAL RECORD OF 100 YARDS FOR A KICKOFF RETURN. MINNESOTA HAS TWO BEARERS OF THIS DISTINCTION. RICK UPCHURCH DID HIS PART AGAINST WISCONSIN IN 1974.
Bobby Weber
27
40
Rick Upchurch
IN 1977 BOBBY WEBER RETURNED THE 100 AGAINST OHIO STATE.
AL PĀPAS Jr.

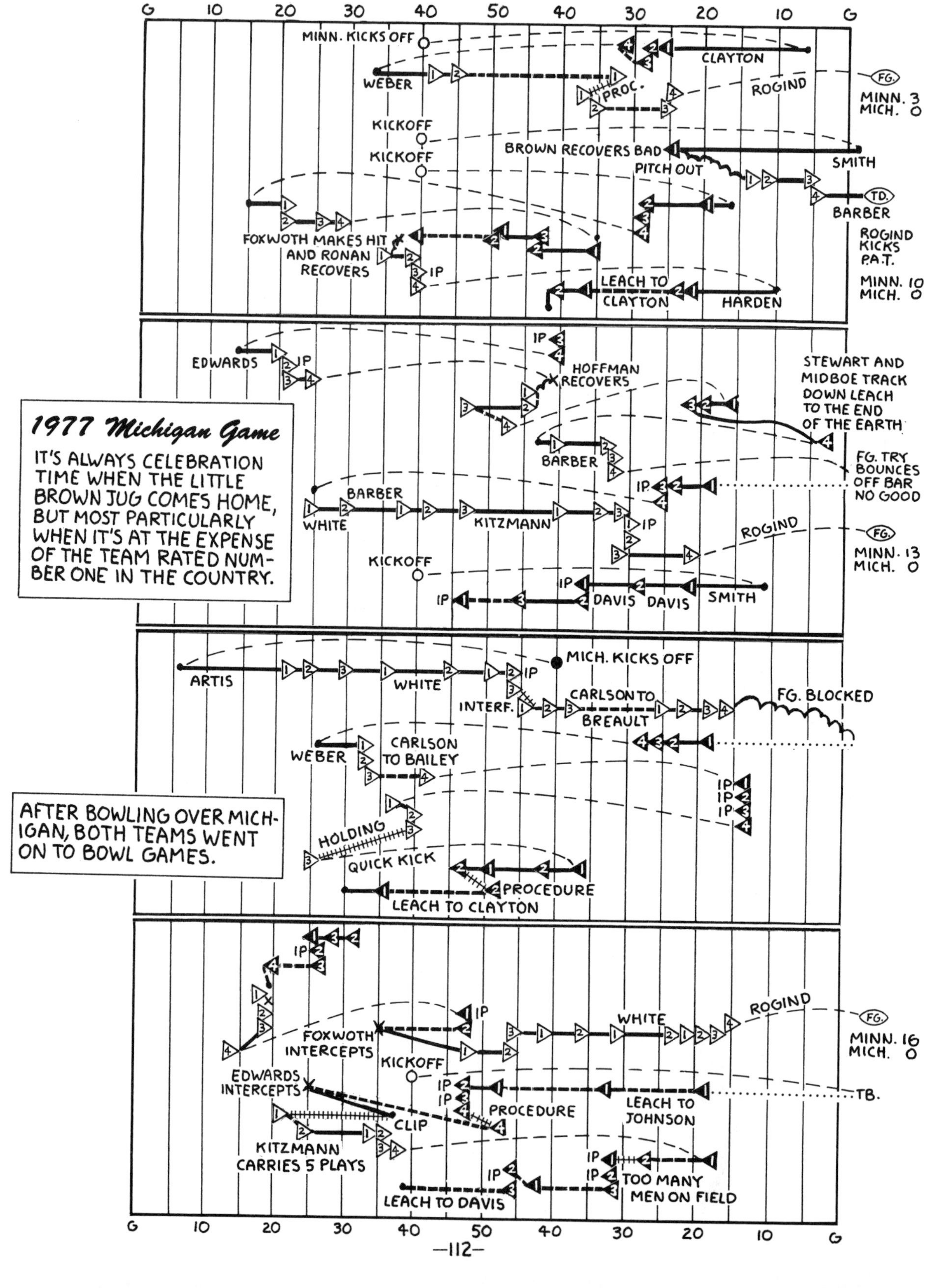
G 10 20 30 40 50 40 30 20 10 G
MINN. KICKS OFF
CLAYTON
WEBER
PROC.
ROGIND
FG.
MINN. 3
MICH. 0
KICKOFF
KICKOFF
BROWN RECOVERS BAD PITCH OUT
SMITH
TD.
BARBER
ROGIND KICKS P.A.T.
FOXWOTH MAKES HIT AND RONAN RECOVERS
IP
LEACH TO CLAYTON
HARDEN
MINN. 10
MICH. 0
EDWARDS
IP
HOFFMAN RECOVERS
STEWART AND MIDBOE TRACK DOWN LEACH TO THE END OF THE EARTH
1977 Michigan Game
IT'S ALWAYS CELEBRATION TIME WHEN THE LITTLE BROWN JUG COMES HOME, BUT MOST PARTICULARLY WHEN IT'S AT THE EXPENSE OF THE TEAM RATED NUMBER ONE IN THE COUNTRY.
BARBER
FG. TRY BOUNCES OFF BAR NO GOOD
IP
BARBER
WHITE
KITZMANN
IP
ROGIND
FG.
MINN. 13
MICH. 0
KICKOFF
IP
IP
DAVIS
DAVIS
SMITH
MICH. KICKS OFF
ARTIS
WHITE
IP
INTERF.
CARLSON TO BREAULT
FG. BLOCKED
WEBER
CARLSON TO BAILEY
IP
IP
IP
AFTER BOWLING OVER MICHIGAN, BOTH TEAMS WENT ON TO BOWL GAMES.
HOLDING
QUICK KICK
PROCEDURE
LEACH TO CLAYTON
IP
IP
ROGIND
WHITE
FOXWOTH INTERCEPTS
FG.
MINN. 16
MICH. 0
KICKOFF
EDWARDS INTERCEPTS
IP
IP
PROCEDURE
LEACH TO JOHNSON
TB.
CLIP
KITZMANN CARRIES 5 PLAYS
IP
IP
IP
TOO MANY MEN ON FIELD
LEACH TO DAVIS
G 10 20 30 40 50 40 30 20 10 G

John Gutekunst

AS DEFENSIVE COORDINATOR, JOHN GUTEKUNST GUIDED VIRGINIA TECH TO LEAD THE NATION IN LEAST POINTS ALLOWED IN 1983. MINNESOTA WAS LEADING THE NATION IN MOST POINTS ALLOWED DURING THE SAME PERIOD.

WHEN "GUTE" CAME TO MINNESOTA THE FOLLOWING YEAR, HE TURNED THE DEFENSE AROUND FOR THE GOPHERS. IN TWO YEARS THE GOPHERS WERE WINNING IN THE INDEPENDENCE BOWL WITH HIM IN HIS FIRST GAME AS HEAD COACH.

HIS FIRST FULL SEASON AT THE HELM SAW THE RETURN OF THE LITTLE BROWN JUG AND A TRIP TO THE LIBERTY BOWL.

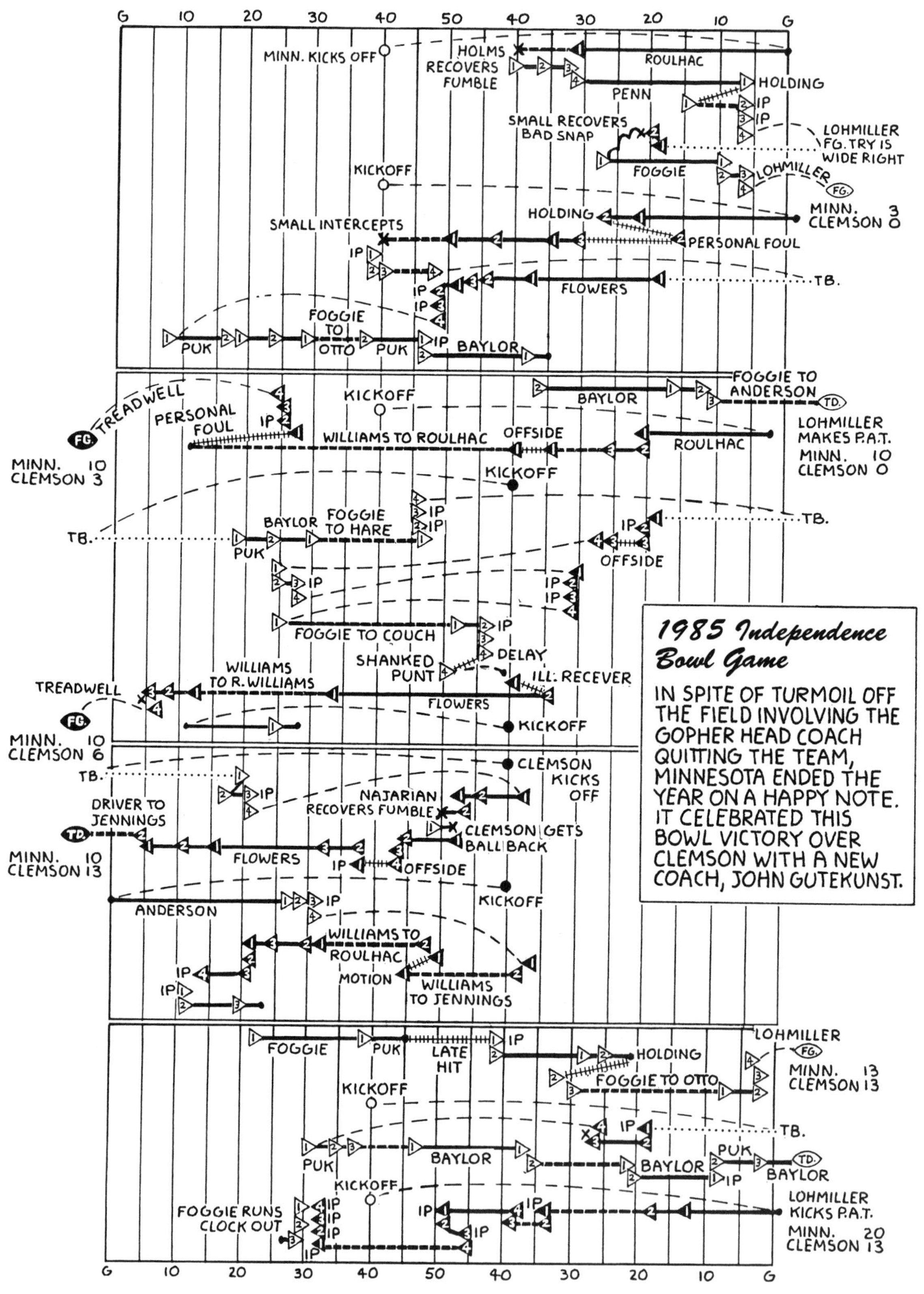

1985 Independence Bowl Game

IN SPITE OF TURMOIL OFF THE FIELD INVOLVING THE GOPHER HEAD COACH QUITTING THE TEAM, MINNESOTA ENDED THE YEAR ON A HAPPY NOTE. IT CELEBRATED THIS BOWL VICTORY OVER CLEMSON WITH A NEW COACH, JOHN GUTEKUNST.

Rickey Foggie
BEFORE ENDING HIS DAYS FOR THE MAROON AND GOLD IN 1987, RICKEY FOGGIE WAS A THREAT EVERY TIME HE TOUCHED THE BALL. PLAYING FROM THE OPTION, HE BECAME ONLY THE THIRD QUARTER-BACK IN COLLEGE HISTORY TO RUN OVER 2,000 YARDS AND PASS FOR OVER 4,000.
14
AL PĀPAS Jr.

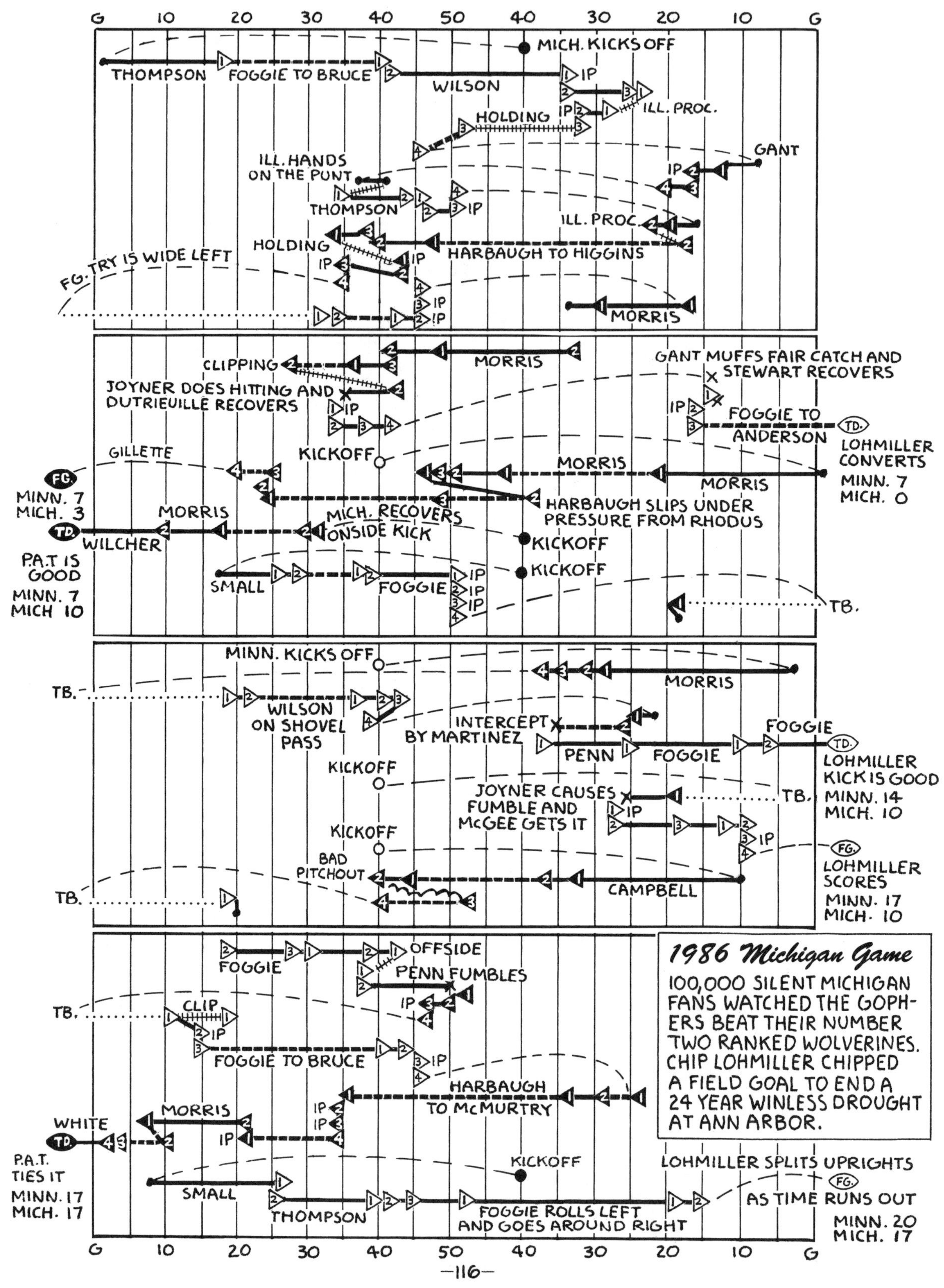

G 10 20 30 40 50 40 30 20 10 G
MICH. KICKS OFF
THOMPSON
FOGGIE TO BRUCE
WILSON
IP
HOLDING
ILL. PROC.
GANT
ILL. HANDS ON THE PUNT
THOMPSON
IP
ILL. PROC.
HOLDING
HARBAUGH TO HIGGINS
FG. TRY IS WIDE LEFT
IP
MORRIS
CLIPPING
MORRIS
GANT MUFFS FAIR CATCH AND STEWART RECOVERS
JOYNER DOES HITTING AND DUTRIEUILLE RECOVERS
FOGGIE TO ANDERSON
TD.
LOHMILLER CONVERTS
MINN. 7
MICH. 0
GILLETTE
KICKOFF
MORRIS
MORRIS
FG.
MINN. 7
MICH. 3
HARBAUGH SLIPS UNDER PRESSURE FROM RHODUS
MORRIS
MICH. RECOVERS ONSIDE KICK
TD.
WILCHER
KICKOFF
P.A.T IS GOOD
KICKOFF
SMALL
FOGGIE
MINN. 7
MICH 10
TB.
MINN. KICKS OFF
MORRIS
TB.
WILSON ON SHOVEL PASS
INTERCEPT BY MARTINEZ
FOGGIE
PENN
FOGGIE
TD.
LOHMILLER KICK IS GOOD
MINN. 14
MICH. 10
KICKOFF
JOYNER CAUSES FUMBLE AND McGEE GETS IT
TB.
KICKOFF
FG.
LOHMILLER SCORES
MINN. 17
MICH. 10
BAD PITCHOUT
CAMPBELL
TB.
OFFSIDE
FOGGIE
PENN FUMBLES
TB.
CLIP
IP
FOGGIE TO BRUCE
HARBAUGH TO McMURTRY
MORRIS
WHITE
TD.
P.A.T. TIES IT
MINN. 17
MICH. 17
KICKOFF
LOHMILLER SPLITS UPRIGHTS AS TIME RUNS OUT
FG.
SMALL
THOMPSON
FOGGIE ROLLS LEFT AND GOES AROUND RIGHT
MINN. 20
MICH. 17
G 10 20 30 40 50 40 30 20 10 G
1986 Michigan Game
100,000 SILENT MICHIGAN FANS WATCHED THE GOPHERS BEAT THEIR NUMBER TWO RANKED WOLVERINES. CHIP LOHMILLER CHIPPED A FIELD GOAL TO END A 24 YEAR WINLESS DROUGHT AT ANN ARBOR.

Darrell Thompson
AS A ROOKIE THIS POPULAR RUNNING BACK, FROM ROCHESTER JOHN MARSHALL, WAS ELECTED M.V.P. BY HIS TEAMMATES. HE PERSONALLY BOUGHT AND PRESENTED TROPHIES TO HIS LINEMEN IN GRATITUDE FOR HELPING HIM GET THROUGH THE LINE.
HE SET A NATIONAL RECORD FOR MOST YARDS (205) RUSHING BY A FRESHMAN IN A FIRST GAME.
AGAINST MICHIGAN HE SET A BIG TEN MARK IN 1987 WITH A 98 YARD RUN. HIS OVER 200 YARDS FOR THE DAY IS THE HIGHEST TOTAL ANYONE HAS EVER MADE AGAINST A MICHIGAN TEAM.
THOMPSON CHALKED UP THREE 1000 YARD SEASONS IN RUSHING AND BARELY MISSED THE FOURTH, DUE TO INJURY. HE RAN FARTHER (4518 YARDS) THAN ANY GOPHER IN HISTORY AND SCORED THE MOST TOUCHDOWNS (43) FOR THE MOST POINTS (260).
HE ATTEMPTED TWO PASSES IN HIS MINNESOTA CAREER... BOTH GOOD FOR TOUCHDOWNS.
GREEN BAY DRAFTED HIM IN THE FIRST ROUND.
AL PAPAS JR.

OVER THE LONG STRETCH THE MOST FAMILIAR VOICES TO MINNESOTA FANS WERE HALSEY "HOLY COW" HALL AND JULES PERLT.

HALSEY'S FRIENDLY VOICE AND INFECTIOUS LAUGHTER, COUPLED WITH HIS DEEP KNOWLEDGE OF THE GAME, WERE A JOY TO LISTEN TO. HE WAS A SPORTS WRITER AS WELL AS SPORTSCASTER.

IN 1934 HE WAS CREDITED WITH GIVING THE GOPHERS THE NICKNAME "GOLDEN GOPHERS." THIS WAS DUE TO THEIR ALL-GOLD UNFORMS. COACH BIERMAN DECIDED ON THE ALL-GOLD LOOK BECAUSE HE THOUGHT THE COLOR WOULD BEST HIDE THE BALL.

JULES PERLT'S DISTINCTIVE AND DRAMATIC VOICE WAS "THE" VOICE OF U OF M SPORTS FOR OVER 50 YEARS. FROM BRONKO NAGURSKI TO DARRELL THOMPSON, HE KEPT STADIUM FANS INFORMED OF WHAT WAS HAPPENING ON THE FIELD. SOMEHOW THINGS WEREN'T OFFICIAL UNTIL HE SPOKE.

AL PĀPAS JR.

Extra Points

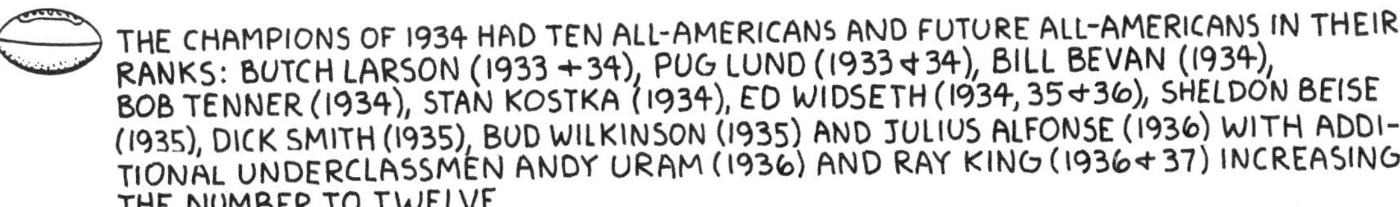

THE CHAMPIONS OF 1934 HAD TEN ALL-AMERICANS AND FUTURE ALL-AMERICANS IN THEIR RANKS: BUTCH LARSON (1933 + 34), PUG LUND (1933 + 34), BILL BEVAN (1934), BOB TENNER (1934), STAN KOSTKA (1934), ED WIDSETH (1934, 35 + 36), SHELDON BEISE (1935), DICK SMITH (1935), BUD WILKINSON (1935) AND JULIUS ALFONSE (1936) WITH ADDITIONAL UNDERCLASSMEN ANDY URAM (1936) AND RAY KING (1936 + 37) INCREASING THE NUMBER TO TWELVE.

THE 1933 TEAM HAD A 4-WIN 4-TIE SEASON WHILE SCORING ONLY 64 POINTS TO THEIR OPPONENTS' 32. STILL, THEY WERE RATED THIRD NATIONALLY BEHIND MICHIGAN AND NEBRASKA.

THE "MINNESOTA SHIFT" WAS THE FIRST GREAT SHIFT IN THE HISTORY OF FOOTBALL. PLAYERS WOULD MOVE TO ANY NUMBER OF POSITIONS, AS THIS DIAGRAM SHOWS, JUST AS THE BALL WAS BEING HIKED. IT WAS SO EFFECTIVE THAT IT WAS EVENTUALLY BANNED. OUT OF THIS EVOLVED THE RULE WHERE THE PLAYERS MUST BE MOTIONLESS IN A SET POSITION FOR AT LEAST ONE SECOND BEFORE THE BALL IS SNAPPED.

WHEN THE TRAINING TABLE BEGAN IT WAS CONSIDERED A "PHENOMENAL ENTERPRISE."

THE FOLLOWING IS THE MINNESOTA FAN'S RETALIATION FOR WISCONSIN'S "OLE" CHEER IN 1909:

OLE OLSON! YON YONSON!
VE SKIN VISKONSIN!
YAH-H-H!

MINNESOTA WON THE CHEERS AND THE GAME.

"GHOST BALL" WAS A NAME REFERRING TO NIGHT PRACTICE BEFORE THE 1911 CHICAGO GAME. THE LIGHTING TECHNIQUE WAS NOT MENTIONED BUT SEARCH LIGHTS WERE USED IN 1922 "GHOST BALL."

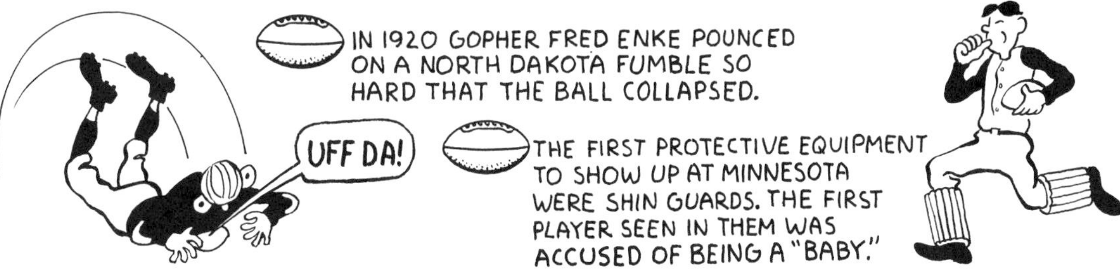

IN 1920 GOPHER FRED ENKE POUNCED ON A NORTH DAKOTA FUMBLE SO HARD THAT THE BALL COLLAPSED.

THE FIRST PROTECTIVE EQUIPMENT TO SHOW UP AT MINNESOTA WERE SHIN GUARDS. THE FIRST PLAYER SEEN IN THEM WAS ACCUSED OF BEING A "BABY."

IN 1889 MICHIGAN WAS CHALLENGED TO A GAME. THEY INSISTED ON $200 TRAVEL EXPENSES TO COME TO MINNESOTA. THIS IDEA WAS DECLINED AND THE GAME WAS NOT PLAYED.

THE FIRST OUT-OF-STATE GAME FOR MINNESOTA WAS IN 1890 AGAINST GRINNELL COLLEGE IN IOWA. (MINNESOTA 18 – GRINNELL 13).

HALL OF FAMER ED ROGERS PLAYED END IN THE DAYS BEFORE THE FORWARD PASS. SINCE HIS OUTPOST POSITION WAS CONSIDERED TOO FAR AWAY TO RUN AND GET THE BALL HE NEVER BECAME A BALL CARRIER.

A POST-SEASON GAME WAS OFFERED TO THE GOPHERS IN 1941. THE REGENTS RESPONDED THAT THEY WOULDN'T CONSIDER AN INVITATION FOR EITHER "COMMERCIAL OR CHARITABLE PURPOSES."

GOPHER M.J. LUBY WAS ONE OF THE FOUNDERS OF A PUBLICATION CALLED "FOOTBALL" IN 1899. "FOOTBALL" EVOLVED INTO THE "MINNESOTA DAILY" WITH LUBY AS ITS FIRST MANAGER.

COACH BILL SPAULDING HAD SOME RATHER DEFINITE OPINIONS IN 1923. HE SAID THAT FOOTBALL "IS A WONDERFUL REMEDY FOR MALE EFFEMINACY WHICH ABOUNDS ON MANY A COLLEGE AND UNIVERSITY CAMPUS. IT TAKES BOYS OUT OF THE PARLORS AND POOL ROOMS AND MAKES MEN OF THEM IF SUCH A THING IS POSSIBLE. EVERY MINNESOTA MAN WHO IS PHYSICALLY ABLE SHOULD PLAY FOOTBALL."

MINNESOTA PLAYED IN DOUBLE HEADERS IN 1899 AND 1905.

OUTSIDE OF FOOTBALL HENRY WILLIAMS MADE HIS MARK IN TRACK AS WELL. UPON GRADUATION FROM YALE HE HELD THE COLLEGE RECORD IN THE LOW HURDLES AND WORLD RECORD IN THE HIGH HURDLES.

WILLIAMS' 1903 PLAYERS WERE KNOWN AS THE "GIANTS OF THE NORTH." THEY AVERAGED, HOWEVER, ONLY 185 POUNDS. THEY WERE ALSO KNOWN AS "SWEDES" THOUGH THERE WEREN'T ANY ON THE TEAM. EGIL BOECKMANN WAS CLOSEST, HAVING BEEN BORN IN NORWAY.

DR. WILLIAMS' TEAMS OF 1903-04 SKUNKED 13 STRAIGHT OPPONENTS.

AFTER HIS OFFICIAL COACHING DAYS WERE OVER, WILLIAMS WOULD STILL SIT ON THE GOPHER BENCH DURING GAMES AND ASSIST HIS SUCCESSOR, BILL SPAULDING.

IN 1916 WISCONSIN WAS HELD TO NO GAINS DURING THE FIRST QUARTER. THE GOPHERS HELD THEM TO MINUS 30 YARDS FOR THE DAY.

DR. HENRY WILLIAMS

YOU COULD SAY THAT THE GOPHERS WERE UPSET FROM BEING UPSET BY NEBRASKA IN 1902. A COUPLE OF WEEKS AFTER THAT GAME THEY TOOK ON GRINNELL WHO HAD LOST TO THE CORNHUSKERS 17-0. MINNESOTA PROCEEDED TO SCORE 17 TOUCHDOWNS ON THEM; ONE FOR EVERY POINT MADE BY NEBRASKA. THE GRINNELL CAPTAIN PLEADED, "LET UP ON US, CAN'T YOU; WE'LL TAKE YOUR WORD FOR IT THAT YOU COULD LICK NEBRASKA."

STANFORD INVITED THE SUCCESSFUL 1903 GOPHERS TO PLAY IN THE SECOND-EVER ROSE BOWL GAME. AFTER THE CONTRACT WAS SET ADDITIONAL CONCESSIONS WERE PUT TO MINNESOTA. THE GOPHERS WOULDN'T AGREE TO THEM AND SO THE 1904 ROSE BOWL CONTEST WAS CANCELLED. THE NEW YEAR'S DAY GAMES WEREN'T TAKEN UP AGAIN UNTIL 1916.

HOW THINGS HAVE CHANGED. THE QUARTERBACK WAS A BLOCKING BACK AND NOT A BALL CARRIER ON THE 1934 TEAM. GLEN SIDEL CARRIED ONLY FIVE TIMES IN SIX GAMES.

IN THE 1965 INDIANA GAME THERE WERE NO PUNTS BY EITHER THE GOPHERS OR HOOSIERS.

A SHOULDER INJURY RESULTED IN ED WIDSETH HAVING HIS ARM STRAPPED TO HIS SIDE FOR THE LAST HALF OF HIS FINAL SEASON. HE STILL MADE CONSENSUS ALL-AMERICAN.

KNUTE ROCKNE PROMISED A NEW SUIT OF CLOTHES TO THE FIRST OF HIS PLAYERS WHO COULD THROW HERB JOESTING FOR A LOSS... BUT NEVER HAD TO PAY OFF.

OHIO STATE AND NEBRASKA WERE CO-NATIONAL CHAMPIONS IN 1970. MINNESOTA HAD THE DISTINCTION OF PLAYING THEM EACH WITHIN 14 DAYS.

MINNESOTA'S BEST 5-YEAR RECORD IS 54-3-3 (.925%) FROM 1900-1904.

ART CLARKSON PLAYED ON THE 1934 TEAM. HE WAS BORN IN CHINA TO CANADIAN PARENTS, SPOKE CHINESE AND JAPANESE AND WAS AMBIDEXTROUS AT PASSING AND KICKING.

GUARD LES PULKRABECK PLAYED IN THE EARLY 1920'S. DURING ONE PRACTICE HE STUFFED HIS NOSE SO FULL OF GRAVEL AND MUD TO STOP BLEEDING THAT IT TOOK A TRAINER AND AIDES OVER TWO HOURS TO CLEAR OUT HIS NOSTRILS, MOUTH AND THROAT.

OF PRESENT DIVISION I-A FOOTBALL TEAMS, ONLY MICHIGAN AND NAVY HAVE PLAYED LONGER THAN MINNESOTA.

MINNESOTA ALMOST STARTED ITS INTERCOLLEGIATE COMPETITION TWO YEARS EARLIER THAN IT DID. CARLETON, HOWEVER, DECLINED AN INVITATION TO PLAY.

IN 1903 MINNESOTA OUT SCORED ITS OPPONENTS 661-12. THE 1904 SEASON IMPROVED TO 725-12. THESE BACK-TO-BACK SEASONS TOTALED 1,386-24.

MIKE HOHENSEE, IN 1981, ATTEMPTED 67 PASSES AGAINST OHIO STATE. FIVE OF THEM WERE FOR TOUCHDOWNS IN THE VICTORY.

THE FIRST HOMECOMING BONFIRE AT MINNESOTA DATES BACK TO 1915.

MINNESOTA WAS THE FIRST TEAM EVER TO BE SEEN ON TELEVISION. THIS HAPPENED ON SEPTEMBER 10, 1939 WHEN KSTP EXPERIMENTED ON A PRACTICE SESSION.

MINNESOTA'S FIRST GAME APPEARANCE ON TELEVISION WAS AGAINST PITTSBURGH IN 1953.

THE 1962 MAROON AND GOLD VICTORY IN THE ROSE BOWL WAS THE FIRST COLLEGE FOOTBALL GAME TO BE TELEVISED NATIONALLY IN COLOR.

BECAUSE OF GOOD SEASONS, MINNESOTA PROCLAIMED ITSELF AS "CHAMPIONS OF THE NORTHWEST" IN 1890 AND 1891.

MINNESOTA WAS THE FIRST TO PLAY EIGHT CONFERENCE GAMES IN THE BIG 10. THEY DID SO IN 1957, MISSING ONLY OHIO STATE.

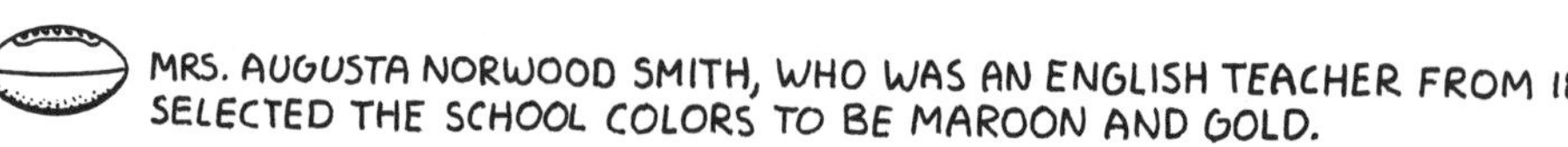
MRS. AUGUSTA NORWOOD SMITH, WHO WAS AN ENGLISH TEACHER FROM 1876-1880, SELECTED THE SCHOOL COLORS TO BE MAROON AND GOLD.

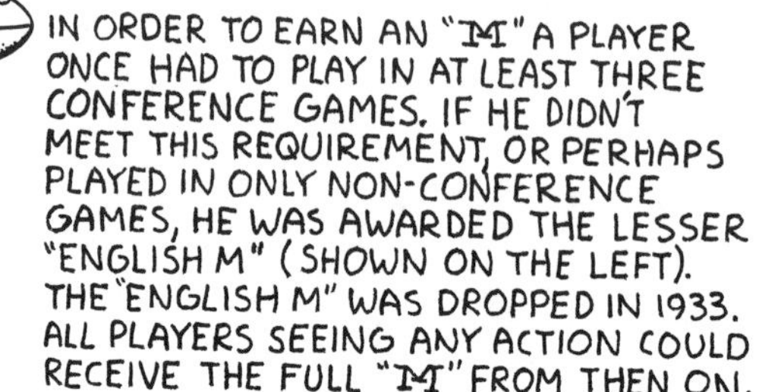
IN ORDER TO EARN AN "M" A PLAYER ONCE HAD TO PLAY IN AT LEAST THREE CONFERENCE GAMES. IF HE DIDN'T MEET THIS REQUIREMENT, OR PERHAPS PLAYED IN ONLY NON-CONFERENCE GAMES, HE WAS AWARDED THE LESSER "ENGLISH M" (SHOWN ON THE LEFT). THE "ENGLISH M" WAS DROPPED IN 1933. ALL PLAYERS SEEING ANY ACTION COULD RECEIVE THE FULL "M" FROM THEN ON.

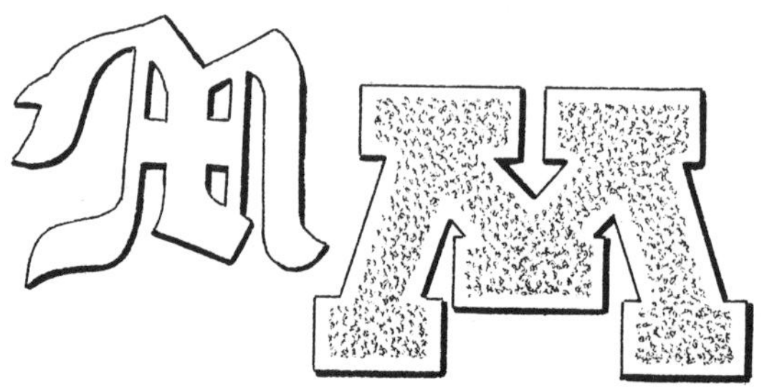

AFTER THE PRESEASON PRACTICE FOR THE 1918 SEASON WAS ENDED THE ENTIRE BACKFIELD WAS CALLED INTO THE ARMED SERVICES.

THE TRAINING TABLE AND QUARTERS WERE BROUGHT TO MINNESOTA IN 1890. SINCE THEY HAD BUT ONE BATHTUB THEIR MAIN CONCERN WAS, "SHALL THE OTHER STUDENTS BE PERMITTED TO SHARE THE BATH-TUB WITH THE TEAM?"

THE FIRST FOOTBALL PLAYED AT THE U OF M WAS ON OCTOBER 12, 1878. IT WAS AN INTRAMURAL GAME FEATURING THE FRESHMEN AGAINST THE SOPHOMORES. THE FRESHMEN WON ON THE STRENGTH OF HAVING MORE PLAYERS.

DURING THE SAME YEAR C.C. CAMP, FROM YALE, INTRODUCED FOOTBALL AT SHATTUCK MILITARY ACADAMY IN FARIBAULT. HE LAID OUT THE FIRST REGULATION FIELD IN THE NORTHWEST. USING THE RUGBY STYLE OF PLAY THE HIGH SCHOOL ORGANIZED A TEAM OF STUDENTS AND FACULTY. THEY WON THEIR FIRST GAME AGAINST SEABURY DIVINITY. THEY CHALLENGED MANY COLLEGES INCLUDING MINNESOTA. THEY ENDED THEIR PLAYING DAYS AGAINST THE GOPHERS WITH A 4-3-0 WINNING EDGE.

MINNESOTA MAY NOW PLAY IN THE DOME, BUT THE FIRST INDOOR GAME HAD PENN PLAYING RUTGERS IN 1887 AT MADISON SQUARE GARDEN, N.Y.

THE MINNEAPOLIS PARK BOARD, IN 1933, RECEIVED A SUGGESTION THAT IT BUILD A COVERED FIELDHOUSE FOR PROFESSIONAL FOOTBALL DURING THE WINTER MONTHS.

1926 SAW THE GOPHERS PLAY MICHIGAN TWICE. THEY PLAYED AT HOME AND AWAY. REPORTS OF THE ANN ARBOR GAME WERE TELEGRAPHED BACK TO MINNESOTA WHERE SCRUBS ACTED OUT THE PLAYS BEFORE HOME FANS.

MINNESOTA WOULD NOT COMPLY WITH BIG TEN "RECOMMENDATIONS" FOR PLAYERS TO WEAR NUMERALS IN 1914. BY 1921 THE BIG TEN "URGED" THAT THEY BE USED. COACH WILLIAMS DID NOT WANT HIS PLAYERS TO BE IDENTIFIED AND SO PUT FOUR-DIGIT NUMBERS ON THEM TO BE UNREADABLE.

IN 1920 MINNESOTA LOST 225 YARDS TO NORTH DAKOTA IN PENALTIES. IT DIDN'T MAKE ANY DIFFERENCE, THOUGH, AS THEY MANAGED TO WIN ANYWAY... 41-3.

BECAUSE OF THE WORLD WAR, ATHLETICS WERE TAKEN OVER BY THE MILITARY IN 1918. THERE WAS LITTLE INTEREST SHOWN BY UNIVERSITY FANS BUT THERE WERE ENOUGH PLAYERS TO FIELD 16 COMPANY TEAMS.

THE INDIANA GAME OF 1906 WAS PLAYED ON A SLIPPERY FIELD. EACH TEAM PUNTED 28 TIMES FOR A GAME TOTAL OF 56! INDIANA SCORED ON A MISJUDGED PUNT OVER A GOPHER RECEIVER. MINNESOTA CAME BACK ON A PUNT WHERE THE INDIANA RECEIVER WAS CARRIED OVER THE GOAL FOR A SAFETY (LEGAL THEN). AFTER A GOPHER FIELD GOAL, INDIANA WAS HELD DEEP NEAR THEIR OWN GOAL. A BAD SNAP ON A PUNT TRY HAD INDIANA COUGHING UP ANOTHER SAFETY, AS WELL AS THE GAME 8-6.

EARLY PLAYERS OF THE 1880'S PAID FOR THEIR OWN UNIFORMS AND TRAVEL EXPENSES AS WELL AS CONDITIONED THE FIELD THEMSELVES.

ED ROGERS ALMOST COMPLETELY MISSED THE 1903 BELOIT GAME. HE WAS LOCKED UP WITH JURY DUTY.

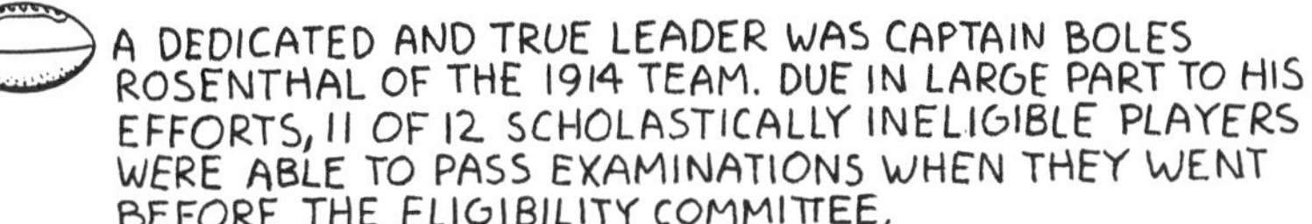

A DEDICATED AND TRUE LEADER WAS CAPTAIN BOLES ROSENTHAL OF THE 1914 TEAM. DUE IN LARGE PART TO HIS EFFORTS, 11 OF 12 SCHOLASTICALLY INELIGIBLE PLAYERS WERE ABLE TO PASS EXAMINATIONS WHEN THEY WENT BEFORE THE ELIGIBILITY COMMITTEE.

JOHN PHILIP SOUSA

JOHN PHILIP SOUSA CAME TO TOWN IN 1926 TO GIVE A CONCERT. A UNIVERSITY COMMITTEE ASKED HIM TO COMPOSE A TUNE FOR THE U OF M. HE ANSWERED BY WRITING THE STIRRING "MINNESOTA MARCH." THE WORDS WERE THEN ADDED TO IT BY MICHAEL M. JALMA, DIRECTOR OF THE MINNESOTA BAND.

TRUMAN E. RICKARD COMPOSED "HAIL MINNESOTA" IN 1904 FOR A SENIOR CLASS PLAY. ADDITIONS TO ITS LYRICS BY ARTHUR UPSON HAVE MADE IT AN ENDURING SCHOOL SONG. IN 1945 IT WAS ADOPTED BY THE LEGISLATURE AS THE MINNESOTA STATE SONG.

THE "MINNESOTA ROUSER" (SEE NEXT PAGE FOR ORIGINAL VERSION) WAS WRITTEN BY FLOYD M. HUTSELL IN 1909. IT WAS THE WINNER OF A CONTEST SPONSORED BY THE MINNEAPOLIS TRIBUNE. THE AWARD WAS $100. A COUPLE OF THE CONTEST JUDGES WERE U OF M PRESIDENT CYRUS W. NORTHROP AND MINNESOTA GOVERNOR A.O. EBERHART.

HUNGRY FOR THAT SAME $100 WAS A SONG WRITER NAMED WILLIAM PURDY. HE CAME UP WITH A TUNE STARTING WITH THE WORDS "MINNESOTA! MINNESOTA!" HIS ROOMMATE, CARL BECK, CONVINCED HIM TO GIVE UP THE CONTEST AND CHANGE THE WORDS TO SUIT A UNIVERSITY THAT BECK HAD PREVIOUSLY ATTENDED. THE TUNE BECAME REBORN AS "ON, WISCONSIN!"

THE U. OF M. ROUSER.

Dedicated to B. A. Rose, Band Master, U. of M.

REFRAIN.
Min - ne - so - ta, hats off to thee, To your col - ors
true we shall ev - er be...... Firm and strong, u - ni - ted are we.
Rah, rah, rah, for Ski - U - Ma, Rah, rah, rah, rah, rah, rah, rah, Rah, for the U of
M. Ah.................. Rah for the U. of M...............

IKE ARMSTRONG WAS MINNESOTA ATHLETIC DIRECTOR FROM 1950–1963. BEFORE COMING TO MINNESOTA HE COACHED UTAH FOR 25 YEARS AND LEFT A 140-55-15 RECORD, FOR A WINNING PERCENTAGE OF .702. IT EARNED HIM ENTRANCE INTO THE HALL OF FAME AS A COACH.

IKE ARMSTRONG

FLOYD OF ROSEDALE WASN'T JUST ANY HOG. HE WAS THE BROTHER OF A MOVIE STAR WHO APPEARED IN THE 1933 MOVIE "STATE FAIR" WITH WILL ROGERS. FAME DIDN'T SAVE POOR FLOYD, THOUGH. HE WAS GIVEN TO AN AUSTIN LAD WHO WON HIM IN AN ESSAY CONTEST AND WAS PROBABLY LAST SEEN ON A DINNER TABLE.

AT ONE TIME ROCKET DISPLAYS WOULD FOLLOW GOPHER TOUCHDOWNS.

IN 1947 LEO NOMELLINI WAS SENT DOWN TO THE SECOND TEAM AFTER TURNING IN HIS "WORST" PERFORMANCE OF THE SEASON AGAINST IOWA. IOWA, HOWEVER, VOTED HIM ON THEIR ALL-OPPONENTS TEAM OF THE SEASON.

A MOVIE, "SMITH OF MINNESOTA" WAS MADE OF THE LIFE OF HEISMAN TROPHY WINNER BRUCE SMITH.

SMITH ONCE COLLAPSED FROM EXHAUSTION AFTER BREAKING FREE FOR A SURE TOUCHDOWN. HE HAD BEEN RUNNING CIRCLES AROUND THE OPPOSITION ALL DAY, UNTIL HE DROPPED.

TWO OF THE MOST GOLDEN OF GOPHERS HAVE HAD THEIR NUMERALS RETIRED: BRUCE SMITH (54) AND BRONKO NAGURSKI (72).

IN 1951 PAUL GIEL SET A THEN-BIG TEN RECORD BY RUSHING AND PASSING FOR 1,078 YARDS. WHAT'S MORE AMAZING IS HE DID IT ON A TEAM WITH A 1-4-1 RECORD. AGAINST WISCONSIN HE MADE 106 YARDS, THOUGH THE BADGERS LED THE NATION IN DEFENSE.

ALL-AMERICAN BOB McNAMARA AND HIS BROTHER PINKY GANGED UP ON MICHIGAN STATE IN 1954. THEY BOTH PLAYED THE FULL GAME AND COMBINED FOR OVER 100 YARDS RUSHING. THEY CAUGHT ALL THE GOPHER PASSES ON THE DAY FOR 91 YARDS. BOB SCORED ON AN INTERCEPTION AS THEY SETTLED FOR A SATISFYING WIN.

SOME TIME AFTER HIS PLAYING DAYS GEORGE HAUSER RAN INTO WALTER CAMP, THE MOST RECOGNIZED AUTHORITY IN NAMING ALL-AMERICANS. IT SEEMED CAMP HAD STARTED TO PUT HAUSER ON HIS ALL-AMERICAN TEAM OF 1916 BUT WITHDREW HIM AT THE REQUEST OF COACH WILLIAMS. WILLIAMS DIDN'T WANT A JUNIOR TO WIN THE HONOR BECAUSE IT MIGHT NOT GIVE HIM SOMETHING TO "SHOOT AT" IN HIS SENIOR YEAR. IN 1917, IN RESPECT TO THOSE WHO WENT TO WAR, CAMP DIDN'T MAKE ALL-AMERICAN SELECTIONS. HE DID HAVE AN HONOR ROLL. HE TOLD HAUSER HE WAS RETHINKING THIS AND WOULD MAKE A RETROACTIVE TEAM FOR THAT YEAR WHICH WOULD INCLUDE HIM. BEFORE CAMP OFFICIALLY HAD A CHANCE TO DO IT, HE DIED. GEORGE HAUSER WAS A TWO-TIME WALTER CAMP ALL-AMERICAN WHO NEVER GOT CREDIT FOR IT.

AGAINST MICHIGAN, IN 1935, TUFFY THOMPSON RETURNED KICKOFFS FOR 93 AND 95 YARDS.

ROBERT LIGGETT SCORED SEVEN TOUCHDOWNS AGAINST GRINNELL IN 1902.

HOWARD T. ABBOTT WAS CAPTAIN IN 1885 THOUGH NO GAMES WERE PLAYED THAT YEAR.

ALL-BIG TEN PLAYER CHUCK ORTMANN OF MICHIGAN, SET A BIG TEN RECORD BY LOSING AN OVERALL 38 YARDS TO MINNESOTA IN 1950.

TULANE MADE GOOD USE OF FORMER GOPHER PLAYERS BY HAVING THEM AS THEIR HEAD COACHES: CLARK SHAUGHNESSY, BERNIE BIERMAN AND TED COX.

ADAM KELLY GOT OFF A PUNT OF 83 YARDS AGAINST IOWA IN 1984.

THINGS MUST HAVE BEEN ROUGH FOR PLAYERS IN 1923-24. CARL LINDBERG RELATED, "ONCE I EVEN SOLD BLOOD SO I COULD EAT BEFORE A GAME."

IN THEIR FIRST EVER GAME WITH MICHIGAN, IN 1892, THE GOPHERS CAME OUT THE VICTOR. THIS ELEVATED MINNESOTA FROM A SMALL COLLEGE TO ONE OF THE BIGGIES BECAUSE THEY HAD DEFEATED SUCH A PRESTIGIOUS COLLEGE. THE CELEBRATIONS LASTED INTO THE SPRING. IT WAS THE ONLY TIME THE GOPHERS HELD THE EDGE IN THIS SCHOOL SERIES.

MINNESOTA HAS HAD MORE THAN ALL-AMERICAN PLAYERS. GEORGE AAGAARD WAS AN ALL-AMERICAN DRUM MAJOR. FROM 1932-36 HE WOULD KICK OFF THE HALFTIME CEREMONIES BY TOSSING HIS BATON OVER THE GOAL POST.

GEORGE AAGAARD

A SECOND TIER WAS PROPOSED FOR MEMORIAL STADIUM IN 1946 TO INCREASE SEATING TO 80,000.

INDIANA FUMBLED 12 TIMES AGAINST THE GOPHERS IN 1946. MINNESOTA GOBBLED UP SEVEN OF THEM.

THE CHICAGO COLLEGE OF PHYSICIANS & SURGEONS CAME TO PLAY IN 1901. THE "GOPHER" YEARBOOK SAID OF THE FUTURE DOCTORS OF OUR HEALTH..."THE CHICAGO TEAM WAS A HEAVY ONE, BUT IN SUCH POOR PHYSICAL CONDITION THAT THE VARSITY WERE GIVEN BUT POOR PRACTICE."

CLARK SHAUGHNESSY BERNIE BIERMAN

FORMER GOPHER TEAMMATES, BERNIE BIERMAN AND CLARK SHAUGHNESSY, HAVE THE DISTINCTION OF BOTH COACHING NATIONAL CHAMPIONS AT THE SAME TIME FOR DIFFERENT TEAMS. IN 1940 BIERMAN'S MINNESOTA SQUAD WAS DECLARED CHAMPIONS WITH AN 8-0 RECORD. SHAUGHNESSY'S STANFORD TEAM RECEIVED THE SAME HONOR WITH A 9-0 RECORD, WHICH INCLUDED A VICTORY IN THE ROSE BOWL. SHAUGHNESSY TOOK OVER A TEAM THAT HAD A 1-7-1 RECORD THE PREVIOUS SEASON.

- ALL-AMERICAN JAMES WALKER WAS 6'3" TALL AND WEIGHED BETWEEN 230-250 POUNDS. HIS FOLKS OBJECTED TO HIS PLAYING, SO HE QUIT AFTER HIS SOPHOMORE YEAR AND WENT OUT EAST TO CONTINUE THERE.

- IN 1978 WASHINGTON TURNED OVER FIVE INTERCEPTIONS AND FOUR FUMBLES TO MINNESOTA.

- MINNESOTA'S LONGEST UNDEFEATED STRING IS AGAINST IOWA STATE WITH 20 GAMES. THE LONGEST WIN STRING IS 18 AGAINST NORTH DAKOTA.

- THE INDIAN WAR DRUM WAS A GIFT FROM ED ROGERS. HE SAID IT WAS USED IN TIME OF DANGER AND SHOULD BE BEATEN WHEN THE TEAM NEEDED EXTRA ENCOURAGEMENT TO PULL A GAME OUT. CHIPPEWA FROM LEECH LAKE WORE FULL CEREMONIAL COSTUMES WHEN IT WAS PRESENTED AT HOMECOMING IN 1917. UNIVERSITY STUDENTS WORE SIMILAR COSTUMES LATER ON AND USED THE DRUM WHEN OPPONENTS ENTERED MINNESOTA TERRITORY. IT WENT OUT OF USE IN THE 1930'S.

- THE HIGHEST SCORE BY A LOSING TEAM, IN THE BIG TEN, IS 43 BY INDIANA AGAINST MINNESOTA IN 1973.

- A QUESTIONNAIRE TO FORMER PLAYERS WAS SENT OUT IN 1914. MOST RETURNED COMMENTS WERE POSITIVE BUT THERE WERE A COUPLE OF COMPLAINTS. ONE WAS, "SECRET PRACTICE AND THE PAID PROFESSIONAL COACH MUST GO IF FOOTBALL IS TO REMAIN A COLLEGE AND AN AMATEUR SPORT."

- ALMOST FIVE COMPLETE SEASONS HAD PASSED BEFORE A BIERMAN TEAM FIRST ATTEMPTED A FIELD GOAL. HORACE BELL THEN KICKED ONE, GOOD FROM 45 YARDS.

- FOR THREE STRAIGHT YEARS, 1934, 35 AND 36, THE GOPHERS CAME IN SECOND FOR BEING THE GREATEST TEAM IN ALL SPORTDOM BY THE ASSOCIATED PRESS.

- MINNESOTA ADVANCED THE BALL 1,183 YARDS IN THE 1904 WISCONSIN GAME.

- FOOTBALL IS MEANT TO BE A FUN GAME. IT CAN ALSO END IN SERIOUS TRAGEDY. IN 1923 AN IOWA STATE TACKLE, JACK TRICE, WAS TAKEN FROM THE GAME IN THE THIRD QUARTER DUE TO INJURIES. UP TO THEN HE HAD PLAYED BRILLIANTLY. HIS INJURIES, NOT CONSIDERED SERIOUS AT THE TIME, ENDED HIS LIFE THE DAY AFTER THE GAME.

- COACH THOMAS PEEBLES WOULD YELL "SIS-BOOM-AH, PRINCETON!" WHENEVER HIS MINNESOTA SQUAD WOULD SCORE.

  TEAM CAPTAIN, JOHN ADAMS, MUST HAVE DECIDED IT WAS TIME MINNESOTA TOOK ON ITS OWN IDENTITY. ONE EVENING HE WORKED TO COME UP WITH A DISTINCTIVE MINNESOTA CHEER.

  SOMETHING WOULD HAVE TO GO WITH "RAH, RAH, RAH!" HE THOUGHT. HE STARTED WITH "SKI-OO" WHICH WAS AN EXPRESSION HE HAD HEARD FROM SIOUX INDIANS AS AN EXULTATION OF VICTORY OR PLEASURE. TO MAKE THIS RYHME WITH "RAH," HE INVENTED THE WORD "MAH." TO FINISH OFF HE TOOK THE "E" OUT OF MINNESOTA. THE CHEER WENT, "RAH-RAH-RAH, SKI-OO-MAH, MINN-SO-TA!"

  ADAMS AND HIS ROOMMATE (THEY LIVED AT 1401 S.E. 6TH ST.) WERE SO PLEASED THEY TRIED IT OUT IN THE LATE NIGHT TO SEE IF ANYONE CARED. THEY WERE ANSWERED WITH, "SHUT UP AND GO TO BED!"

  THE YELL BEGAN ITS USE IN THE FALL OF 1884.

TERRITORIAL SETTLERS LOOKED FOR A PROPER ANIMAL TO SYMBOLIZE THE NEW GREAT STATE OF MINNESOTA. OTHER STATES HAD THEM AND MINNESOTA CERTAINLY POSSESSED AMPLE CREATURES TO CHOOSE FROM FOR ITSELF. THE BEAVER WAS THE MOST FAVORED CHOICE, BUT IN THE END IT LOST TO CIRCUMSTANCES THAT MADE THE CHOICE FOR THEM.

ABOVE IS THE CARTOON THAT DECIDED IT ALL. IT WAS WIDELY DISTRIBUTED AND WAS CRITICAL OF A $5,000,000 BOND ISSUE SUPPORTING A RAILROAD CONSTRUCTION PROPOSAL. THE BOND CAME TO THE LEGISLATURE TWO WEEKS BEFORE STATEHOOD IN 1858. THE CARTOON FEATURED THE LOWLY, DESTRUCTIVE GOPHER WITH HEADS OF PROMINENT PRO-BOND PEOPLE ON THEM. THESE "LOW LIFES" WERE REPRESENTED AS TAKING BRIBES, SUPPORTING CORRUPTION AND CLAIMING POLITICAL POWER TO DO AS THEY PLEASED.

THE BOND WON IN SPITE OF THE MUCH-TALKED-ABOUT CARTOON. BEING MUCH TALKED ABOUT, THOUGH, THE NAME "GOPHER" BECAME LINKED TO MINNESOTA... THE GOPHER STATE.

TWINS PLAYED ON THE GOPHER LINE IN 1931. THEY WERE ALLEN AND ALVIN TEETER WHO WERE NICKNAMED "NIP" AND "TUCK."

THE 1918 CARLETON TEAM PUNTED 50 TIMES TO MINNESOTA.

MINNESOTA SET A "WORLD" HIGH SCORING RECORD BY DRUBBING GRINNELL 146-0 IN 1904. THEY SCORED 73 POINTS IN EACH 25 MINUTE HALF AND OUTGAINED GRINNELL 390-60 YARDS. THE SCORING RECORD HELD FOR 13 YEARS.

THE BIG TEN HAS HAD THE ROSE BOWL CONTRACT SINCE 1947 WITH THE EXCEPTION OF 1961 AND 1962. MINNESOTA WENT BY INVITATION THOSE TWO YEARS.

THE ALL-SHRINE TEAM UP THROUGH 1938 FEATURED THREE GOPHERS: HERB JOESTING (1928), BRONKO NAGURSKI (1930) AND ED WIDSETH (1938).

IF JOHN McGOVERN HAD QUIT PLAYING AT MID-SEASON BECAUSE OF A BROKEN COLLAR BONE, HE WOULD HAVE LOST HIS CHANCE FOR ALL-AMERICAN HONORS IN 1909. HE CONVINCED COACH WILLIAMS TO LET HIM CONTINUE.

MICHIGAN COACH FIELDING YOST, ADMIRED THE SPUNKY McGOVERN. HE ORDERED HIS PLAYERS NOT TO HURT HIM.

AT ONE POINT, DURING THE ENSUING GAME, McGOVERN GOT AWAY A PUNT AS THREE WOLVERINES WERE CLOSING IN ON HIM. THE FIRST BOWLED HIM TO THE GROUND. INSTEAD OF ROLLING OVER McGOVERN AND POSSIBLY AGGRAVATING HIS INJURY, HE MANAGED TO STOP SHORT AND BRIDGE HIMSELF OVER HIS BODY. AT THAT POINT THE OTHER TWO WOLVERINES WERE UNABLE TO STOP THEIR COLLISION COURSE. THE WOLVERINE ON THE GROUND PROCEEDED TO BLOCK HIS OWN PLAYERS OUT OF THE WAY. McGOVERN WAS SAVED AND WENT ON TO ALL-AMERICAN DISTINCTION.

THIS WAS THE BREAD AND BUTTER FORMATION OF THE GOLDEN ERA... THE SINGLE WING WITH THE UNBALANCED LINE TO THE RIGHT.

ITS STRENGTH WAS MASS POWER AND BLOCKING POSITION. BIERMAN BELIEVED THAT THE TEAM THAT BLOCKED BEST WOULD WIN. THE PASS, REVERSE AND QUICK KICK WERE USED TO KEEP THE DEFENSE HONEST.

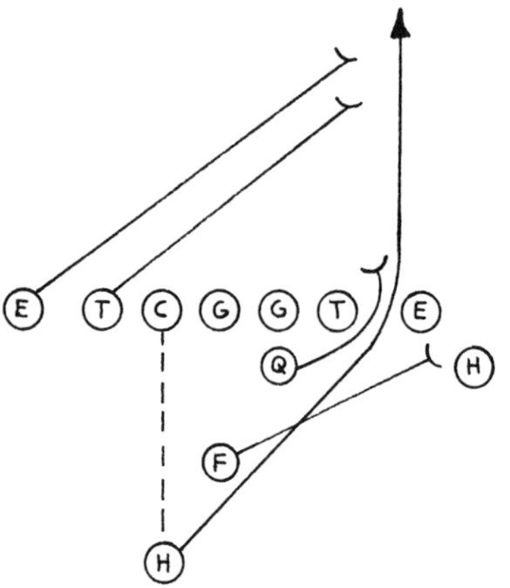

THE LEFT HALFBACK WAS THE CHIEF BALL CARRIER WHILE THE FULLBACK AND QUARTERBACK WERE KEY BLOCKERS. THE RIGHT HALFBACK FOLLOWED THE BALL CARRIER TO RECEIVE A POSSIBLE LATERAL AFTER GOING BEYOND THE LINE OF SCRIMMAGE. THE WEAK LEFT SIDE PLAYERS WERE DEFINITE DOWNFIELD BLOCKERS. IN TIMES PAST DOWNFIELD BLOCKING WAS A MERE HAPPENING RATHER THAN A DELIBERATE ASSIGNMENT.

DISADVANTAGES OF THE FORMATION WERE IN HIDING THE BALL AND THE GREAT LENGTH OF TIME IT TOOK TO SET UP THE PLAY. THAT'S WHY, IN BLOCKING, IT WAS IMPORTANT TO KNOCK DEFENDERS COMPLETELY ON THEIR BACKS.

THE FORMATION WAS DESIGNED TO SCORE A TOUCHDOWN ON EVERY PLAY. BIERMAN STRESSED DISIPLINE AND PERFECTION, WHICH IS WHAT THE SINGLE WING REQUIRED. HE WAS THE MOST CAPABLE COACH AT GETTING IT.

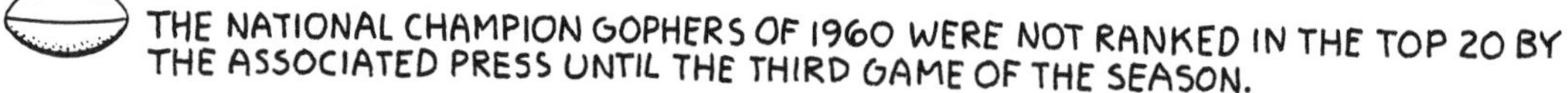

THE NATIONAL CHAMPION GOPHERS OF 1960 WERE NOT RANKED IN THE TOP 20 BY THE ASSOCIATED PRESS UNTIL THE THIRD GAME OF THE SEASON.

ON OCTOBER 19, 1936, THE FIRST-EVER ASSOCIATED PRESS NATIONAL RANKING HAD MINNESOTA AT THE TOP.

IN 1970, AGAINST MICHIGAN STATE, WALTER BOWSER RAN BACK 140 YARDS OF INTERCEPTIONS AND JEFF WRIGHT INTERCEPTED THREE OF HIS OWN.

MINNESOTA BEAT WISCONSIN IN 1926 BY COMING FROM BEHIND IN AN UNUSUAL GAME. THE BADGERS SCORED ON AN 80 YARD RETURN OF A GOPHER FUMBLE. MINNESOTA FOUGHT BACK FOR A TOUCHDOWN WITH HERB JOESTING CARRYING FOUR DEFENDERS ON HIS BACK OVER THE GOAL LINE. LATER ON, MINNESOTA TOOK A LEAD WITH A FIELD GOAL. ANOTHER GOPHER FUMBLE LET WISCONSIN BOOT A FIELD GOAL TO PUT MINNESOTA BEHIND AGAIN. LATE IN THE GAME MINNESOTA RECEIVED A PUNT AND RETURNED 65 YARDS TO WIN 16-10. ON THAT DAY MINNESOTA ALMOST LOST TO A TEAM THEY HAD OUT-FIRST-DOWNED 16-0 AND OUT-GAINED 353 YARDS TO 6.

THE GOPHERS WERE LEADING NEBRASKA 16-12 IN THEIR 1904 CONTEST. DARKNESS WAS FALLING ON THE FINAL MOMENTS AS THE CORNHUSKERS ADVANCED TO THE GOPHER THREE. THERE WAS TIME FOR ONLY ONE MORE PLAY TO DECIDE THE OUTCOME.

MINNESOTA END USHER BURDICK NOTICED HOW SIMILAR HIS SOCKS WERE TO HIS OPPONENTS'. IN THE EXCITEMENT, BETWEEN PLAYS, HE SNEAKED INTO THE NEBRASKA BACKFIELD. AMAZINGLY, NO ONE NOTICED HIM AS THEY LOOKED TO THE GROUND WHILE RECEIVING INSTRUCTIONS. AFTER ALL, DIDN'T THEY ALL LOOK LIKE TEAMMATES FROM THE KNEES DOWN? HE GOT THE PLAY DIRECTLY FROM THE CAPTAIN.

AS THEY LINED UP, BURDICK WAITED AN ETERNITY FOR THE BALL TO BE HIKED. AT LONG LAST IT CAME AND HE CHARGED THE BALL CARRIER. THERE BEING NO FORWARD PROGRESS RULES THEN, HE PICKED HIM UP AND STARTED CARRYING HIM TOWARD THE OPPOSITE GOAL. THE CORNHUSKER WAS BEATING HIM ON THE NECK ALL THE WAY WHILE YELLING "DOWN!" TO STOP THE PLAY. BY THE TIME HE WAS HEARD HE HAD BEEN TAKEN FOR A 12 YARD LOSS. THE GUN SOUNDED TO END THE GAME.

RUSSELL RATHBUN WAS TOO SMALL TO PLAY FOOTBALL BUT STILL MANAGED TO MAKE A UNIQUE CONTRIBUTION. THE 5'5" BIG TEN CHAMPION IN THE MILE RUN WAS VOTED BY THE STUDENT BODY TO BE TEAM CHEERLEADER, OR "ROOTER KING" AS THEY WERE CALLED BACK IN 1910.

HE DIDN'T REALLY WANT THE JOB BUT DECIDED TO DO IT "RIGHT," ANYWAY. TO GET ATTENTION ON THE SIDELINES HE GOT THE IDEA OF WEARING A UNIFORM. HE DRESSED IN ALL WHITE AND PUT AN "M" ON HIS CHEST.

RATHBUN, WHO WAS WELL KNOWN AS "BUNNY" BECAUSE HE RAN AROUND THE TRACK LIKE A RABBIT, DID FLIPS AND GYMNASTICS TO EXCITE THE CROWDS. HIS CHEERLEADING STYLE AND USE OF A UNIFORM WAS HIS INNOVATION HANDED DOWN TO THIS DAY.

THE FORWARD PASS WAS LEGALIZED IN 1906. IF AN ATTEMPTED PASS HIT THE GROUND WITHOUT IT BEING TOUCHED BY A PLAYER ON EITHER TEAM, THE BALL WAS TURNED OVER TO THE DEFENDING TEAM AT THE POINT WHERE IT WAS THROWN. IN THE MEAN TIME THE DEFENSE HAD THE RIGHT TO INTERFERE WITH THE OFFENSIVE RECEIVER.

DURING THE FIRST YEAR OF THE PASS, IN THE NEBRASKA GAME, WILLIAM DOANE BECAME THE FIRST GOPHER TO RECORD AN INTERCEPTION.

THE FIRST INTERCOLLEGIATE POINTS MADE BY MINNESOTA WERE FROM CAPTAIN A. J. BALDWIN. IT WAS IN THE SOCCER STYLE OF PLAY AND HIS SCORE WAS WORTH TWO POINTS. THE GOPHERS BEAT HAMLINE 4-0 IN THAT FIRST GAME ON SEPTEMBER 30, 1882. THE CONTEST TOOK PLACE AT AN EARLY STATE FAIR GROUNDS IN SOUTH MINNEAPOLIS AS SHOWN BELOW. HAMLINE OBJECTED TO PLAYING ON A RACE TRACK.

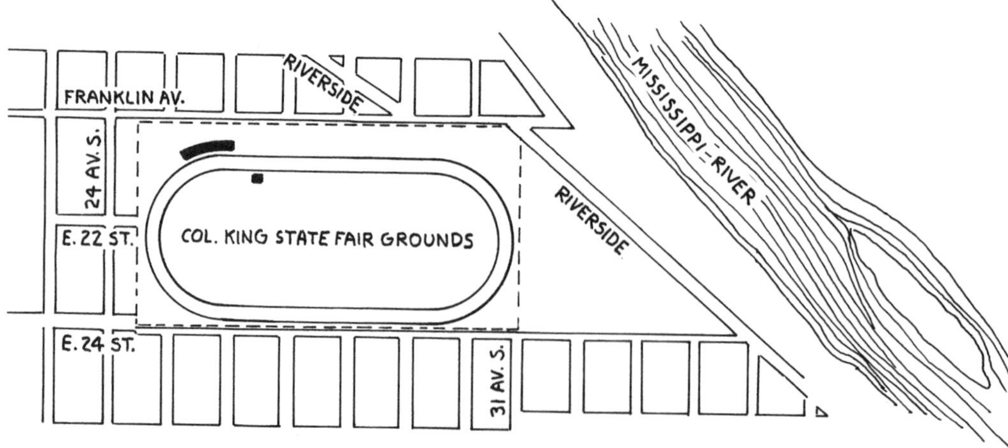

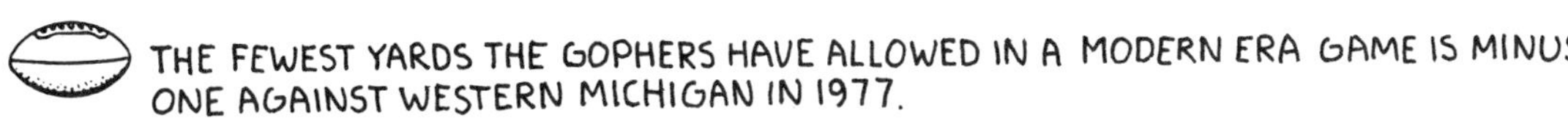

THE FEWEST YARDS THE GOPHERS HAVE ALLOWED IN A MODERN ERA GAME IS MINUS ONE AGAINST WESTERN MICHIGAN IN 1977.

TWO GAMES OF THE 1918 SEASON WERE PLAYED UNDER QUARANTINE DUE TO AN INFLUENZA EPIDEMIC.

MINNESOTA, MICHIGAN AND NORTHWESTERN FORMED THE "INTERCOLLEGIATE ATHLETIC ASSOCIATION OF THE NORTHWEST" IN 1892. IT COVERED FOOTBALL, BASEBALL AND TRACK. THE ASSOCIATION DISBANDED AFTER ITS SECOND SEASON WITH MINNESOTA WINNING THE ONLY TWO FOOTBALL CHAMPIONSHIPS.

1886 WAS THE FIRST YEAR MINNESOTA USED SIGNALS. THEY WERE MILITARY TYPE COMMANDS.

THE 1934 GOPHER CHAMPIONS WERE NOT A PASSING TEAM. THEY THREW ONLY 25 TIMES FOR 15 RECEPTIONS, WHILE ALLOWING THEIR OPPONENTS 28 COMPLETIONS AND INTERCEPTING THEM 21 TIMES.

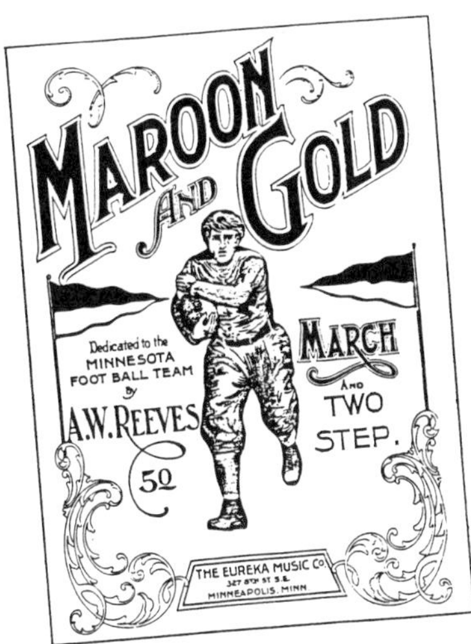

A TUNE PREDATING ALL PRESENT GOPHER SONGS WAS THE "MAROON AND GOLD MARCH AND TWO STEP" OF 1903.

Minnesota's Home Fields

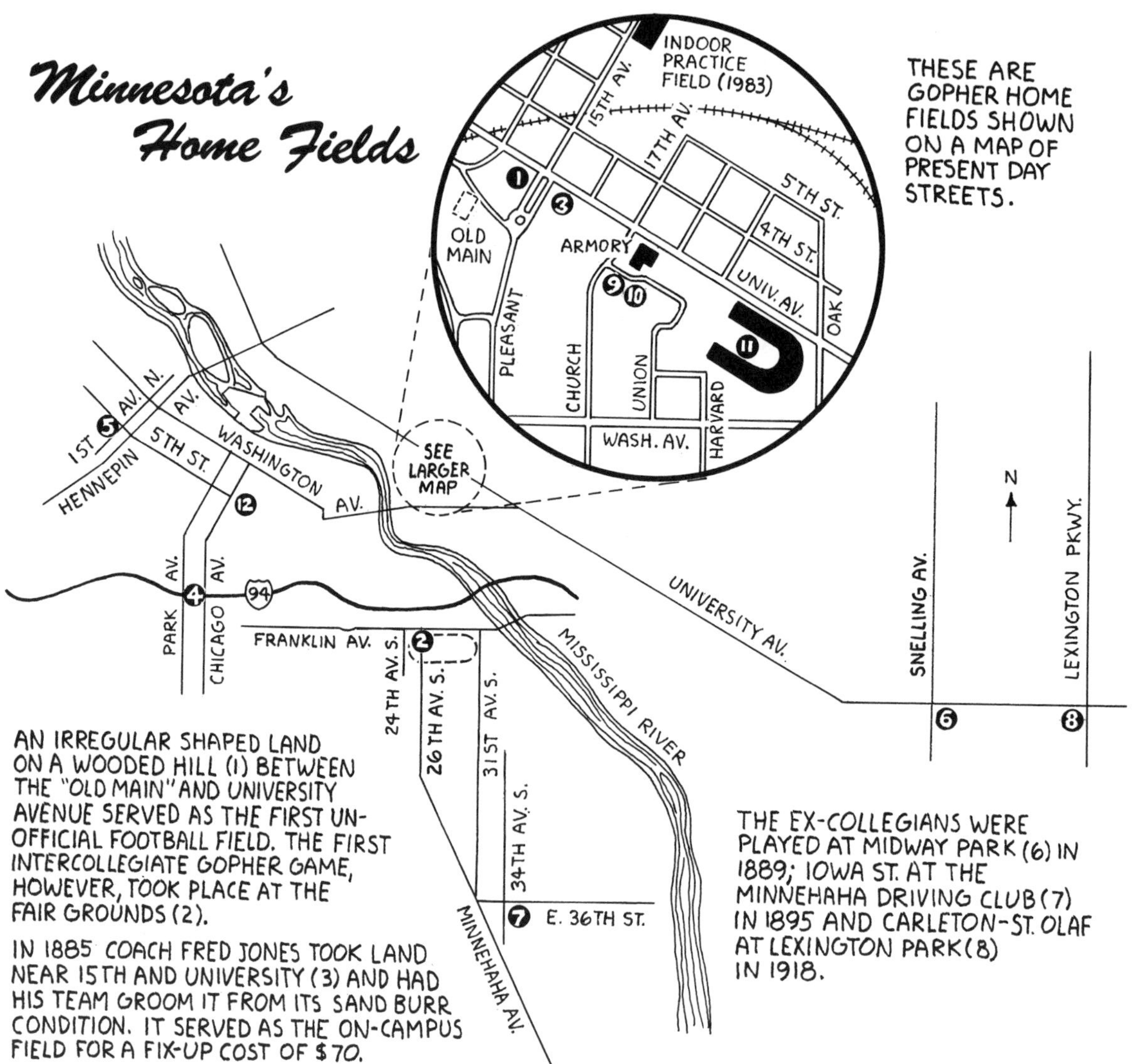

THESE ARE GOPHER HOME FIELDS SHOWN ON A MAP OF PRESENT DAY STREETS.

AN IRREGULAR SHAPED LAND ON A WOODED HILL (1) BETWEEN THE "OLD MAIN" AND UNIVERSITY AVENUE SERVED AS THE FIRST UN-OFFICIAL FOOTBALL FIELD. THE FIRST INTERCOLLEGIATE GOPHER GAME, HOWEVER, TOOK PLACE AT THE FAIR GROUNDS (2).

IN 1885 COACH FRED JONES TOOK LAND NEAR 15TH AND UNIVERSITY (3) AND HAD HIS TEAM GROOM IT FROM ITS SAND BURR CONDITION. IT SERVED AS THE ON-CAMPUS FIELD FOR A FIX-UP COST OF $70.

THE EX-COLLEGIANS WERE PLAYED AT MIDWAY PARK (6) IN 1889; IOWA ST. AT THE MINNEHAHA DRIVING CLUB (7) IN 1895 AND CARLETON-ST. OLAF AT LEXINGTON PARK (8) IN 1918.

IN 1886 OFF-CAMPUS FIELDS WERE LEASED. THE FIRST CHARGED-ADMISSION TOOK PLACE AT THE PARK AVENUE GROUNDS (4). LATER ATHLETIC PARK (5) WAS RENTED AND SERVED AS THE MOST USED HOME. IT SEATED 4000 FANS. NORTHWESTERN PROTESTED THE FIELD IN 1892 BECAUSE IT WASN'T REGULATION SIZE. A FEW FEET WERE ADDED TO MAKE IT RIGHT.

THE CAMPUS ARMORY WAS BUILT IN 1896 AND SERVED AS TRAINING QUARTERS. AT THE SAME TIME A FIELD WAS MADE JUST SOUTH OF IT (9). THIS FIELD HAD ONLY CHAIRS ALONG THE SIDELINE WITH NO ENCLOSED FENCE. BEING INADEQUATE, GAMES WERE CONTINUED AT ATHLETIC PARK UNTIL 1899. THE ARMORY SITE WAS FIXED WITH A GRANDSTAND SEATING 3000 AND THE STUDENTS BUILT A FENCE. IT BECAME THE FIRST NORTHROP FIELD.

THE GREATER NORTHROP FIELD (10) WAS BUILT UNDER FRED JONES' DIRECTION. IT WAS THE FINEST IN THE COUNTRY WITH A SEATING OF 10,000. ANOTHER 10,000 COULD BE ADDED IN BLEACHERS AND STANDING ROOM. THOUGH USED THROUGHOUT THE SEASON, IT WASN'T COMPLETED UNTIL THE HISTORIC 1903 MICHIGAN GAME.

THEN CAME MEMORIAL STADIUM (11) WHICH WAS READY FOR THE 1924 SEASON. FUNDS FOR IT WERE RAISED IN AN OVERWHELMING MANNER BY SUBSCRIPTION AND WAS DEDICATED TO THE MINNESOTANS WHO DIED IN WORLD WAR I. ITS BIGGEST CROWD WAS 66,284 AGAINST PURDUE IN 1961. THE GOPHERS MOVED TO THE METRODOME (12) IN 1982.

The Golden Honor Roll

THE BIG TEN STARTED ITS ALL-CONFERENCE TEAM IN 1947. BEFORE THAT SELECTIONS WERE MADE BY PRESTIGIOUS SPORTS WRITERS AND NEWS SERVICES. PLAYERS IN EARLY TIMES WERE CALLED "ALL-WESTERN." THIS WAS EVEN BEFORE THE BIG TEN WAS CREATED. ALL-AMERICAN SELECTIONS STARTED IN 1889, HEISMAN IN 1935 AND OUTLAND IN 1946.

FORMER GOPHERS MAKING ARMED SERVICE TEAMS DURING WORLD WAR II ARE NOT SHOWN ON THIS CHART. HOWEVER, THOSE PLAYERS INCLUDE BILL DALEY, HERB HEIN, URBAN ODSON, CHARLES W. SCHULTZ, BRUCE SMITH AND GEORGE SVENDSEN.

Key to Symbols

- ● ACCOMPLISHMENT AS A PLAYER AT MINNESOTA
- ■ ACCOMPLISHMENT AS A COACH AT MINNESOTA
- ○ ACCOMPLISHMENT AS A PLAYER AFTER LEAVING MINNESOTA
- □ ACCOMPLISHMENT AS A COACH AFTER LEAVING MINNESOTA
- ▲ ACCOMPLISHMENT AS A TRAINER AT MINNESOTA
- ◉ HALL OF FAME GOLD MEDAL AWARD FOR LIFETIME ACHIEVEMENTS

(MARKS IN THE HALL OF FAME COLUMN FALL IN THE INDIVIDUAL'S LAST YEAR AT MINNESOTA RATHER THAN THE ACTUAL YEAR OF INDUCTION INTO THE HALL)

	ALL-CONF.	ALL-AMER.	CONS. ALL-AMER.	HALL OF FAME
1887				
PUDGE HEFFELFINGER-G				○
1889				
PUDGE HEFFELFINGER-G		○	○	
1890				
PUDGE HEFFELFINGER-G		○	○	
1891				
PUDGE HEFFELFINGER-G		○	○	
JOHN W. ADAMS-C		○	○	
1894				
JOHN HARRISON-LE	●			
1895				
JOHN HARRISON-LE	●			
1896				
JOHN HARRISON-LE	●			
1897				
JOHN HARRISON-LE	●			
1900				
BEYER AUNE-LE	●			
JOHN FLYNN-LG	●			
L.A. PAGE, JR.-C	●			
1901				
GILMORE DOBIE-QB				□
JOHN FLYNN-LG	●			
L.A. PAGE, JR.-C	●			

	ALL-CONF.	ALL-AMER.	CONS. ALL-AMER.	HALL OF FAME
1903				
EARL CURRENT-FB	●			
SIG HARRIS-QB	●			
JAMES IRSFELD-RHB	●			
ED ROGERS-LE	●			●
FRED SCHACHT-RT	●	●	●	
MOSE STRATHERN-C	●			
1904				
MOSE STRATHERN-C	●	●		
WALTON THORP-LG	●			
1905				
WILLIAM ITTNER-LT	●			
BOBBY MARSHALL-LE	●			●
1909				
EARL FARNAM-C	●			
LISLE JOHNSTON-LHB	●			
JOHN McGOVERN-QB		●	●	●
RUBE ROSENWALD-LHB	●			
1910				
LISLE JOHNSTON-FB	●	●		
JOHN McGOVERN-QB	●			
R.M. ROSENWALD-LHB	●			
JAMES WALKER-LT	●	●	●	
1911				
RALPH CAPRON-QB	●			
LUCIUS SMITH-LG	●			
CLIFFORD MORRELL-C	●			
R.M. ROSENWALD-LHB	●			

Year	Player	All-Conf.	Conf. MVP	All-Amer.	Cons. All-Amer.	Heisman	Hall of Fame
1912	CLARK SHAUGHNESSY-RT	●					
1913	CLARK SHAUGHNESSY-FB	●		●			□
	LORIN SOLON-LE	●		●			
1914	LORIN SOLON-FB	●					
1915	BERT BASTON-LE	●		●			
	BERNIE BIERMAN-LHB	●		●			
	MERTON DUNNIGAN-RG, C	●		●			
1916	BERT BASTON-LE	●		●	●		●
	GEORGE HAUSER-RT	●					
	SHORTY LONG-QB			●			
	GILBERT SINCLAIR-LG	●					
	JACK TOWNLEY-C	●					
	ARNOLD WYMAN-FB	●					
1917	GEORGE HAUSER-RT	●		●	●		
1920	FESTUS TIERNEY-RG	●					
1921	DR. HENRY WILLIAMS-COACH						■
1922	EARL MARTINEAU-LHB, RHB	●					
1923	RAY ECKLUND-LE	●		●	●		
	EARL MARTINEAU-RHB, QB	●		●			
1926	HAROLD ALMQUIST-QB	●					
	MIKE GARY-RT	●					
	HERB JOESTING-FB			●	●		
	GEORGE MAC KINNON-C	●					
	MALLY NYDAHL-QB	●					
1927	HAROLD HANSON-LG			●			
	HERB JOESTING-FB			●	●		●
1928	GEORGE GIBSON-LG	●		●			
	KENNETH HAYCRAFT-E	●		●			
	FRED HOVDE-QB	●					◉
	BRONKO NAGURSKI-FB, T	●					
1929	BRONKO NAGURSKI-FB, T	●		●	●		●
	ROBERT TANNER-RE	●					
1930	BIGGIE MUNN-LG	●					
1931	FRITZ CRISLER-COACH						□
	BIGGIE MUNN-LG	●	●	●	●		□
1933	SHELDON BEISE-FB	●					
	BUTCH LARSON-RE	●		●			
	PUG LUND-LHB	●		●			
1934	SHELDON BEISE-FB	●					
	PHIL BENGSTON-RT	●					
	BILL BEVAN-RG	●		●	●		
	STAN KOSTKA-FB			●			
	BUTCH LARSON-RE	●		●	●		
	PUG LUND-LHB	●	●	●	●		●
	BOB TENNER-LE	●		●			
	ED WIDSETH-LT	●		●			
1935	SHELDON BEISE-FB	●		●			
	BABE LEVOIR-B	●		●			
	DICK SMITH-RT	●		●			
	ED WIDSETH-LT	●		●	●		
	BUD WILKINSON-LG	●		●			
1936	JULIUS ALFONSE-RHB			●			
	RAY KING-RE			●			
	ANDY URAM-FB	●		●			
	ED WIDSETH-LT	●	●	●	●		●
	BUD WILKINSON-QB						□
1937	RUDY GMITRO-RHB	●					
	RAY KING-RE	●		●			
	LEW MIDLER-RT	●					
	FRANCIS TWEDELL-RG	●					
	ANDY URAM-FB			●			
	HAROLD VAN EVERY-LHB			●			
1938	WILBER MOORE-HB	●					
	BUTCH NASH-RE	●		●			
	FRANCIS TWEDELL-RG	●		●			
1939	GEORGE FRANCK-LHB	●					
	WIN PEDERSON-LT	●					
	HAROLD VAN EVERY-RHB	●					
1940	GEORGE FRANCK-LHB	●		●	●		
	URBAN ODSON-RT	●		●	●		
	HELGE PUKEMA-RG	●					
1941	BILL DALEY-FB	●					
	ROBERT FITCH-LE	●					
	BILL GARNAAS-QB, HB			●			
	LEONARD LEVY-LG	●					
	URBAN ODSON-RT	●					
	BRUCE SMITH-LHB	●		●	●	●	●
	DICK WILDUNG-RT	●		●	●		
1942	DICK WILDUNG-RT	●		●	●		●
1943	BILL DALEY-FB	○		○	○		
	HERB HEIN-RE	○		○			
	PAUL MITCHELL-RT	●					

	ALL-CONF.	CONF. MVP	ALL-AMER.	CONS. ALL-AMER.	HEISMAN	OUTLAND	HALL OF FAME
1947							
LEO NOMELLINI - RG, LT	●						
1948							
BUD GRANT - LE	●						
LEO NOMELLINI - RG, LT	●		●	●			
1949							
BUD GRANT - LE	●						
LEO NOMELLINI - RG, LT	●		●	●			●
CLAYTON TONNEMAKER - C	●		●	●			●
1950							
BERNIE BIERMAN - COACH							■
1952							
PAUL GIEL - LHB	●	●	●				
BOB McNAMARA - RHB, FB	●						
PERCY ZACHARY - G	●						
1953							
PAUL GIEL - LHB	●	●	●	●			●
1954							
BOB McNAMARA - RHB, FB	●		●				
1956							
BOB HOBERT - RT	●		●				
1958							
MIKE SVENDSON - C	●						
1960							
TOM BROWN - RG	●	●	●	●		●	
GREG LARSON - C	●						
1961							
BOBBY BELL - RT	●		●				
TOM HALL - E	●						
SANDY STEPHENS - QB	●	●	●	●			
1962							
BOBBY BELL - RT	●		●	●		●	
JOHN CAMPBELL - RE	●						
JULIAN HOOK - LG	●						
1963							
CARL ELLER - LT	●		●	●			
1964							
AARON BROWN - RE	●						
KRAIG LOFQUIST - LHB	●						
1965							
AARON BROWN - ORE, DLE	●		●	●			
1967							
McKINLEY BOSTON - DRT	●						
TOM SAKAL - RHB	●						
BOB STEIN - DLE	●		●				
JOHN WILLIAMS - ORT	●						
1968							
DICK ENDERLE - ORG	●						
NOEL JENKE - DLB	●						
BOB STEIN - DRE	●		●				
1969							
RAY PARSON - ORE	●						
1970							
BILL LIGHT - DLB	●						
JEFF WRIGHT - DRB	●						
1971							
DOUG KINGSRITER - TE	●		●				
BILL LIGHT - DLB	●						
1972							
JOHN KING - FB	●						
1973							
KEITH FAHNHORST - ORE	●						
STEVE NEILS - DLE	●						
1975							
RON KULLAS - SPE	●						
KEITH SIMONS - DRT	●						
LLOYD STEIN - TRAINER							▲
1976							
GEORGE ADZICK - SS	●						
1977							
STEVE MIDBOE - DLT	●						
PAUL ROGIND - K	●						
1978							
MARION BARBER - TB	●						
KEITH BROWN - SS	●						
PAUL ROGIND - K	●						
STAN SYTSMA - DRE	●						
1979							
ELMER BAILEY - ORE	●						
MARION BARBER - TB	●						
1980							
MARION BARBER - TB	●						
JEFF SCHUH - DRE	●						
GARRY WHITE - FB	●						
1981							
KEN DALLAFIOR - OLT	●						
JIM FAHNHORST - DLB	●						
1986							
BRUCE HOLMES - DLB	●						
CHIP LOHMILLER - PK	●						
DARRELL THOMPSON - TB	●						
1987							
JON LEVERENZ - DLB	●						
TROY WOLKOW - ORG	●						

Final Score

IN ORDER TO RECORD THE FOLLOWING GAME STATISTICS OLD GOPHER YEARBOOKS, HISTORICAL BIOGRAPHIES, PROGRAMS, PRESS GUIDES ETC. HAVE BEEN STUDIED. IF THERE WAS A DISCREPANCY IN ANYTHING A SEARCH WAS MADE FOR THAT GAME THROUGH OLD NEWSPAPERS. HUNDREDS OF PAPERS, MAINLY FROM THE MINNEAPOLIS STAR, JOURNAL AND TRIBUNE, WERE CONSULTED.

ADDED, HERE, ARE SIX GAMES NORMALLY NOT COUNTED ELSEWHERE. ONE IS THE MINNEAPOLIS FOOTBALL ASSOCIATION GAME OF 1883. THE 1956-60 ALUMNI GAMES ARE ALSO COUNTED BECAUSE THEY WERE TRUE BATTLES JUST AS THE ALUMNI AND EX-COLLEGIATE GAMES BEFORE 1900 WERE. THE ALUMNI OF THE 1950'S WEREN'T ENTIRELY OLD MEN USING THEIR SCRAPBOOKS FOR PADDING. SOME WERE STILL ACTIVE IN PRO BALL AND MANAGED TO WIN THREE OF FIVE GAMES. ONE OF THOSE VICTORIES WAS AGAINST A GOPHER SQUAD WHICH WAS NATIONALLY RANKED.

SOME HIGH SCHOOL GAMES, AROUND THE TURN OF THE CENTURY, HAD MINNESOTA PLAY ONE TEAM FOR THE FIRST HALF AND ANOTHER FOR THE SECOND. OFFICIALLY, SOME OF THESE CONTESTS WERE COUNTED AS TWO GAMES AND SOMETIMES AS ONLY ONE. THIS RECORD SHALL COUNT THESE TYPE OF GAMES AS ONE.

BECAUSE OF THESE CHANGES, THE TEAM AND COACH RECORDS ARE DIFFERENT FROM OFFICIAL RECORDS.

Key to Symbols

MINNESOTA SCORE IS ALWAYS SHOWN FIRST

- H HOME GAME
- HC HOMECOMING GAME
- A AWAY GAME
- ▼ OPPONENT WAS CONFERENCE CHAMPION
- ★ OPPONENT WAS RANKED FIRST NATIONALLY WHILE GOING AGAINST MINNESOTA BUT DIDN'T FINISH THE SEASON SO RANKED
- ☆ OPPONENT WAS RANKED FIRST NATIONALLY SOMETIME DURING THE SEASON BUT NOT WHILE GOING AGAINST MINNESOTA
- [ ] OPPONENT NATIONAL RANKING AT SEASON END
- [ ] GOPHER NATIONAL RANKING FOLLOWS OVERALL W-L-T RECORD
- [u] UNRANKED
- ( ) GOPHER CONFERENCE RANKING FOLLOWS CONFERENCE W-L-T RECORD

COACH: NONE

1882

Date		Score	Opponent
SEP. 30	H	4 - 0	HAMLINE
OCT. 16	A	0 - 2	HAMLINE
		4 - 2	1-1-0 [?]

COACH: THOMAS PEEBLES

1883

Date		Score	Opponent
?	A	2 - 4	CARLETON
OCT. 29	?	W - L	MPLS. FOOTBALL ASSN.
NOV. 3	A	5 - 0	HAMLINE
?	?	2 - 4	EX-COLLEGIANS
		9 - 8	2-2-0 [?]

1884
NO INTERCOLLEGIATE GAMES PLAYED

1885
NO INTERCOLLEGIATE GAMES PLAYED

COACH: FREDERICK S. JONES

1886

Date		Score	Opponent
OCT. 25	A	5 - 9	SHATTUCK
NOV. ?	H	8 - 18	SHATTUCK
		13 - 27	0-2-0 [?]

1887

Date		Score	Opponent
OCT. ?	H	8 - 0	MINNEAPOLIS HIGH
OCT. ?	H	14 - 0	ALUMNI
		22 - 0	2-0-0 [?]

1888

Date		Score	Opponent
OCT. 27	A	8 - 16	SHATTUCK
OCT. 31	H	14 - 0	SHATTUCK
		22 - 16	1-1-0 [?]

COACH: D.W. & AL McCORD, FRANK HEFFELFINGER & "BILLY" MORSE

1889

Date		Score	Opponent
OCT. 5	H	2 - 0	EX-COLLEGIANS
OCT. 26	H	10 - 0	EX-COLLEGIANS
NOV. 11	A	8 - 28	SHATTUCK
NOV. 20	H	26 - 0	SHATTUCK
		46 - 28	3-1-0 [?]

COACH: TOM ECK

1890

Date		Score	Opponent
OCT. 27	?	44 - 0	HAMLINE
NOV. 3	A	58 - 0	SHATTUCK
NOV. 5	H	0 - 0	EX-COLLEGIANS
NOV. 8	H	18 - 14	GRINNELL
NOV. 15	H	63 - 0	WISCONSIN
NOV. 19	H	11 - 14	EX-COLLEGIANS
NOV. 29	H	14 - 6	EX-COLLEGIANS
		208 - 34	5-1-1 [?]

(CHAMPIONS OF THE NW)

COACH: EDWARD MOULTON

1891

Date		Score	Opponent
OCT. 17	H	0 - 4	EX-COLLEGIANS
OCT. 24	H	26 - 12	WISCONSIN
OCT. 31	A	12 - 12	GRINNELL
NOV. 2	A	42 - 4	IOWA
NOV. 14	H	22 - 14	GRINNELL
		102 - 46	3-1-1 [?]

(CHAMPIONS OF THE NW)

COACH: NONE

1892

Date		Score	Opponent
OCT. 1	H	18–10	EX-COLLEGIANS
OCT. 17	H	14–6	MICHIGAN
OCT. 22	H	40–24	GRINNELL
OCT. 29	A	32–4	WISCONSIN
NOV. 8	H	18–12	NORTHWESTERN
		122–56	5-0-0 [?]
			3-0-0 (1)

COACH: "WALLIE" WINTER

1893

Date		Score	Opponent
OCT. 14	H	12–6	KANSAS
OCT. 21	H	36–6	GRINNELL
OCT. 24	A	10–6	HAMLINE
OCT. 28	A	34–20	MICHIGAN
OCT. 30	A	16–0	NORTHWESTERN
NOV. 11	H	40–0	WISCONSIN
		148–38	6-0-0 [?]
			3-0-0 (1)

COACH: THOMAS COCHRANE, JR.

1894

Date		Score	Opponent
OCT. 13	H	10–2	GRINNELL
OCT. 27	H	24–0	PURDUE
NOV. 10	H	40–0	BELOIT
NOV. 17	A	0–6	WISCONSIN
		74–8	3-1-0 [?]

COACH: WALTER "PUDGE" HEFFELFINGER

1895

Date		Score	Opponent
SEP. 29	H	20–0	MPLS. CENTRAL
OCT. 5	H	4–6	GRINNELL
OCT. 12	A	6–0	MINN. BOAT CLUB
OCT. 19	H	24–0	IOWA ST.
OCT. 25	A	10–6	CHICAGO
OCT. 29	A	4–16	PURDUE
NOV. 2	H	40–0	MACALESTER
NOV. 16	H	14–10	WISCONSIN
NOV. 23	A	0–20	MICHIGAN
NOV. 28	H	14–0	EX-COLLEGIANS
		136–58	7-3-0 [?]

COACH: ALEXANDER N. JERREMS

1896

Date		Score	Opponent
SEP. 19	H	34–0	MPLS. SOUTH
SEP. 26	H	50–0	MPLS. CENTRAL
OCT. 3	H	16–6	CARLETON
OCT. 10	H	12–0	GRINNELL
OCT. 17	H	14–0	PURDUE
OCT. 24	H	18–6	IOWA ST.
OCT. 31	H	8–0	EX-COLLEGIANS
NOV. 7	H	4–6	MICHIGAN
NOV. 21	A	0–6	WISCONSIN▼
NOV. 28	A	12–0	KANSAS
		168–24	8-2-0 [?]
			1-2-0 (5)

1897

Date		Score	Opponent
SEP. 25	H	22–0	MPLS. SOUTH
OCT. 2	H	26–0	MACALESTER
OCT. 9	H	48–6	CARLETON
OCT. 16	H	6–0	GRINNELL
OCT. 23	H	10–12	IOWA ST.
OCT. 30	H	0–39	WISCONSIN▼
NOV. 13	A	0–14	MICHIGAN
NOV. 26	A	0–6	PURDUE
		112–77	4-4-0 [?]
			0-3-0 (6)

"WALLIE" WINTER

"PUDGE" HEFFELFINGER

COACH: JACK MINDS

1898

Date		Score	Opponent
OCT. 1	H	32–0	CARLETON
OCT. 5	H	0–5	ALUMNI
OCT. 8	H	12–0	RUSH MED. COL. OF CHI.
OCT. 15	H	6–16	GRINNELL
OCT. 22	H	0–6	IOWA ST.
OCT. 29	A	0–28	WISCONSIN
NOV. 5	H	15–0	NO. DAKOTA
NOV. 12	H	17–6	NORTHWESTERN
NOV. 24	H	10–11	ILLINOIS
		92–72	4-5-0 [?]
			1-2-0 (5)

COACH: WILLIAM C. LEARY & JOHN M. HARRISON

1899

Date		Score	Opponent
SEP. 26	H	20–0	MPLS. CENTRAL
OCT. 3	H	29–0	MACALESTER
OCT. 7	H	40–0	SHATTUCK
OCT. 14	H	35–5	CARLETON
OCT. 21	H	6–0	IOWA ST.
OCT. 28	H	5–5	GRINNELL
NOV. 4	H	5–11	NORTHWESTERN
NOV. 4	H	6–5	ALUMNI
NOV. 11	H	5–5	BELOIT
NOV. 18	H	0–19	WISCONSIN
NOV. 25	A	0–29	CHICAGO▼
		151–79	6-3-2 [?]
			0-3-0 (6)

COACH: DR. HENRY L. WILLIAMS

1900

Date		Score	Opponent
SEP. 15	H	0–0	MPLS. CENTRAL
SEP. 22	H	26–0	ST. PAUL CENTRAL
SEP. 26	H	66–0	MACALESTER
SEP. 29	H	44–0	CARLETON
OCT. 6	H	27–0	IOWA ST.
OCT. 13	H	6–6	CHICAGO
OCT. 20	H	26–0	GRINNELL
OCT. 27	H	34–0	NO. DAKOTA
NOV. 3	H	6–5	WISCONSIN
NOV. 10	H	23–0	ILLINOIS
NOV. 12	H	21–0	NORTHWESTERN
NOV. 29	A	20–12	NEBRASKA
		299–23	10-0-2 [?]
			3-0-1 (1)

1901

Date		Score	Opponent
SEP. 21	H	0–0	MPLS. CENTRAL (1ST ½)
		16–0	ST. P. CENTRAL (2ND ½)
SEP. 28	H	35–0	CARLETON
OCT. 5	H	27–0	CHICAGO COLLEGE
OCT. 12	H	19–0	NEBRASKA
OCT. 26	H	16–0	IOWA
NOV. 4	H	28–0	HASKELL
NOV. 9	H	10–0	NO. DAKOTA
NOV. 16	A	0–18	WISCONSIN▼
NOV. 23	A	16–0	NORTHWESTERN
NOV. 28	A	16–0	ILLINOIS
		183–18	9-1-0 [?]
			3-1-0 (3)

1902

Date		Score	Opponent
SEP. 22	H	0–0	ST. P. CENTRAL (1ST ½)
		28–0	MPLS. CENTRAL (2ND ½)
SEP. 27	H	33–0	CARLETON
OCT. 4	H	16–0	IOWA ST.
OCT. 7	H	59–0	HAMLINE
OCT. 11	H	29–0	BELOIT
OCT. 18	H	0–6	NEBRASKA
OCT. 25	A	34–0	IOWA
NOV. 1	H	102–0	GRINNELL
NOV. 8	H	17–5	ILLINOIS
NOV. 15	H	11–0	WISCONSIN
NOV. 27	A	6–23	MICHIGAN▼ [1]
		335–34	9-2-0 [15]
			3-1-0 (3)

1903

Date		Score	Opponent
SEP. 19	H	21–6	MPLS. CENTRAL (1ST ½)
		36–0	ST. P. CENTRAL (2ND ½)
SEP. 23	H	37–0	MPLS. EAST
SEP. 26	H	29–0	CARLETON
SEP. 30	H	112–0	MACALESTER
OCT. 3	H	39–0	GRINNELL
OCT. 7	H	65–0	HAMLINE
OCT. 10	H	46–0	IOWA ST.
OCT. 17	H	75–0	IOWA
OCT. 24	H	46–0	BELOIT
OCT. 31	H	6–6	MICHIGAN▼★
NOV. 7	A	46–0	LAWRENCE
NOV. 14	A	32–0	ILLINOIS
NOV. 21	A	49–0	N.D. STATE
NOV. 26	A	17–0	WISCONSIN
		656–12	13-0-1 [?]
			3-0-1 (1)

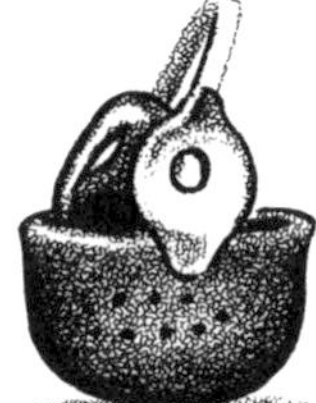

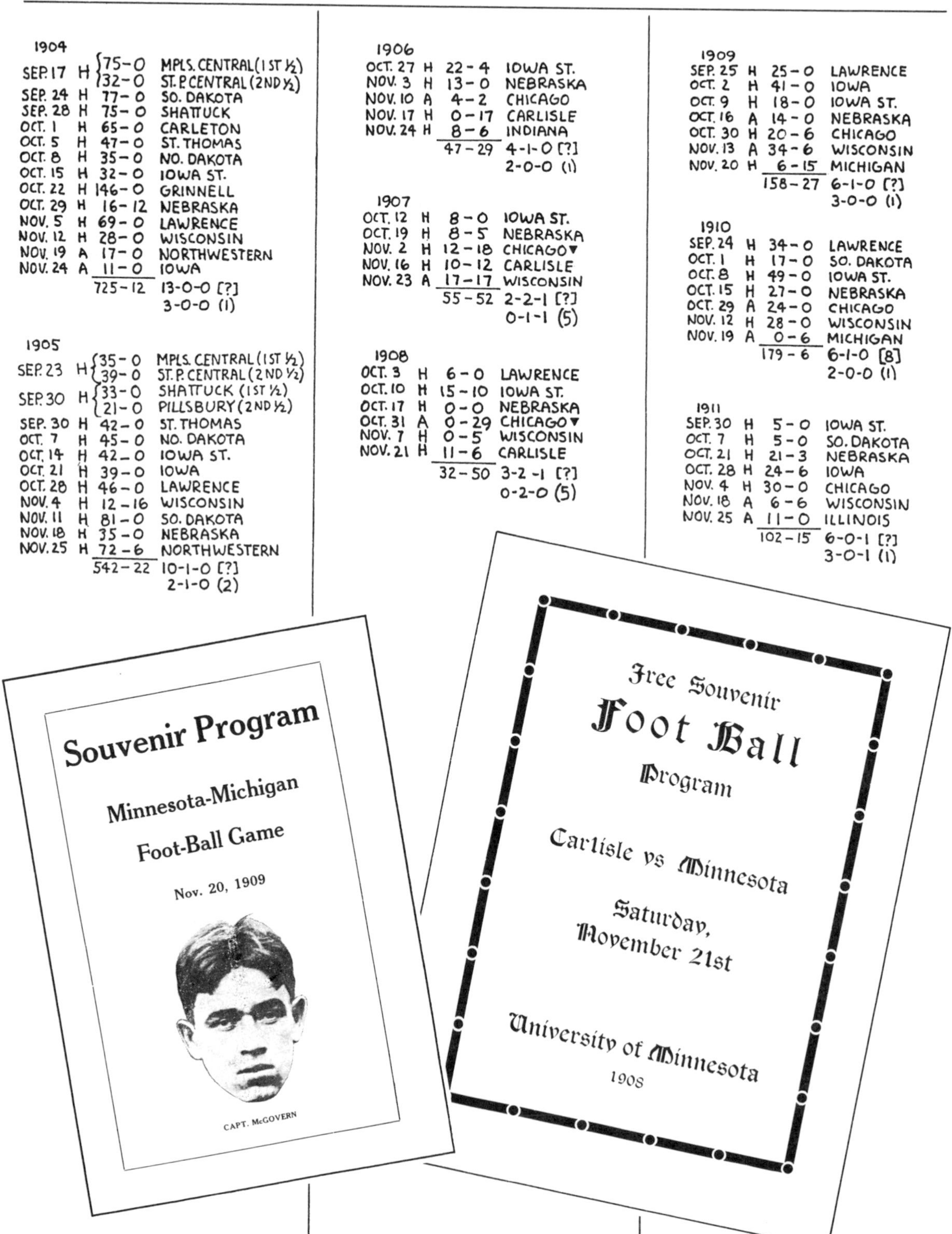

1904

Date		Score	Opponent
SEP. 17	H	75–0	MPLS. CENTRAL (1ST ½)
		32–0	ST. P. CENTRAL (2ND ½)
SEP. 24	H	77–0	SO. DAKOTA
SEP. 28	H	75–0	SHATTUCK
OCT. 1	H	65–0	CARLETON
OCT. 5	H	47–0	ST. THOMAS
OCT. 8	H	35–0	NO. DAKOTA
OCT. 15	H	32–0	IOWA ST.
OCT. 22	H	146–0	GRINNELL
OCT. 29	H	16–12	NEBRASKA
NOV. 5	H	69–0	LAWRENCE
NOV. 12	H	28–0	WISCONSIN
NOV. 19	A	17–0	NORTHWESTERN
NOV. 24	A	11–0	IOWA
		725–12	13-0-0 [?]
			3-0-0 (1)

1905

Date		Score	Opponent
SEP. 23	H	35–0	MPLS. CENTRAL (1ST ½)
		39–0	ST. P. CENTRAL (2ND ½)
SEP. 30	H	33–0	SHATTUCK (1ST ½)
		21–0	PILLSBURY (2ND ½)
SEP. 30	H	42–0	ST. THOMAS
OCT. 7	H	45–0	NO. DAKOTA
OCT. 14	H	42–0	IOWA ST.
OCT. 21	H	39–0	IOWA
OCT. 28	H	46–0	LAWRENCE
NOV. 4	H	12–16	WISCONSIN
NOV. 11	H	81–0	SO. DAKOTA
NOV. 18	H	35–0	NEBRASKA
NOV. 25	H	72–6	NORTHWESTERN
		542–22	10-1-0 [?]
			2-1-0 (2)

1906

Date		Score	Opponent
OCT. 27	H	22–4	IOWA ST.
NOV. 3	H	13–0	NEBRASKA
NOV. 10	A	4–2	CHICAGO
NOV. 17	H	0–17	CARLISLE
NOV. 24	H	8–6	INDIANA
		47–29	4-1-0 [?]
			2-0-0 (1)

1907

Date		Score	Opponent
OCT. 12	H	8–0	IOWA ST.
OCT. 19	H	8–5	NEBRASKA
NOV. 2	H	12–18	CHICAGO ▼
NOV. 16	H	10–12	CARLISLE
NOV. 23	A	17–17	WISCONSIN
		55–52	2-2-1 [?]
			0-1-1 (5)

1908

Date		Score	Opponent
OCT. 3	H	6–0	LAWRENCE
OCT. 10	H	15–10	IOWA ST.
OCT. 17	H	0–0	NEBRASKA
OCT. 31	A	0–29	CHICAGO ▼
NOV. 7	H	0–5	WISCONSIN
NOV. 21	H	11–6	CARLISLE
		32–50	3-2-1 [?]
			0-2-0 (5)

1909

Date		Score	Opponent
SEP. 25	H	25–0	LAWRENCE
OCT. 2	H	41–0	IOWA
OCT. 9	H	18–0	IOWA ST.
OCT. 16	A	14–0	NEBRASKA
OCT. 30	H	20–6	CHICAGO
NOV. 13	A	34–6	WISCONSIN
NOV. 20	H	6–15	MICHIGAN
		158–27	6-1-0 [?]
			3-0-0 (1)

1910

Date		Score	Opponent
SEP. 24	H	34–0	LAWRENCE
OCT. 1	H	17–0	SO. DAKOTA
OCT. 8	H	49–0	IOWA ST.
OCT. 15	H	27–0	NEBRASKA
OCT. 29	A	24–0	CHICAGO
NOV. 12	H	28–0	WISCONSIN
NOV. 19	A	0–6	MICHIGAN
		179–6	6-1-0 [8]
			2-0-0 (1)

1911

Date		Score	Opponent
SEP. 30	H	5–0	IOWA ST.
OCT. 7	H	5–0	SO. DAKOTA
OCT. 21	H	21–3	NEBRASKA
OCT. 28	H	24–6	IOWA
NOV. 4	H	30–0	CHICAGO
NOV. 18	A	6–6	WISCONSIN
NOV. 25	A	11–0	ILLINOIS
		102–15	6-0-1 [?]
			3-0-1 (1)

1912			
SEP. 28	H	0 – 10	SO. DAKOTA
OCT. 5	H	5 – 0	IOWA ST.
OCT. 19	H	13 – 0	NEBRASKA
OCT. 26	H	56 – 7	IOWA
NOV. 2	H	13 – 0	ILLINOIS
NOV. 16	H	0 – 14	WISCONSIN ▼
NOV. 23	A	0 – 7	CHICAGO
		87 – 38	4-3-0 [?]
			2-2-0 (3)

1913			
SEP. 27	H	14 – 0	SO. DAKOTA
OCT. 4	H	25 – 0	IOWA ST.
OCT. 18	A	0 – 7	NEBRASKA
OCT. 25	H	30 – 0	NO. DAKOTA
NOV. 1	A	21 – 3	WISCONSIN
NOV. 15	H	7 – 13	CHICAGO ▼
NOV. 22	A	19 – 9	ILLINOIS
		116 – 32	5-2-0 [?]
			2-1-0 (2)

1914			
OCT. 3	H	28 – 6	NO. DAKOTA
OCT. 10	H	26 – 0	IOWA ST.
OCT. 17	H	29 – 7	SO. DAKOTA
OCT. 24	A	7 – 0	IOWA
OCT. 31	H	6 – 21	ILLINOIS ▼
NOV. 14	HC	14 – 3	WISCONSIN
NOV. 21	A	13 – 7	CHICAGO
		123 – 44	6-1-0 [?]
			3-1-0 (2)

1915			
OCT. 2	H	41 – 0	NO. DAKOTA
OCT. 9	H	34 – 6	IOWA ST.
OCT. 16	H	19 – 0	SO. DAKOTA
OCT. 23	H	51 – 13	IOWA
OCT. 30	A	6 – 6	ILLINOIS ▼
NOV. 13	HC	20 – 7	CHICAGO
NOV. 20	A	20 – 3	WISCONSIN
		191 – 35	6-0-1 [?]
			3-0-1 (1)

1916			
OCT. 7	H	41 – 7	SO. DAKOTA ST.
OCT. 14	H	47 – 7	NO. DAKOTA
OCT. 21	H	81 – 0	SO. DAKOTA
OCT. 28	H	67 – 0	IOWA
NOV. 4	H	9 – 14	ILLINOIS
NOV. 18	HC	54 – 0	WISCONSIN
NOV. 25	A	49 – 0	CHICAGO
		348 – 28	6-1-0 [?]
			3-1-0 (3)

1917			
OCT. 13	H	64 – 0	SO. DAKOTA ST.
OCT. 20	H	33 – 9	INDIANA
NOV. 3	A	7 – 10	WISCONSIN
NOV. 17	HC	33 – 0	CHICAGO
NOV. 24	A	27 – 6	ILLINOIS
		164 – 25	4-1-0 [?]
			3-1-0 (2)

1918			
OCT. 5	H	0 – 0	ALL STARS
OCT. 19	H	30 – 0	OVERLAND STATION
OCT. 26	A	25 – 7	ST. THOMAS
NOV. 2	H	59 – 6	CARLETON-ST. OLAF
NOV. 9	A	0 – 6	IOWA
NOV. 16	HC	6 – 0	WISCONSIN
NOV. 23	H	6 – 20	CHI. MUNICIPAL PIER
NOV. 30	A	7 – 0	CHICAGO
		133 – 39	5-2-1 [?]
			2-1-0 (4)

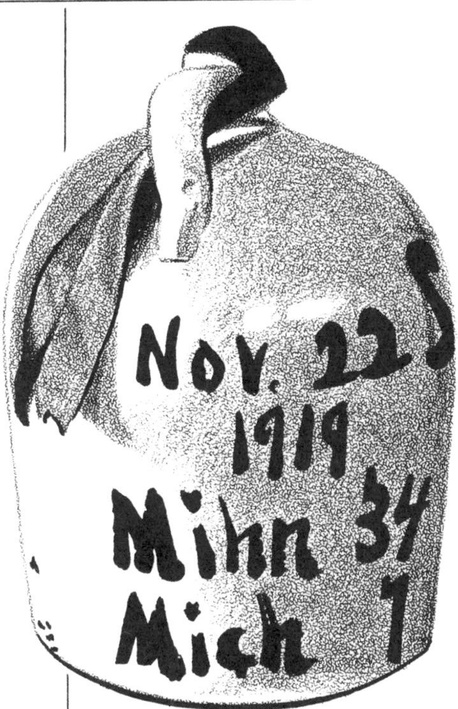

A FRESHLY PAINTED "LITTLE BROWN JUG" COMES HOME AFTER A STAY IN MICHIGAN

1919			
OCT. 4	H	39 – 0	NO. DAKOTA
OCT. 11	H	6 – 6	NEBRASKA
OCT. 18	A	20 – 6	INDIANA
OCT. 25	H	6 – 9	IOWA
NOV. 1	A	19 – 7	WISCONSIN
NOV. 8	HC	6 – 10	ILLINOIS ▼
NOV. 22	A	34 – 7	MICHIGAN
		130 – 45	4-2-1 [?]
			3-2-0 (4)

1920			
OCT. 2	H	41 – 3	NO. DAKOTA
OCT. 9	A	0 – 17	NORTHWESTERN
OCT. 16	H	7 – 21	INDIANA
OCT. 30	A	7 – 17	ILLINOIS
NOV. 6	H	0 – 3	WISCONSIN
NOV. 13	A	7 – 28	IOWA
NOV. 20	HC	0 – 3	MICHIGAN
		62 – 92	1-6-0 [?]
			0-6-0 (9)

1921			
OCT. 1	H	19 – 0	NO. DAKOTA
OCT. 8	H	28 – 0	NORTHWESTERN
OCT. 15	A	0 – 27	OHIO ST.
OCT. 22	H	6 – 0	INDIANA
OCT. 29	A	0 – 35	WISCONSIN
NOV. 5	HC	7 – 41	IOWA ▼
NOV. 19	A	0 – 38	MICHIGAN
		60 – 141	3-4-0 [?]
			2-4-0 (6)

COACH: WILLIAM SPAULDING

1922			
OCT. 7	H	22 – 0	NO. DAKOTA
OCT. 14	A	20 – 0	INDIANA
OCT. 21	A	7 – 7	NORTHWESTERN
OCT. 28	H	9 – 0	OHIO ST.
NOV. 4	HC	0 – 14	WISCONSIN
NOV. 11	A	14 – 28	IOWA ▼
NOV. 25	H	7 – 16	MICHIGAN ▼
		79 – 65	3-3-1 [?]
			2-3-1 (6)

1923			
OCT. 6	H	20 – 17	IOWA ST
OCT. 13	H	13 – 12	HASKELL
OCT. 20	H	27 – 0	NO. DAKOTA
OCT. 27	A	0 – 0	WISCONSIN
NOV. 3	H	34 – 14	NORTHWESTERN
NOV. 17	HC	20 – 7	IOWA
NOV. 24	A	0 – 10	MICHIGAN ▼
		114 – 60	5-1-1 [?]
			2-1-1 (4)

1924			
OCT. 4	H	14 – 0	NO. DAKOTA
OCT. 11	H	20 – 0	HASKELL
OCT. 18	A	7 – 7	WISCONSIN
OCT. 25	A	0 – 13	IOWA
NOV. 1	HC	0 – 13	MICHIGAN
NOV. 8	H	7 – 7	IOWA ST. [6]
NOV. 15	H	20 – 7	ILLINOIS ★ [4]
NOV. 22	H	0 – 16	VANDERBILT
		68 – 63	3-3-2 [U]
			1-2-1 (6)

COACH: DR. CLARENCE W. SPEARS

1925			
OCT. 3	H	25 – 6	NO. DAKOTA
OCT. 10	H	34 – 6	GRINNELL
OCT. 17	H	32 – 6	WABASH
OCT. 24	H	7 – 19	NOTRE DAME
OCT. 31	H	12 – 12	WISCONSIN [8]
NOV. 7	H	33 – 7	BUTLER
NOV. 14	HC	33 – 0	IOWA
NOV. 21	A	0 – 35	MICHIGAN ▼ [2]
		176 – 91	5-2-1 [U]
			1-1-1 (4)

1926			
OCT. 2	H	51 – 0	NO. DAKOTA
OCT. 9	H	7 – 20	NOTRE DAME [3]
OCT. 16	A	0 – 20	MICHIGAN ▼ [3]
OCT. 23	H	67 – 7	WABASH
OCT. 30	A	16 – 10	WISCONSIN
NOV. 6	A	41 – 0	IOWA
NOV. 13	H	81 – 0	BUTLER
NOV. 20	HC	6 – 7	MICHIGAN ▼
		269 – 64	5-3-0 [U]
			2-2-0 (6)

1927			
OCT. 1	H	57 – 10	NO. DAKOTA U.
OCT. 8	H	40 – 0	OKLAHOMA A&M
OCT. 15	A	14 – 14	INDIANA
OCT. 22	HC	38 – 0	IOWA
OCT. 29	H	13 – 7	WISCONSIN
NOV. 5	A	7 – 7	NOTRE DAME [4]
NOV. 12	H	27 – 6	DRAKE
NOV. 19	A	13 – 7	MICHIGAN [7]
		209 – 51	6-0-2 [3]
			3-0-1 (2)

1928

OCT. 6	H	40–0	CREIGHTON
OCT. 13	H	15–0	PURDUE
OCT. 20	HC	33–7	CHICAGO
OCT. 27	A	6–7	IOWA
NOV. 3	A	9–10	NORTHWESTERN
NOV. 10	H	20–12	INDIANA
NOV. 17	H	52–0	HASKELL
NOV. 24	A	6–0	WISCONSIN ★ [4]
		181–36	6-2-0 [U]
			4-2-0 (3)

1929

OCT. 5	H	39–0	COE
OCT. 12	H	15–6	VANDERBILT
OCT. 19	A	26–14	NORTHWESTERN
OCT. 26	H	54–0	RIPON
NOV. 2	H	19–7	INDIANA
NOV. 9	A	7–9	IOWA
NOV. 16	HC	6–7	MICHIGAN
NOV. 23	H	13–12	WISCONSIN
		179–55	6-2-0 [U]
			3-2-0 (3)

COACH: FRITZ CRISLER

1930

SEP. 27	H	48–0	SO. DAKOTA ST.
OCT. 4	H	7–33	VANDERBILT
OCT. 11	H	0–0	STANFORD [7]
OCT. 18	H	6–0	INDIANA
NOV. 1	HC	6–27	NORTHWESTERN ▼ [4]
NOV. 8	H	59–0	SO. DAKOTA
NOV. 15	A	0–7	MICHIGAN ▼ [5]
NOV. 22	A	0–14	WISCONSIN
		126–81	3-4-1 [U]
			1-3-0 (6)

1931

SEP. 26	H	13–7	NO. DAKOTA ST.
SEP. 26	H	30–0	RIPON
OCT. 3	H	20–0	OKLAHOMA A&M
OCT. 10	A	0–13	STANFORD
OCT. 24	H	34–0	IOWA
OCT. 31	HC	14–0	WISCONSIN
NOV. 7	A	14–32	NORTHWESTERN ▼ [4]
NOV. 14	H	47–7	CORNELL (IOWA)
NOV. 21	A	0–6	MICHIGAN ▼ (POST
NOV. 28	H	19–7	OHIO ST. – SEASON)
		191–72	7-3-0 [U]
			3-2-0 (5)

COACH: BERNIE BIERMAN

1932

OCT. 1	H	12–0	SO. DAKOTA ST.
OCT. 8	H	0–7	PURDUE ▼ [4]
OCT. 15	H	7–6	NEBRASKA
OCT. 22	A	21–6	IOWA
OCT. 29	HC	7–0	NORTHWESTERN
NOV. 5	H	26–0	MISSISSIPPI
NOV. 12	A	13–20	WISCONSIN [11]
NOV. 19	H	0–3	MICHIGAN ▼ [1]
		86–42	5-3-0 [U]
			2-3-0 (5)

1933

SEP. 30	H	19–6	SO. DAKOTA ST.
OCT. 7	H	6–6	INDIANA
OCT. 14	H	7–7	PURDUE [10]
OCT. 21	H	7–3	PITTSBURGH [4]
OCT. 28	HC	19–7	IOWA
NOV. 4	A	0–0	NORTHWESTERN
NOV. 18	A	0–0	MICHIGAN ▼ [1]
NOV. 25	H	6–3	WISCONSIN
		64–32	4-0-4 [3]
			2-0-4 (2)

1934

SEP. 29	H	56–12	NO. DAKOTA ST.
OCT. 6	H	20–0	NEBRASKA
OCT. 20	A	13–7	PITTSBURGH ★ [2]
OCT. 27	A	48–12	IOWA
NOV. 3	HC	34–0	MICHIGAN
NOV. 10	H	30–0	INDIANA
NOV. 17	H	35–7	CHICAGO
NOV. 24	A	34–0	WISCONSIN
		270–38	8-0-0 [1]
			5-0-0 (1)

1935

SEP. 28	H	26–6	NO. DAKOTA ST.
OCT. 12	A	12–7	NEBRASKA
OCT. 19	H	20–0	TULANE
OCT. 26	HC	21–13	NORTHWESTERN
NOV. 2	H	29–7	PURDUE
NOV. 9	A	13–6	IOWA
NOV. 16	A	40–0	MICHIGAN
NOV. 23	H	33–7	WISCONSIN
		194–46	8-0-0 [1]
			5-0-0 (1)

1936

SEP. 26	A	14–7	WASHINGTON [4]
OCT. 10	H	7–0	NEBRASKA [9]
OCT. 17	H	26–0	MICHIGAN
OCT. 24	H	33–0	PURDUE
OCT. 31	A	0–6	NORTHWESTERN ▼☆ [6]
NOV. 7	HC	52–0	IOWA
NOV. 14	H	47–19	TEXAS
NOV. 21	A	24–0	WISCONSIN
		203–32	7-1-0 [1]
			4-1-0 (2)

1937

SEP. 25	H	69–7	NO. DAKOTA ST.
OCT. 2	A	9–14	NEBRASKA [5]
OCT. 9	H	6–0	INDIANA
OCT. 16	A	39–6	MICHIGAN
OCT. 30	H	6–7	NOTRE DAME [9]
NOV. 6	A	35–10	IOWA
NOV. 13	HC	7–0	NORTHWESTERN
NOV. 20	H	13–6	WISCONSIN
		184–50	6-2-0 [5]
			5-0-0 (1)

1938

SEP. 24	H	15–0	WASHINGTON
OCT. 1	H	16–7	NEBRASKA
OCT. 8	H	7–0	PURDUE
OCT. 15	HC	7–6	MICHIGAN [6]
OCT. 29	A	3–6	NORTHWESTERN [17]
NOV. 5	H	28–0	IOWA
NOV. 12	A	0–19	NOTRE DAME [1]
NOV. 19	A	21–0	WISCONSIN
		97–38	6-2-0 [7]
			4-1-0 (1)

1939

SEP. 30	H	62–0	ARIZONA
OCT. 7	A	0–6	NEBRASKA [18]
OCT. 14	H	13–13	PURDUE
OCT. 21	HC	20–23	OHIO ST. ▼ [15]
NOV. 4	H	7–14	NORTHWESTERN
NOV. 11	A	20–7	MICHIGAN [7]
NOV. 18	A	9–13	IOWA [9]
NOV. 25	H	23–6	WISCONSIN
		154–82	3-4-1 [U]
			2-3-1 (7)

1940
SEP. 28 H 19–14 WASHINGTON [10]
OCT. 5 H 13–7 NEBRASKA [7]
OCT. 19 A 13–7 OHIO ST.
OCT. 26 HC 34–6 IOWA
NOV. 2 A 13–12 NORTHWESTERN [8]
NOV. 9 H 7–6 MICHIGAN [2]
NOV. 16 H 33–6 PURDUE
NOV. 23 A 22–13 WISCONSIN
154–71 8-0-0 [1]
6-0-0 (1)

1941
SEP. 28 A 14–6 WASHINGTON
OCT. 11 H 34–6 ILLINOIS
OCT. 18 H 39–0 PITTSBURGH
OCT. 25 A 7–0 MICHIGAN [5]
NOV. 1 HC 8–7 NORTHWESTERN [11]
NOV. 8 H 9–0 NEBRASKA
NOV. 15 A 34–13 IOWA
NOV. 22 H 41–6 WISCONSIN
186–38 8-0-0 [1]
5-0-0 (1)

COACH: DR. GEORGE HAUSER

1942
SEP. 26 H 50–7 PITTSBURGH
OCT. 3 H 6–7 IOWA SEAHAWKS [2]*
OCT. 10 A 13–20 ILLINOIS
OCT. 17 A 15–2 NEBRASKA
OCT. 24 HC 16–14 MICHIGAN [9]
OCT. 31 H 19–7 NORTHWESTERN
NOV. 7 H 0–7 INDIANA
NOV. 14 H 27–7 IOWA
NOV. 21 A 6–20 WISCONSIN [1]
152–91 5-4-0 [19]
3-3-0 (5)

1943
SEP. 25 H 26–13 MISSOURI
OCT. 2 H 54–0 NEBRASKA
OCT. 16 H 13–7 CAMP GRANT
OCT. 23 A 6–49 MICHIGAN ▼ [3]
OCT. 30 A 6–42 NORTHWESTERN [9]
NOV. 6 HC 7–14 PURDUE ▼ [5]
NOV. 13 H 33–14 IOWA
NOV. 20 H 25–13 WISCONSIN
NOV. 27 H 0–32 IOWA SEAHAWKS [2]**
170–184 5-4-0 [U]
2-3-0 (4)

* ARMED SERVICES RANKING IN 1942
** ARMED SERVICES RANKED WITH COLLEGE TEAMS IN 1943 & 44

1944
SEP. 23 H 13–19 IOWA SEAHAWKS [6]**
SEP. 30 H 39–0 NEBRASKA
OCT. 7 H 13–28 MICHIGAN [8]
OCT. 14 H 39–27 MISSOURI
OCT. 28 A 14–34 OHIO ST. ▼ [2]
NOV. 4 HC 14–14 NORTHWESTERN
NOV. 11 H 19–14 INDIANA
NOV. 18 A 46–0 IOWA
NOV. 25 A 28–26 WISCONSIN
225–162 5-3-1 [U]
3-2-1 (4)

COACH: BERNIE BIERMAN

1945
SEP. 22 H 34–0 MISSOURI
OCT. 6 A 61–7 NEBRASKA
OCT. 13 H 14–0 FORT WARREN
OCT. 20 HC 30–7 NORTHWESTERN
OCT. 27 H 7–20 OHIO ST. [12]
NOV. 3 A 0–26 MICHIGAN [6]
NOV. 10 H 0–49 INDIANA ▼ [4]
NOV. 17 A 19–20 IOWA
NOV. 24 H 12–26 WISCONSIN
177–155 4-5-0 [U]
1-5-0 (8)

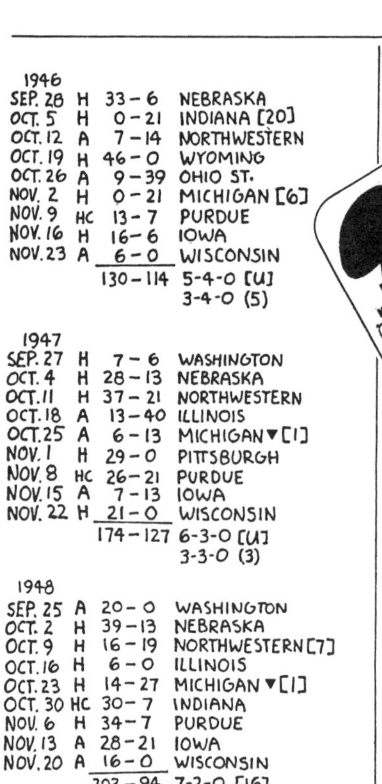

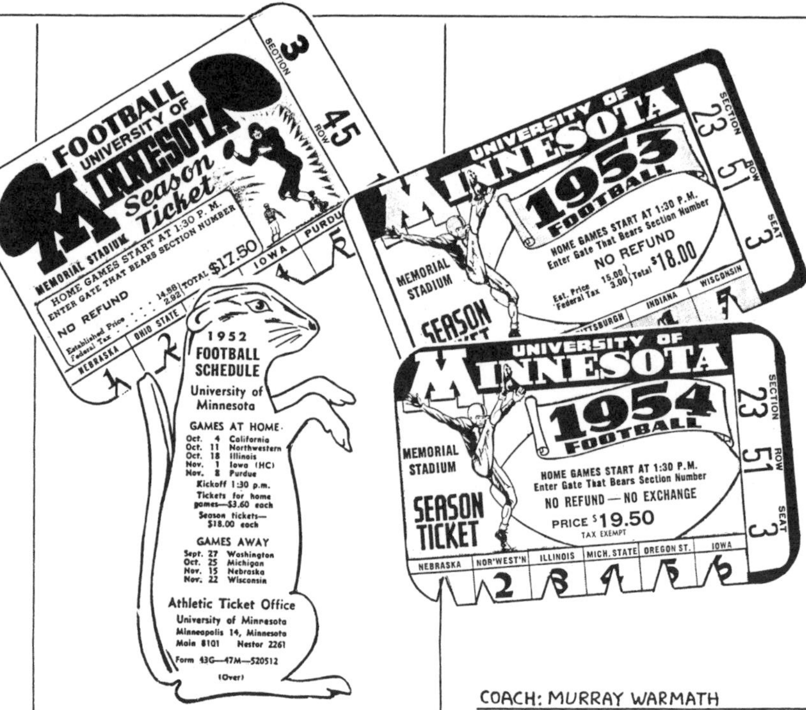

1946

SEP. 28	H	33 – 6	NEBRASKA
OCT. 5	H	0 – 21	INDIANA [20]
OCT. 12	A	7 – 14	NORTHWESTERN
OCT. 19	H	46 – 0	WYOMING
OCT. 26	A	9 – 39	OHIO ST.
NOV. 2	H	0 – 21	MICHIGAN [6]
NOV. 9	HC	13 – 7	PURDUE
NOV. 16	H	16 – 6	IOWA
NOV. 23	A	6 – 0	WISCONSIN
		130 – 114	5-4-0 [U]
			3-4-0 (5)

1947

SEP. 27	H	7 – 6	WASHINGTON
OCT. 4	H	28 – 13	NEBRASKA
OCT. 11	H	37 – 21	NORTHWESTERN
OCT. 18	A	13 – 40	ILLINOIS
OCT. 25	A	6 – 13	MICHIGAN ▼ [1]
NOV. 1	H	29 – 0	PITTSBURGH
NOV. 8	HC	26 – 21	PURDUE
NOV. 15	A	7 – 13	IOWA
NOV. 22	H	21 – 0	WISCONSIN
		174 – 127	6-3-0 [U]
			3-3-0 (3)

1948

SEP. 25	A	20 – 0	WASHINGTON
OCT. 2	H	39 – 13	NEBRASKA
OCT. 9	H	16 – 19	NORTHWESTERN [7]
OCT. 16	H	6 – 0	ILLINOIS
OCT. 23	H	14 – 27	MICHIGAN ▼ [1]
OCT. 30	HC	30 – 7	INDIANA
NOV. 6	H	34 – 7	PURDUE
NOV. 13	A	28 – 21	IOWA
NOV. 20	A	16 – 0	WISCONSIN
		203 – 94	7-2-0 [16]
			5-2-0 (3)

1949

SEP. 24	H	48 – 20	WASHINGTON
OCT. 1	A	28 – 6	NEBRASKA
OCT. 8	H	21 – 7	NORTHWESTERN
OCT. 15	A	27 – 0	OHIO ST. ▼ [6]
OCT. 22	A	7 – 14	MICHIGAN ▼ ☆ [7]
OCT. 29	HC	7 – 13	PURDUE
NOV. 5	H	55 – 7	IOWA
NOV. 12	A	24 – 7	PITTSBURGH
NOV. 19	H	14 – 6	WISCONSIN
		231 – 80	7-2-0 [7]
			4-2-0 (3)

1950

SEP. 30	A	13 – 28	WASHINGTON [11]
OCT. 7	H	26 – 32	NEBRASKA [17]
OCT. 14	A	6 – 13	NORTHWESTERN
OCT. 21	H	0 – 48	OHIO ST. ☆ [10]
OCT. 28	H	7 – 7	MICHIGAN ▼ [6]
NOV. 4	HC	0 – 13	IOWA
NOV. 11	A	0 – 27	MICHIGAN ST. [8] ✤
NOV. 18	H	27 – 14	PURDUE
NOV. 25	A	0 – 14	WISCONSIN [20]
		79 – 196	1-7-1 [U]
			1-4-1 (7)

✤ THE MICHIGAN ST. LOSS IS NOT COUNTED AGAINST MINNESOTA IN THE ABOVE CONFERENCE STANDINGS. MICHIGAN ST. WAS A NEW BIG TEN MEMBER BUT BECAUSE THEY DIDN'T YET PLAY A FULL BIG TEN SCHEDULE THEY WERE NOT COUNTED IN THE CONFERENCE STANDINGS FROM 1950–1952

COACH: WES FESLER

1951

SEP. 29	H	20 – 25	WASHINGTON
OCT. 6	A	14 – 55	CALIFORNIA ☆ [12]
OCT. 13	H	7 – 21	NORTHWESTERN
OCT. 20	HC	39 – 20	NEBRASKA
OCT. 27	A	27 – 54	MICHIGAN
NOV. 3	A	20 – 20	IOWA
NOV. 10	H	16 – 14	INDIANA
NOV. 17	A	13 – 19	PURDUE [14]
NOV. 24	H	6 – 30	WISCONSIN [8]
		162 – 258	2-6-1 [U]
			1-4-1 (7)

1952

SEP. 27	A	13 – 19	WASHINGTON
OCT. 4	H	13 – 49	CALIFORNIA
OCT. 11	H	27 – 26	NORTHWESTERN
OCT. 18	H	13 – 7	ILLINOIS
OCT. 25	A	0 – 21	MICHIGAN
NOV. 1	HC	17 – 7	IOWA
NOV. 8	H	14 – 14	PURDUE ▼ [12]
NOV. 15	A	13 – 7	NEBRASKA
NOV. 22	A	21 – 21	WISCONSIN ▼ ☆ [10]
		131 – 171	4-3-2 [U]
			3-1-2 (4)

1953

SEP. 26	A	7 – 17	USC
OCT. 3	H	0 – 21	MICHIGAN ST. ▼ [3]
OCT. 10	A	30 – 13	NORTHWESTERN
OCT. 17	A	7 – 27	ILLINOIS ▼ [7]
OCT. 24	H	22 – 0	MICHIGAN [19]
OCT. 31	H	35 – 14	PITTSBURGH
NOV. 7	HC	28 – 20	INDIANA
NOV. 14	A	0 – 27	IOWA [9]
NOV. 21	H	21 – 21	WISCONSIN [14]
		150 – 160	4-4-1 [U]
			3-3-1 (5)

COACH: MURRAY WARMATH

1954

SEP. 25	H	19 – 7	NEBRASKA
OCT. 2	A	46 – 7	PITTSBURGH
OCT. 9	H	26 – 7	NORTHWESTERN
OCT. 16	H	19 – 6	ILLINOIS
OCT. 23	A	0 – 34	MICHIGAN [15]
OCT. 30	HC	19 – 13	MICHIGAN ST.
NOV. 6	H	44 – 6	OREGON ST.
NOV. 13	H	22 – 20	IOWA
NOV. 20	A	0 – 27	WISCONSIN [9]
		195 – 127	7-2-0 [20]
			4-2-0 (4)

1955

SEP. 24	H	0 – 30	WASHINGTON
OCT. 1	H	6 – 7	PURDUE
OCT. 8	A	18 – 7	NORTHWESTERN
OCT. 15	A	13 – 21	ILLINOIS
OCT. 22	H	13 – 14	MICHIGAN ★ [12]
OCT. 29	HC	25 – 19	USC
NOV. 5	A	0 – 26	IOWA [19]
NOV. 12	A	14 – 42	MICHIGAN ST. [2]
NOV. 19	H	21 – 6	WISCONSIN
		110 – 172	3-6-0 [U]
			2-5-0 (8)

1956

MAY 19	H	24 – 38	ALUMNI
SEP. 29	A	34 – 14	WASHINGTON
OCT. 6	H	21 – 14	PURDUE
OCT. 13	H	0 – 0	NORTHWESTERN
OCT. 20	H	16 – 13	ILLINOIS
OCT. 27	A	20 – 7	MICHIGAN [7]
NOV. 3	HC	9 – 6	PITTSBURGH [13]
NOV. 10	H	0 – 7	IOWA ▼ [3]
NOV. 17	H	14 – 13	MICHIGAN ST. ☆ [9]
NOV. 24	A	13 – 13	WISCONSIN
		151 – 125	6-2-2 [9]
			4-1-2 (2)

1957

MAY 18	H	7-10	ALUMNI
SEP. 28	H	46-7	WASHINGTON
OCT. 5	H	21-17	PURDUE
OCT. 12	A	41-6	NORTHWESTERN
OCT. 19	A	13-34	ILLINOIS
OCT. 26	H	7-24	MICHIGAN
NOV. 2	HC	34-0	INDIANA
NOV. 9	A	20-44	IOWA [5]
NOV. 16	A	13-42	MICHIGAN ST. [1]
NOV. 23	H	6-14	WISCONSIN [14]
		208-198	4-6-0 [U]
			3-5-0 (8)

1958

MAY 17	H	2-26	ALUMNI
SEP. 27	A	21-24	WASHINGTON
OCT. 4	H	7-13	PITTSBURGH
OCT. 11	H	3-7	NORTHWESTERN [17]
OCT. 18	HC	8-20	ILLINOIS
OCT. 25	A	19-20	MICHIGAN
NOV. 1	A	0-6	INDIANA
NOV. 8	H	6-28	IOWA ▼ [1]
NOV. 15	H	39-12	MICHIGAN ST.
NOV. 22	A	12-27	WISCONSIN [6]
		117-183	1-9-0 [U]
			1-6-0 (9)

1959

MAY 16	H	13-7	ALUMNI
SEP. 26	H	12-32	NEBRASKA
OCT. 3	H	24-14	INDIANA
OCT. 10	A	0-6	NORTHWESTERN [16]
OCT. 17	A	6-14	ILLINOIS [11]
OCT. 24	H	6-14	MICHIGAN
OCT 31	HC	20-6	VANDERBILT
NOV. 7	A	0-33	IOWA
NOV. 14	A	23-29	PURDUE
NOV. 21	H	7-11	WISCONSIN ▼ [6]
		111-166	3-7-0 [U]
			1-6-0 (10)

1960

MAY 14	H	19-7	ALUMNI
SEP. 24	A	26-14	NEBRASKA
OCT. 1	H	42-0	INDIANA
OCT. 8	H	7-0	NORTHWESTERN
OCT. 15	HC	21-10	ILLINOIS
OCT. 22	A	10-0	MICHIGAN
OCT. 29	H	48-7	KANSAS ST.
NOV. 5	H	27-10	IOWA ▼ [1]
NOV. 12	H	14-23	PURDUE [15]
NOV. 19	A	26-7	WISCONSIN [5]
JAN. 2	A	7-17	WASHINGTON [1] (1961 ROSE BOWL)
		247-95	9-2-0 [1]
			6-1-0 (1)

1961

SEP. 30	H	0-6	MISSOURI [11]
OCT. 7	H	14-7	OREGON
OCT. 14	A	10-3	NORTHWESTERN
OCT. 21	A	33-0	ILLINOIS
OCT. 28	HC	23-20	MICHIGAN
NOV. 4	H	13-0	MICHIGAN ST. ★ [8]
NOV. 11	A	16-9	IOWA ☆
NOV. 18	H	10-7	PURDUE [11]
NOV. 25	H	21-23	WISCONSIN [18]
JAN. 1	A	21-3	UCLA (1962 ROSE BOWL)
		161-78	8-2-0 [6]
			6-1-0 (2)

1962

SEP. 29	H	0-0	MISSOURI [12]
OCT. 6	H	21-0	NAVY
OCT. 13	H	22-34	NORTHWESTERN ☆ [16]
OCT. 20	HC	17-0	ILLINOIS [18]
OCT. 27	A	17-0	MICHIGAN
NOV. 3	A	28-7	MICHIGAN ST.
NOV. 10	H	10-0	IOWA
NOV. 17	H	7-6	PURDUE
NOV. 24	A	9-14	WISCONSIN ▼ [2]
		131-61	6-2-1 [10]
			5-2-0 (2)

1963

SEP. 28	H	7-14	NEBRASKA [5]
OCT. 5	H	24-8	ARMY
OCT. 12	A	8-15	NORTHWESTERN
OCT. 19	A	6-16	ILLINOIS ▼ [3]
OCT. 26	HC	6-0	MICHIGAN [10]
NOV. 2	H	6-24	INDIANA
NOV. 9	A	13-27	IOWA
NOV. 16	A	11-13	PURDUE
NOV. 28	H	14-0	WISCONSIN
		95-117	3-6-0 [U]
			2-5-0 (9)

1964

SEP. 26	H	21-26	NEBRASKA [6]
OCT. 3	A	26-20	CALIFORNIA
OCT. 10	H	21-18	NORTHWESTERN
OCT. 17	HC	0-14	ILLINOIS
OCT. 24	A	12-19	MICHIGAN ▼ [1]
OCT. 31	A	21-0	INDIANA
NOV. 7	H	14-13	IOWA
NOV. 14	H	14-7	PURDUE
NOV. 21	A	7-14	WISCONSIN
		136-131	5-4-0 [U]
			4-3-0 (4)

1965

SEP. 17	A	20-20	USC [9]
SEP. 25	H	13-14	WASHINGTON ST.
OCT. 2	H	6-17	MISSOURI [6]
OCT. 9	H	42-18	INDIANA
OCT. 16	A	14-3	IOWA
OCT. 23	HC.	14-13	MICHIGAN
OCT. 30	A	10-11	OHIO ST. [11]
NOV. 6	H	27-22	NORTHWESTERN
NOV. 13	A	0-35	PURDUE [13]
NOV. 20	H	42-7	WISCONSIN
		188-160	5-4-1 [U]
			5-2-0 (3)

MURRAY WARMATH

1966

SEP. 17	A	0-24	MISSOURI
SEP. 24	H	35-21	STANFORD
OCT. 1	H	14-16	KANSAS
OCT. 8	A	7-7	INDIANA
OCT. 15	HC	17-0	IOWA
OCT. 22	A	0-49	MICHIGAN
OCT. 29	H	17-7	OHIO ST.
NOV. 5	A	28-13	NORTHWESTERN
NOV. 12	H	0-16	PURDUE [6]
NOV. 19	A	6-7	WISCONSIN
		124-160	4-5-1 [U]
			3-3-1 (5)

1967

SEP. 23	H	13-12	UTAH
SEP. 30	A	0-7	NEBRASKA
OCT. 7	H	23-3	SOUTHERN METH.
OCT. 14	A	10-7	ILLINOIS
OCT. 21	HC	21-0	MICHIGAN ST.
OCT. 28	H	20-15	MICHIGAN
NOV. 4	A	10-0	IOWA
NOV. 11	A	12-41	PURDUE ▼ [9]
NOV. 18	H	33-7	INDIANA ▼ [4]
NOV. 25	H	21-14	WISCONSIN
		163-106	8-2-0 [14]
			6-1-0 (1)

1968

SEP. 21	H	20-29	U.S.C. ★ [2]
SEP. 28	H	14-17	NEBRASKA
OCT. 5	H	24-19	WAKE FOREST
OCT. 12	HC	17-10	ILLINOIS
OCT. 19	A	14-13	MICHIGAN ST.
OCT. 26	A	20-33	MICHIGAN [15]
NOV. 2	H	28-35	IOWA
NOV. 9	H	27-13	PURDUE ☆ [10]
NOV. 16	A	20-6	INDIANA
NOV. 23	A	23-15	WISCONSIN
		207-190	6-4-0 [18]
			5-2-0 (3)

1969

SEP. 20	A	26-48	ARIZONA ST.
SEP. 27	H	35-35	OHIO U.
OCT. 4	H	14-42	NEBRASKA [12]
OCT. 11	A	7-17	INDIANA
OCT. 18	HC	7-34	OHIO ST. ★ [4]
OCT. 25	H	9-35	MICHIGAN ▼ [8]
NOV. 1	A	35-7	IOWA
NOV. 8	H	28-21	NORTHWESTERN
NOV. 15	A	14-10	MICHIGAN ST.
NOV. 22	H	35-10	WISCONSIN
		210-259	4-5-1 [U]
			4-3-0 (4)

1970

SEP. 19	A	12-34	MISSOURI
SEP. 26	H	49-7	OHIO U.
OCT. 3	H	10-35	NEBRASKA [1]
OCT. 10	H	23-0	INDIANA
OCT. 17	A	8-28	OHIO ST. ▼ [1]
OCT. 24	A	13-39	MICHIGAN [7]
OCT. 31	HC	14-14	IOWA
NOV. 7	A	14-28	NORTHWESTERN
NOV. 14	H	23-13	MICHIGAN ST.
NOV. 21	A	14-39	WISCONSIN
		180-237	3-6-1 [U]
			2-4-1 (7)

1971

Date	Site	Score	Opponent
SEP. 11	H	28 – 0	INDIANA
SEP. 18	A	7 – 35	NEBRASKA [1]
SEP. 25	H	20 – 31	WASHINGTON ST.
OCT. 2	H	38 – 20	KANSAS
OCT. 9	A	13 – 27	PURDUE
OCT. 16	A	19 – 14	IOWA
OCT. 23	HC	7 – 35	MICHIGAN ▼ [4]
OCT. 30	H	12 – 14	OHIO ST.
NOV. 6	A	20 – 41	NORTHWESTERN
NOV. 13	A	25 – 40	MICHIGAN ST.
NOV. 20	H	23 – 21	WISCONSIN
		212 – 278	4-7-0 [U]
			3-5-0 (6)

COACH: CAL STOLL

1972

Date	Site	Score	Opponent
SEP. 16	A	23 – 27	INDIANA
SEP. 23	H	6 – 38	COLORADO [14]
SEP. 30	A	0 – 49	NEBRASKA ☆ [4]
OCT. 7	H	28 – 34	KANSAS
OCT. 14	H	3 – 28	PURDUE
OCT. 21	HC	43 – 14	IOWA
OCT. 28	A	0 – 42	MICHIGAN ▼ [6]
NOV. 4	A	19 – 27	OHIO ST. ▼ [3]
NOV. 11	H	35 – 29	NORTHWESTERN
NOV. 18	H	14 – 10	MICHIGAN ST.
NOV. 25	A	14 – 6	WISCONSIN
		185 – 304	4-7-0 [U]
			4-4-0 (5)

1973

Date	Site	Score	Opponent
SEP. 15	A	7 – 56	OHIO ST. ▼ ☆ [2]
SEP. 22	H	41 – 14	NO. DAKOTA
SEP. 29	A	19 – 34	KANSAS
OCT. 6	H	7 – 48	NEBRASKA [7]
OCT. 13	H	24 – 3	INDIANA
OCT. 20	A	31 – 23	IOWA
OCT. 27	HC	7 – 34	MICHIGAN ▼ [6]
NOV. 3	A	52 – 43	NORTHWESTERN
NOV. 10	H	34 – 7	PURDUE
NOV. 17	A	19 – 16	ILLINOIS
NOV. 24	H	19 – 17	WISCONSIN
		260 – 295	7-4-0 [U]
			6-2-0 (3)

1974

Date	Site	Score	Opponent
SEP. 14	H	19 – 34	OHIO ST. ▼ [3]
SEP. 21	H	42 – 30	NO. DAKOTA
SEP. 28	H	9 – 7	TEXAS CHRISTIAN
OCT. 5	A	0 – 54	NEBRASKA [8]
OCT. 12	A	3 – 34	INDIANA
OCT. 19	HC	23 – 17	IOWA
OCT. 26	A	0 – 49	MICHIGAN ▼ [3]
NOV. 2	H	13 – 21	NORTHWESTERN
NOV. 9	A	24 – 20	PURDUE
NOV. 16	H	14 – 17	ILLINOIS
NOV. 23	A	14 – 49	WISCONSIN
		161 – 332	4-7-0 [U]
			2-6-0 (7)

1975

Date	Site	Score	Opponent
SEP. 13	A	14 – 20	INDIANA
SEP. 20	H	38 – 0	WESTERN MICH.
SEP. 27	H	10 – 7	OREGON
OCT. 4	H	21 – 0	OHIO U.
OCT. 11	A	23 – 42	ILLINOIS
OCT. 18	HC	15 – 38	MICHIGAN ST.
OCT. 25	A	31 – 7	IOWA
NOV. 1	H	21 – 28	MICHIGAN [8]
NOV. 8	H	33 – 9	NORTHWESTERN
NOV. 15	A	6 – 38	OHIO ST. ▼ ★ [4]
NOV. 22	H	24 – 3	WISCONSIN
		236 – 192	6-5-0 [U]
			3-5-0 (7)

1976

Date	Site	Score	Opponent
SEP. 11	H	32 – 13	INDIANA
SEP. 18	H	28 – 14	WASHINGTON ST.
SEP. 25	H	21 – 10	WESTERN MICH.
OCT. 2	A	7 – 38	WASHINGTON
OCT. 9	HC	29 – 14	ILLINOIS
OCT. 16	A	14 – 10	MICHIGAN ST.
OCT. 23	H	12 – 22	IOWA
OCT. 30	A	0 – 45	MICHIGAN ▼ ★ [3]
NOV. 6	A	38 – 10	NORTHWESTERN
NOV. 13	H	3 – 9	OHIO ST. ▼ [5]
NOV. 20	A	17 – 26	WISCONSIN
		201 – 211	6-5-0 [U]
			4-4-0 (3)

1977

Date	Site	Score	Opponent
SEP. 10	H	10 – 7	WESTERN MICH.
SEP. 17	A	7 – 38	OHIO ST. ▼ [12]
SEP. 24	H	27 – 13	UCLA
OCT. 1	H	19 – 17	WASHINGTON [9]
OCT. 8	A	6 – 18	IOWA
OCT. 15	HC	10 – 7	NORTHWESTERN
OCT. 22	H	16 – 0	MICHIGAN ▼ ★ [8]
OCT. 29	A	22 – 34	INDIANA
NOV. 5	H	10 – 29	MICHIGAN ST.
NOV. 12	A	21 – 0	ILLINOIS
NOV. 19	H	13 – 7	WISCONSIN
DEC. 22	A	7 – 17	MARYLAND (HALL OF FAME BOWL)
		168 – 187	7-5-0 [U]
			4-4-0 (5)

1978

Date	Site	Score	Opponent
SEP. 16	H	38 – 12	TOLEDO
SEP. 23	H	10 – 27	OHIO ST.
SEP. 30	A	3 – 17	UCLA [12]
OCT. 7	H	14 – 17	OREGON ST.
OCT. 14	H	22 – 20	IOWA
OCT. 21	A	38 – 14	NORTHWESTERN
OCT. 28	A	10 – 42	MICHIGAN ▼ [5]
NOV. 4	HC	32 – 31	INDIANA
NOV. 11	A	9 – 33	MICHIGAN ST. ▼
NOV. 18	H	24 – 6	ILLINOIS
NOV. 25	A	10 – 48	WISCONSIN
		210 – 267	5-6-0 [U]
			4-4-0 (5)

COACH: JOE SALEM

1979

Date	Site	Score	Opponent
SEP. 8	H	24 – 10	OHIO
SEP. 15	H	17 – 21	OHIO ST. ▼ ☆ [4]
SEP. 22	A	14 – 48	USC ★ [2]
SEP. 29	A	38 – 8	NORTHWESTERN
OCT. 6	H	31 – 14	PURDUE [10]
OCT. 13	A	21 – 31	MICHIGAN [19]
OCT. 20	A	24 – 7	IOWA
OCT. 27	HC	17 – 17	ILLINOIS
NOV. 3	H	24 – 42	INDIANA [16]
NOV. 10	A	17 – 31	MICHIGAN ST.
NOV. 17	H	37 – 42	WISCONSIN
		264 – 271	4-6-1 [U]
			3-5-1 (6)

1980

Date	Site	Score	Opponent
SEP. 13	H	38 – 14	OHIO
SEP. 20	A	0 – 47	OHIO ST. ☆ [15]
SEP. 27	H	7 – 24	USC [12]
OCT. 4	A	49 – 21	NORTHWESTERN
OCT. 11	A	7 – 21	PURDUE [16]
OCT. 18	HC	14 – 37	MICHIGAN ▼ [4]
OCT. 25	H	24 – 6	IOWA
NOV. 1	A	21 – 18	ILLINOIS
NOV. 8	H	31 – 7	INDIANA
NOV. 15	H	12 – 30	MICHIGAN ST.
NOV. 22	A	7 – 25	WISCONSIN
		210 – 250	5-6-0 [U]
			4-5-0 (5)

1981

Date	Site	Score	Opponent
SEP. 12	H	19 – 17	OHIO
SEP. 19	H	16 – 13	PURDUE
SEP. 26	H	42 – 12	OREGON ST.
OCT. 3	A	29 – 38	ILLINOIS
OCT. 10	HC	35 – 23	NORTHWESTERN
OCT. 17	A	16 – 17	INDIANA
OCT. 24	A	12 – 10	IOWA ▼ [15]
OCT. 31	H	13 – 34	MICHIGAN ☆ [10]
NOV. 7	H	35 – 31	OHIO ST. ▼ [12]
NOV. 14	A	36 – 43	MICHIGAN ST.
NOV. 21	H	21 – 26	WISCONSIN
		274 – 264	6-5-0 [U]
			4-5-0 (6)

1982

Date	Site	Score	Opponent
SEP. 11	H	57 – 3	OHIO
SEP. 18	A	36 – 10	PURDUE
SEP. 25	H	41 – 11	WASHINGTON ST.
OCT. 2	H	24 – 42	ILLINOIS
OCT. 9	A	21 – 31	NORTHWESTERN
OCT. 16	HC	21 – 40	INDIANA
OCT. 23	H	16 – 21	IOWA
OCT. 30	A	14 – 52	MICHIGAN ▼ [15]
NOV. 6	A	10 – 35	OHIO ST. [12]
NOV. 13	H	7 – 26	MICHIGAN ST.
NOV. 20	A	0 – 24	WISCONSIN
		247 – 295	3-8-0 [U]
			1-8-0 (10)

1983

Date	Site	Score	Opponent
SEP. 10	A	21 – 17	RICE
SEP. 17	H	13 – 84	NEBRASKA ★ [2]
SEP. 24	H	20 – 32	PURDUE
OCT. 1	A	18 – 64	OHIO ST. [8]
OCT. 8	A	31 – 38	INDIANA
OCT. 15	HC	17 – 56	WISCONSIN
OCT. 22	A	8 – 19	NORTHWESTERN
OCT. 29	A	10 – 34	MICHIGAN ST.
NOV. 5	H	23 – 50	ILLINOIS ▼ [10]
NOV. 12	H	10 – 58	MICHIGAN [8]
NOV. 19	A	10 – 61	IOWA [14]
		181 – 513	1-10-0 [U]
			0-9-0 (10)

COACH: LOU HOLTZ

1984

SEP. 8	H	31 – 24	RICE
SEP. 15	A	7 – 38	NEBRASKA★[3]
SEP. 22	A	10 – 34	PURDUE
SEP. 29	H	22 – 35	OHIO ST.▼[12]
OCT. 6	A	33 – 24	INDIANA
OCT. 13	A	17 – 14	WISCONSIN
OCT. 20	HC	28 – 31	NORTHWESTERN
OCT. 27	H	13 – 20	MICHIGAN ST.
NOV. 3	A	3 – 48	ILLINOIS
NOV. 10	A	7 – 31	MICHIGAN
NOV. 17	H	23 – 17	IOWA [15]
		194 – 316	4-7-0 [U]
			3-6-0 (8)

1985

SEP. 14	H	28 – 14	WICHITA ST.
SEP. 21	H	62 – 17	MONTANA
SEP. 28	H	7 – 13	OKLAHOMA [1]
OCT. 5	H	45 – 15	PURDUE
OCT. 12	A	21 – 10	NORTHWESTERN
OCT. 19	A	22 – 7	INDIANA
OCT. 26	HC	19 – 23	OHIO ST. [11]
NOV. 2	A	26 – 31	MICHIGAN ST.
NOV. 9	H	27 – 18	WISCONSIN
NOV. 16	H	7 – 48	MICHIGAN [2]
NOV. 23	A	9 – 31	IOWA▼ [9]

COACH: JOHN GUTEKUNST

DEC. 21	A	20 – 13	CLEMSON (INDEP. BOWL)
		293 – 240	7-5-0 [U]
			4-4-0 (6)

1986

SEP. 13	H	31 – 7	BOWLING GREEN
SEP. 20	A	0 – 63	OKLAHOMA [1]
SEP. 27	H	20 – 24	PACIFIC
OCT. 4	A	36 – 9	PURDUE
OCT. 11	HC	44 – 23	NORTHWESTERN
OCT. 18	H	19 – 17	INDIANA
OCT. 25	A	0 – 33	OHIO ST.▼ [6]
NOV. 1	H	23 – 52	MICHIGAN ST.
NOV. 8	A	27 – 20	WISCONSIN
NOV. 15	A	20 – 17	MICHIGAN▼ [7]
NOV. 22	H	27 – 30	IOWA [15]
DEC. 29	A	14 – 21	TENNESSEE (LIBERTY BOWL)
		261 – 316	6-6-0 [U]
			5-3-0 (3)

1987

SEP. 12	H	24 – 7	NO. IOWA
SEP. 19	H	32 – 23	U. OF CALIFORNIA
SEP. 26	H	30 – 10	CENTRAL MICHIGAN U.
OCT. 3	H	21 – 19	PURDUE
OCT. 10	A	45 – 33	NORTHWESTERN
OCT. 16	HC	17 – 18	INDIANA [20]
OCT. 24	A	9 – 42	OHIO ST.
OCT. 31	A	17 – 27	ILLINOIS
NOV. 7	H	20 – 30	MICHIGAN [18]
NOV. 14	H	22 – 19	WISCONSIN
NOV. 21	A	20 – 34	IOWA [16]
		239 – 239	6-5-0 [U]
			3-5-0 (6)

1988

SEP. 10	H	9 – 41	WASHINGTON ST. [16]
SEP. 17	H	35 – 3	MIAMI OF OHIO
SEP. 24	H	31 – 20	NO. ILLINOIS
OCT. 1	A	10 – 14	PURDUE
OCT. 8	HC	28 – 28	NORTHWESTERN
OCT. 15	A	13 – 33	INDIANA [20]
OCT. 22	H	6 – 13	OHIO ST.
OCT. 29	H	27 – 27	ILLINOIS
NOV. 5	A	7 – 22	MICHIGAN [4]
NOV. 12	A	7 – 14	WISCONSIN
NOV. 19	H	22 – 31	IOWA
		195 – 246	2-7-2 [U]
			0-6-2 (9)

1989

SEP. 16	A	30 – 20	IOWA ST.
SEP. 23	H	0 – 48	NEBRASKA [11]
SEP. 30	H	34 – 14	INDIANA ST.
OCT. 7	HC	35 – 15	PURDUE
OCT. 14	A	20 – 18	NORTHWESTERN
OCT. 21	A	18 – 28	INDIANA
OCT. 28	H	37 – 41	OHIO ST. [24]
NOV. 4	H	24 – 22	WISCONSIN
NOV. 11	A	7 – 21	MICHIGAN ST. [16]
NOV. 18	H	15 – 49	MICHIGAN [7]
NOV. 25	A	43 – 7	IOWA
		263 – 283	6-5-0 [U]
			4-4-0 (5)

1990

SEP. 8	H	29 – 35	UTAH
SEP. 15	H	20 – 16	IOWA ST.
SEP. 22	A	–	NEBRASKA
OCT. 6	A	–	PURDUE
OCT. 13	H	–	NORTHWESTERN
OCT. 20	H	–	INDIANA
OCT. 27	A	–	OHIO ST.
NOV. 3	A	–	WISCONSIN
NOV. 10	H	–	MICHIGAN ST.
NOV. 17	A	–	MICHIGAN
NOV. 24	H	–	IOWA
		–	

1991

SEP. 14	H	–	SAN JOSE ST.
SEP. 21	A	–	COLORADO
SEP. 28	H	–	PITTSBURGH
OCT. 5	A	–	ILLINOIS
OCT. 12	H	–	PURDUE
OCT. 19	A	–	MICHIGAN ST.
OCT. 26	H	–	MICHIGAN
NOV. 2	A	–	INDIANA
NOV. 9	H	–	OHIO ST.
NOV. 16	H	–	WISCONSIN
NOV. 23	A	–	IOWA
		–	

1992

SEP. 12	H	–	SAN JOSE ST.
SEP. 19	H	–	COLORADO
SEP. 26	A	–	PITTSBURGH
OCT. 3	H	–	ILLINOIS
OCT. 10	A	–	PURDUE
OCT. 17	H	–	MICHIGAN ST.
OCT. 24	A	–	MICHIGAN
OCT. 31	H	–	INDIANA
NOV. 7	A	–	OHIO ST.
NOV. 14	A	–	WISCONSIN
NOV. 21	H	–	IOWA
		–	

1993

SEP. 11	H	–	INDIANA ST.
SEP. 18	H	–	KANSAS ST.
SEP. 25	A	–	SAN DIEGO ST.
OCT. 2	A	–	INDIANA
OCT. 9	H	–	PURDUE
OCT. 16	A	–	NORTHWESTERN
OCT. 23	H	–	WISCONSIN
OCT. 30	H	–	OHIO ST.
NOV. 6	A	–	ILLINOIS
NOV. 13	H	–	MICHIGAN
NOV. 20	A	–	IOWA
		–	

1994

SEP. 10	H	–	TBA
SEP. 17	H	–	SAN JOSE ST.
SEP. 24	A	–	KANSAS CITY
OCT. 1	H	–	INDIANA
OCT. 8	A	–	PURDUE
OCT. 15	H	–	NORTHWESTERN
OCT. 22	A	–	WISCONSIN
OCT. 29	A	–	OHIO ST.
NOV. 5	H	–	ILLINOIS
NOV. 12	A	–	MICHIGAN
NOV. 19	H	–	IOWA
		–	

1995

SEP. 16	H	–	BALL ST.
SEP. 23	A	–	SYRACUSE
SEP. 30	H	–	TBA
OCT. 7	A	–	MICHIGAN ST.
OCT. 14	H	–	PURDUE
OCT. 21	A	–	NORTHWESTERN
OCT. 28	H	–	OHIO ST.
NOV. 4	A	–	ILLINOIS
NOV. 11	H	–	WISCONSIN
NOV. 18	H	–	MICHIGAN
NOV. 25	A	–	IOWA
		–	

Big Ten

PRESIDENT JAMES H. SMART OF PURDUE CALLED A MEETING AT THE PALMER HOUSE IN CHICAGO ON JANUARY 11, 1895. THIS HISTORIC MEETING MARKED THE BIRTH OF THE BIG TEN, THE FIRST INTERCOLLEGIATE CONFERENCE. ITS ORIGINAL NAME WAS THE INTERCOLLEGIATE CONFERENCE OF FACULTY REPRESENTATIVES AND SERVED AS THE PATTERN FOR THE YET-TO-BE-CREATED N.C.A.A.— THE FOUNDING MEMBERS WERE PURDUE, MINNESOTA, MICHIGAN, WISCONSIN, NORTHWESTERN, ILLINOIS AND CHICAGO. LAKE FOREST COLLEGE WAS ALSO PRESENT BUT DIDN'T JOIN.

Standings

IN EARLY BIG TEN STANDINGS TIES WERE NOT COUNTED AGAINST A TEAM. IF IT HAD FOUR WINS, TWO TIES AND NO LOSSES IT HAD A 1000% RECORD JUST LIKE A TEAM WHO HAD WON ALL THEIR GAMES. TIES WERE COMPLETELY IGNORED.

THIS BUSINESS COULD CAUSE TROUBLE.

IN 1927 ILLINOIS HAD A PERFECT 5-0-0 RECORD AND MINNESOTA WAS 3-0-1. BOTH HAD A 1000% WIN RECORD AND A SHARE IN THE TITLE. UNIVERSITY OF MINNESOTA PRESIDENT LOTUS COFFMAN, HOWEVER, CONCEDED THE CHAMPIONSHIP TO ILLINOIS WITHOUT CONSULTATION WITH ANYONE ELSE. IT CAUSED A GREAT UPROAR AMONG GOPHER FOLLOWERS. A RECOGNITION RALLY WAS PUT ON AT THE MINNEAPOLIS AUDITORIUM FOR THE TEAM AND TO SHOW CONTEMPT FOR COFFMAN'S BOO-BOO. MINNESOTA LOST AN OFFICIAL FIRST PLACE IN THE STANDINGS, JUST THE SAME.

IN 1933 THE GOPHERS COMPILED A 2-0-4 RECORD TO SHARE A BIG TEN TITLE WITH 5-0-1 MICHIGAN. HEAD TO HEAD THESE TWO TEAMS TIED 0-0. ONCE AGAIN MINNESOTA DID NOT RECEIVE CREDIT.

BECAUSE OF THESE TWO SEASONS, OFFICIAL RECORDS TODAY SHOW MINNESOTA WITH TWO LESS CHAMPIONSHIPS THAN THEY, BY DEFINITION AND RIGHT, SHOULD HAVE. UNDER SIMILAR CIRCUMSTANCES, OTHER TEAMS IN BIG TEN HISTORY HAVE RETAINED THEIR FIRST PLACE STATUS.

IN 1946 THE SYSTEM WAS CHANGED TO WHERE A TIE WAS COUNTED AS A HALF-GAME WON AND HALF-GAME LOST. THE FOLLOWING CHART SHOWS HOW TEAMS ACTUALLY PLACED IN THE STANDINGS, TO THE LEFT OF THEIR NAME. TO THEIR RIGHT IS INDICATED THEIR FINISH IF TODAY'S SYSTEM HAD BEEN USED.

★ NATIONAL CHAMPIONS

1896		
1	WI	
2	NW	
2	MI	
4	CH	
5	MN	
6	IL	
6	PU	

1897		
1	WI	
2	CH	
3	MI	
4	IL	
5	PU	
6	NW	
6	MN	

1898		
1	MI	
2	CH	
3	WI	
4	IL	
5	MN	
6	NW	
6	PU	

1899		
1	CH	
2	WI	
3	NW	
3	MI	
5	PU	
6	MN	
6	IL	

1900		
1	MN	
1	IA	2
3	WI	
3	NW	4
5	MI	4
6	CH	
7	IN	
8	IL	
9	PU	

1901		
1	MI★	
1	WI	
3	MN	
4	IL	
5	NW	
6	IN	
7	CH	
7	PU	8
7	IA	9

1902		
1	MI★	
2	CH	
3	MN	
4	IL	
5	PU	
6	WI	
7	IA	
7	NW	
7	IN	

1903		
1	MN	
1	MI	
1	NW	4
4	CH	3
5	IA	
6	IN	
7	IL	
8	WI	
8	PU	9

1904		
1	MN	
1	MI	
3	CH	
4	IL	
5	NW	
5	PU	
7	IA	
7	WI	
7	IN	

1905		
1	CH★	
2	MI	
2	MN	
4	PU	
5	WI	
6	IN	
6	IA	7
6	NW	7
6	IL	7

1906		
1	WI	
1	MN	
1	MI	
4	CH	
5	IA	
6	IL	
6	IN	
6	PU	

1907		
1	CH	
2	WI	
3	IL	
4	IA	
5	MN	
5	IN	6
5	PU	6

1908		
1	CH	
2	IL	
3	WI	
4	PU	
4	IN	
6	MN	
6	NW	
6	IA	

1909		
1	MN	
2	CH	
3	IL	
4	WI	
5	IN	
5	NW	
7	IA	
7	PU	

1910		
1	IL	
1	MN	2
3	IN	
4	IA	
5	WI	
5	NW	
5	CH	7
8	PU	

1911		
1	MN	
2	CH	
3	WI	
4	IL	
4	IA	
6	PU	
7	NW	
8	IN	

1912		
1	WI	
2	CH	
3	PU	
3	MN	
5	NW	
6	IL	
6	IA	7
8	IN	
–	OS	

1913		
1	CH	
2	MN	
2	IA	
2	PU	4
5	IL	
6	WI	
6	IN	7
6	OS	7
9	NW	

1914		
1	IL	
2	MN	
3	CH	
4	WI	
4	OS	
4	PU	
7	IA	
8	IN	
9	NW	

1915		
1	MN	
1	IL	2
3	CH	
3	OS	4
5	PU	
6	WI	
7	IA	
8	IN	
9	NW	

1916		
1	OS	
2	NW	
3	MN	
4	IL	
4	CH	
6	WI	
6	IA	7
8	IN	
8	PU	9

1917		
1	OS	
2	MN	
3	NW	
3	WI	
5	IL	
5	CH	
7	IN	
8	MI	
8	IA	
8	PU	

1918	1919	1920	1921	1922	1923	1924	1925	1926	1927	1928
1 IL	1 IL	1 OS	1 IA	1 IA	1 IL★	1 CH	1 MI	1 MI	1 IL★	1 IL
1 MI	2 OS	2 WI	2 CH	1 MI	1 MI	2 IL	2 NW	1 NW	2 MN	2 WI
1 PU	3 CH	3 IN	2 OS	3 CH	3 CH	2 IA	2 WI	3 OS	3 MI	3 MN
4 MN	4 WI	4 IL	4 WI	4 WI	4 MN	4 MI	4 MN	4 PU	4 PU	4 IA
4 IA	4 MN	5 IA	5 MI	5 MN	5 IA	5 PU	4 IA	5 WI	4 CH	4 OS
6 NW	6 IA	6 MI	6 MN	6 IL	5 IN	6 MN	4 IL	6 IL	6 OS	6 PU
7 WI	7 MI	7 NW	6 IN	7 NW	7 WI	7 OS	4 CH	6 MN	6 NW	7 NW
8 OS	7 NW	8 CH	8 IL	8 OS	8 OS	7 NW 8	8 OS	8 IN	8 IN	7 MI
8 CH	9 IN	9 PU	8 PU	9 IN	8 PU	7 IN 8	9 IN	8 IA	9 IA	9 IN
– IN	9 PU	9 MN	10 NW	9 PU 10	10 NW	10 WI 8	9 PU	8 CH	9 WI	10 CH

1929	1930	1931	1932	1933	1934	1935	1936	1937	1938
1 PU	1 MI	1 PU	1 MI★	1 MI★	1 MN★	1 MN★	1 NW	1 MN	1 MN
2 IL	1 NW	1 MI	1 PU 2	2 MN 4	2 OS	1 OS	2 MN★	2 OS	2 MI
3 MN	3 PU	1 NW	3 WI	3 OS★2	3 IL	3 IN	2 OS	3 IN	2 PU
3 NW	4 WI	4 OS	4 OS	4 PU 3	4 PU	3 PU	4 IN	4 PU	4 NW
5 OS	4 OS	5 MN	5 NW	5 IA	5 WI	5 NW	4 PU	4 WI	5 WI
5 IA	6 MN	6 WI	5 MN 6	5 IL	5 NW	5 MI 6	6 IL	4 NW	5 OS 6
7 MI	6 IN	7 IN	7 IL	7 NW	7 CH	5 CH 6	7 CH	4 MI	7 IL
7 IN	8 IL	7 CH 8	8 IN	8 CH	8 IN	8 IA	8 IA	8 IL	8 IA
7 CH 9	9 IA	9 IA	8 CH 9	8 IN	8 IA	9 IL	8 WI 9	9 CH	9 IN
10 WI	9 CH	9 IL 10	10 IA	8 WI 9	10 MI	9 WI	8 MI 9	9 IA	10 CH

1939	1940	1941	1942	1943	1944	1945	1946	1947	1948	1949
1 OS	1 MN★	1 MN★	1 OS★	1 PU	1 OS	1 IN	1 IL	1 MI★	1 MI★	1 OS
2 IA	2 MI	2 MI	2 WI★	1 MI	2 MI	2 MI	2 MI	2 WI	2 NW	1 MI
3 PU	3 NW	2 OS	3 MI	3 NW	3 PU	3 OS	3 IN	3 MN	3 MN	3 MN
4 MI	4 WI	4 NW	3 IL	4 IN	4 MN	4 PU	4 IA	3 IL	4 OS	4 WI
4 NW 5	4 OS	5 WI	5 IN	4 MN 5	5 IN	4 NW	5 MN	3 PU	5 IA	5 IL
6 IL	6 IA	6 IA	5 IA	6 IL	6 IL	6 WI	6 OS	6 IN	5 PU	5 IA
7 MN	6 IN	7 PU	5 MN	7 OS	7 WI	7 IL	6 NW	6 IA	5 IN	7 NW
7 IN 8	8 PU	7 IN	8 PU	8 WI	8 NW	8 MN	8 WI	8 NW	8 IL	8 PU
9 WI	9 IL	9 IL	9 NW	9 IA	8 IA 9	8 IA	9 PU	9 OS	9 WI	9 IN
9 CH 10										

1950	1951	1952	1953	1954	1955	1956	1957	1958	1959	1960
1 MI	1 IL	1 WI	1 MS	1 OS★	1 OS	1 IA	1 OS★	1 IA★	1 WI	1 MN★
2 OS	2 PU	1 PU	1 IL	2 WI	2 MS	2 MN	2 MS★	2 WI	2 MS	1 IA★
2 WI	3 WI	3 OS	3 WI	2 MI	3 MI	2 MI	3 IA	3 OS	3 PU	3 OS
4 IL	4 MI	4 MN	4 OS	4 MN	4 PU	4 MS	4 WI	4 PU	3 IL	4 MS
5 NW	5 OS	4 MI	5 MI	5 IA	5 IL	4 OS	4 PU	5 IN	5 NW	5 IL
6 IA	6 NW	6 IL	5 IA	6 PU	6 WI	6 NW	6 MI	6 IL	6 IA	5 MI
7 MN	7 MN	6 NW	5 MN	7 IN	7 IA	7 PU	7 IL	7 NW	7 MI	5 NW
8 IN	8 IN	6 IA	8 PU	8 MS	8 MN	7 IL	8 MN	8 MI	8 IN	5 PU
8 PU	9 IA	9 IN	9 IN	8 NW	9 IN	9 WI	9 IN	9 MN	8 OS	9 WI
– MS	– MS★	– MS★	10 NW	10 IL	10 NW	10 IN	9 NW	10 MS	10 MN	– IN

1961	1962	1963	1964	1965	1966	1967	1968	1969	1970	1971
1 OS★	1 WI	1 IL	1 MI★	1 MS★	1 MS★	1 IN	1 OS★	1 OS	1 OS★	1 MI
2 MN	2 MN	2 MS	2 OS	2 OS	2 PU	1 MN	2 MI	1 MI	2 MI	2 NW
3 MS	3 NW	2 OS	3 PU	3 PU	3 MI	1 PU	3 PU	3 PU	2 NW	3 OS
4 PU	3 OS	4 PU	4 IL	3 MN	3 IL	4 OS	3 MN	4 MN	4 IA	3 MS
5 WI	5 MS	5 NW	4 MN	5 IL	5 MN	5 IL	5 IN	5 IA	5 WI	3 IL
6 MI	5 PU	5 WI	6 MS	6 NW	6 OS	5 MI	5 IA	5 IN	5 MS	6 WI
7 IA	5 IA	5 MI	7 NW	7 MI	7 NW	5 MS	7 MS	5 NW	7 MN	6 MN
7 NW	8 IL	8 IA	7 WI	7 WI	7 WI	8 NW	8 IL	5 WI	8 PU	6 PU
9 IN	9 IN	9 MN	9 IA	9 IN	9 IN	9 IA	8 NW	9 MS	9 IL	9 IN
9 IL	10 MI	10 IN	9 IN	10 IA	10 IA	9 WI	10 WI	10 IL	9 IN	10 IA

1972	1973	1974	1975	1976	1977	1978	1979	1980	1981	1982
1 MI	1 OS	1 MI	1 OS★	1 MI	1 MI	1 MI	1 OS	1 MI	1 OS	1 MI
1 OS	1 MI	1 OS	2 MI	1 OS	1 OS	1 MS	2 PU	2 OS	1 IA	2 OS
3 PU	3 MN	3 MS	3 MS	3 MN	3 MS	3 PU	3 MI	2 PU	3 MI	3 IA
4 MS	4 IL	4 WI	3 IL	3 PU	4 IN	4 OS	4 IN	4 IA	3 IL	4 IL
5 MN	4 MS	5 IL	3 PU	3 IL	5 MN	5 MN	5 IA	5 MN	3 WI	5 WI
6 IN	4 PU	6 PU	6 WI	3 IN	6 PU	6 WI	6 MN	6 IN	6 MN	6 IN
6 IL	4 NW	7 MN	7 MN	7 IA	6 IA	7 IN	7 MS	6 WI	6 MS	7 PU
8 IA	8 WI	7 IA	7 IA	7 WI	8 WI	8 IA	7 WI	6 IL	8 PU	8 NW
9 WI	9 IN	7 NW	9 NW	7 MS	9 IL	9 IL	9 IL	9 MS	8 IN	8 MS
10 NW	9 IA	10 IN	10 IN	10 NW	10 NW	10 NW	10 NW	10 NW	10 NW	10 MN

1983	1984	1985	1986	1987	1988	1989
1 IL	1 OS	1 IA	1 MI	1 MS	1 MI	1 MI
2 MI	2 IL	2 MI	1 OS	2 IA	2 MS	2 IL
3 IA	2 PU	3 IL	3 IA	2 IN	3 IA	3 OS
4 OS	4 IA	4 OS	3 MN	4 MI	3 IL	3 MS
5 WI	4 WI	4 MS	5 MS	5 OS	5 IN	5 MN
6 PU	6 MI	6 MN	6 IN	6 MN	6 PU	6 IN
7 MS	6 MS	7 PU	6 IL	6 PU	7 OS	6 IA
8 IN	8 MN	8 WI	8 NW	8 IL	7 NW	8 PU
8 NW	9 NW	9 IN	8 PU	9 NW	9 MN	9 WI
10 MN	10 IN	9 NW	8 WI	10 WI	9 WI	10 NW

Over-all Big Ten Standings

	AVERAGE STANDING	YEARS IN STANDINGS	NUMBER OF FINISHES PER STANDING										LAST* PLACE
			1	2	3	4	5	6	7	8	9	10	
MICHIGAN	2.98	84	34	15	8	6	7	4	5	3	0	2	4
OHIO STATE	3.18	77	25	12	10	13	4	4	3	5	1	0	2
MINNESOTA	4.31	94	16	10	14	10	15	12	6	4	4	3	10
MICHIGAN STATE	4.41	37	5	5	6	5	4	3	4	2	2	1	1
CHICAGO	4.66	45	6	7	6	6	3	1	5	5	3	2	9
ILLINOIS	4.90	94	13	5	13	13	10	15	6	8	9	2	11
PURDUE	4.98	94	7	7	15	16	10	12	6	15	6	0	18
WISCONSIN	5.26	94	8	10	9	12	12	11	9	9	10	4	16
IOWA	5.68	90	8	4	5	10	14	14	11	11	9	4	25
NORTHWESTERN	6.12	92	5	6	7	6	13	11	15	8	9	12	25
INDIANA	6.75	88	2	1	6	5	10	14	11	15	19	5	27
PENN STATE	-	-	-	-	-	-	-	-	-	-	-	-	-

* LAST PLACE HAS BEEN AS HIGH AS FIFTH IN THE STANDINGS. THE BIG TEN HASN'T ALWAYS CONSISTED OF TEN TEAMS, EITHER. THIS WOULD RESULT IN A HIGHER STANDING NUMBER AND NOT REFLECT LAST PLACE. PURDUE, FOR INSTANCE, HAS FINISHED LAST 18 TIMES BUT HAS NEVER PLACED TENTH IN THE STANDINGS.

Win & Loss Trends at a Glance:

W-L-T

by Game:

by Season:

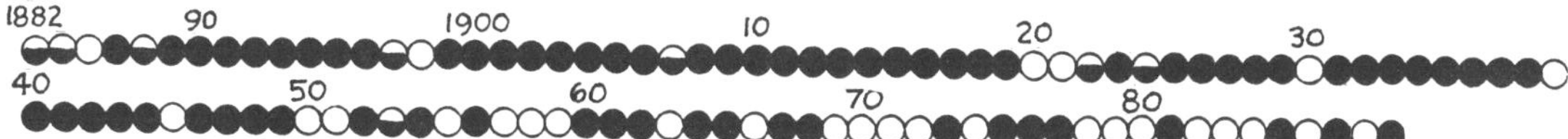

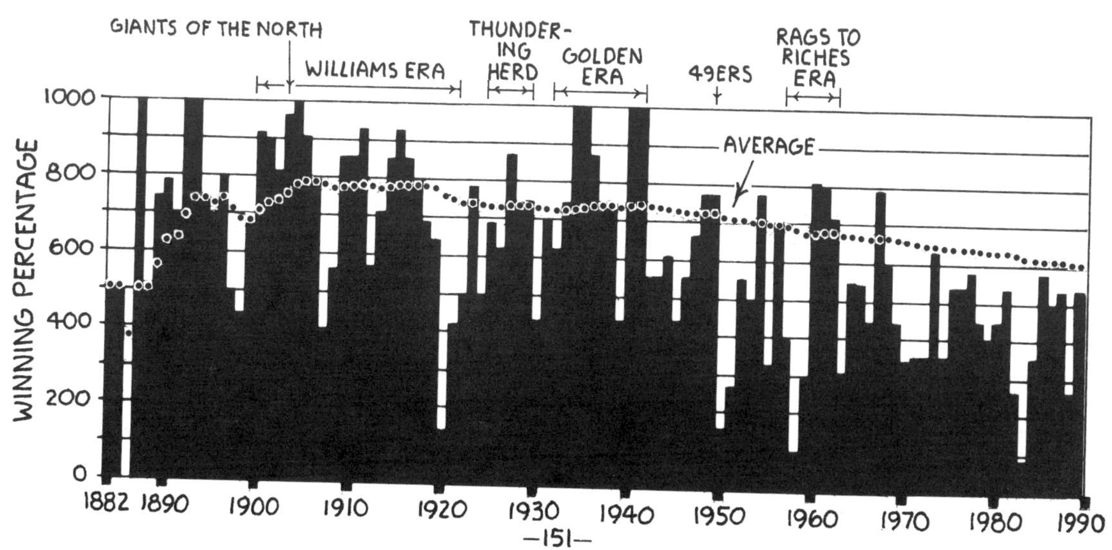

Coach Comparisons

COACH	YEARS COACHED	TOTAL SEASONS	TOTAL GAMES	CAREER GAME RECORD W-L-T	WIN/LOSS SEASONS W-L-T	WIN PERCENTAGE	BEST SINGLE SEASON W-L-T	WORST SINGLE SEASON W-L-T	SHUT-OUTS GIVEN	SHUT-OUTS TAKEN
NO COACH	1882&92	2	7	6-1-0	1-0-1	857	5-0-0	1-1-0	1	1
T. PEEBLES	1883	1	4	2-2-0	0-0-1	500	2-2-0	2-2-0	1	0
F. JONES	1886-88	3	6	3-3-0	1-1-1	500	2-0-0	0-2-0	3	0
D. McCORD A. McCORD F. HEFFELFINGER B. MORSE	1889	1	4	3-1-0	1-0-0	750	3-1-0	3-1-0	3	0
T. ECK	1890	1	7	5-1-1	1-0-0	786	5-1-1	5-1-1	4	1
E. MOULTON	1891	1	5	3-1-1	1-0-0	700	3-1-1	3-1-1	0	1
W. WINTER ☆	1893	1	6	6-0-0	1-0-0	1000	6-0-0	6-0-0	2	0
T. COCHRANE	1894	1	4	3-1-0	1-0-0	750	3-1-0	3-1-0	2	1
W. HEFFELFINGER ☆◇	1895	1	10	7-3-0	1-0-0	700	7-3-0	7-3-0	5	1
A. JERREMS	1896-97	2	18	12-6-0	1-0-1	667	8-2-0	4-4-0	9	4
J. MINDS ☆◇	1898	1	9	4-5-0	0-1-0	444	4-5-0	4-5-0	3	3
W. LEARY J. HARRISON	1899	1	11	6-3-2	1-0-0	636	6-3-2	6-3-2	4	2
H. WILLIAMS ★	1900-21	22	177	135-33-9	19-2-1	788	13-0-0	1-6-0	101	20
W. SPAULDING	1922-24	3	22	11-7-4	1-0-2	591	5-1-1	3-3-1	7	6
C. SPEARS ☆◇	1925-29	5	40	28-9-3	5-0-0	738	6-0-2	5-3-0	12	2
F. CRISLER ★	1930-31	2	18	10-7-1	1-1-0	583	7-3-0	3-4-0	8	5
B. BIERMAN ☆▽★	1932-41 1945-50	16	134	93-35-6	13-3-0	716	8-0-0	1-7-1	36	15
G. HAUSER ☆	1942-44	3	27	15-11-1	3-0-0	574	5-3-1	5-4-0	3	2
W. FESLER ☆◇	1951-53	3	27	10-13-4	1-1-1	444	4-3-2	2-6-1	1	3
M. WARMATH ▼	1954-71	18	177	89-81-7	9-9-0	523	9-2-0	1-9-0	20	17
C. STOLL	1972-78	7	78	39-39-0	4-3-0	500	7-4-0	4-7-0	4	5
J. SALEM	1979-83	5	55	19-35-1	1-4-0	355	6-5-0	1-10-0	0	2
L. HOLTZ	1984-85	2	22	10-12-0	1-1-0	455	6-5-0	4-7-0	0	0
J. GUTEKUNST	1985-	4+	46	21-23-2	2-1-1	479	6-5-0	2-7-2	0	3
TOTALS:	1882-1989	106	914	540-332-42	70-27-9	614			229	94

▽ COACH OF THE YEAR: 1935, 1941
▼ COACH OF THE YEAR: 1960
★ COACHES HALL OF FAME
☆ COACHES WHO WERE ALL-AMERICANS IN THEIR PLAYING DAYS
◇ COACHES WHO MADE THE HALL OF FAME AS PLAYERS

CAREER POINTS MN.-OPP.	LONGEST UNDEFEATED STRING	LONGEST WIN STRING	LONGEST LOSS STRING	POST SEASON GAMES W-L-T	CHAMPIONS OF NW/MIDWEST	CONFERENCE RECORD W-L-T	CONFERENCE WIN PERCENTAGE	CONFERENCE TITLES	AVERAGE STANDING IN THE CONFERENCE	ALL-CONFERENCE PLAYERS	ALL-AMERICAN PLAYERS	NATIONAL TITLES
126-58	5	5	1	–	1	–	–	–	–		0	0
9-8	2	2	1	–	–	–	–	–	–		–	0
57-43	2	2	2	–	–	–	–	–	–		–	0
46-28	2	2	1	–	–	–	–	–	–	–	0	0
208-34	5	2	1	–	1	–	–	–	–	–	0	0
102-46	4	2	1	–	1	–	–	–	–	–	0	0
148-38	6	6	0	–	1	–	–	–	–	–	0	0
74-8	3	3	1	–	0	–	–	–	–	–	0	0
136-58	3	3	1	–	0	–	–	–	–	–	0	0
280-101	7	7	4	–	0	1-5-0	167	0	5.50	1	0	0
92-72	2	2	3	–	0	1-2-0	333	0	5.00	0	0	0
151-79	6	5	2	–	0	0-3-0	000	0	6.00	0	0	0
4727-819	34	24	6	0	3	50-25-5	656	8	2.77	33	12	0
261-188	6	3	3	0	–	5-6-3	464	0	5.33	2	2	0
1014-297	11	8	2	0	–	13-7-1	643	0	3.60	9	5	0
317-153	3	3	2	1-0-0	–	4-5-0	444	0	5.50	1	1	0
2586-1235	28	21	5	0	–	57-28-6	659	6	3.18	33	24	5
547-437	4	3	3	0	–	8-8-1	500	0	4.33	1	0	0
443-589	4	3	4	0	–	7-8-4	474	0	5.33	3	1	0
2946-2843	8	8	11	1-1-0	–	66-57-4	535	2	4.89	24	9	1
1421-1788	4	4	5	0-1-0	–	27-29-0	482	0	5.43	11	0	0
1176-1593	3	3	10	0	–	12-32-1	278	0	7.40	6	0	0
467-543	3	3	4	0	–	7-10-0	412	0	7.00	0	0	0
996-1120	5	5	4	1-1-0	–	12-18-2	406	0	5.75	5	0	0
18,330-12,178				3-3-0	7	270-243-27	525	16	4.31	128*	53*	6

*PLAYERS WHO REPEATED THEIR ACCOMPLISHMENTS ARE COUNTED ONCE AND ONLY UNDER THE FIRST COACH THEY RECEIVED THEIR DISTINCTION. GOPHERS RECEIVING THEIR DISTINCTIONS WHILE AWAY FROM MINNESOTA ARE NOT COUNTED.

We're Number One!

- #1 SELF-PROCLAIMED CHAMPIONS OF THE NORTHWEST: 1890, 1891
- #1 CHAMPIONS OF THE INTERCOLLEGIATE ATHLETIC ASSOCIATION OF THE NORTHWEST: 1892, 1893
- #1 SELF-PROCLAIMED CHAMPIONS OF THE MIDWEST: 1900, 1903, 1911, 1915
- #1 BIG TEN CHAMPIONS: 1900, 1903, 1904, 1906, 1909, 1910, 1911, 1915, 1934, 1935, 1937, 1938, 1940, 1941, 1960, 1967
- #1 NATIONAL CHAMPIONS: 1934, 1935, 1936, 1940, 1941, 1960
- #1 UNDEFEATED SEASONS: 1892 (5-0-0), 1893 (6-0-0), 1900 (10-0-2), 1903 (13-0-1), 1904 (13-0-0), 1911 (6-0-1), 1927 (6-0-2), 1933 (4-0-4), 1934 (8-0-0), 1935 (8-0-0), 1940 (8-0-0), 1941 (8-0-0)
- #1 LONGEST UNDEFEATED STRINGS: 1903-05 (33-0-1), 1933-36 (24-0-4), 1900-01 (17-0-2), 1939-42 (18-0-0), 1891-94 (17-0-1), 1914-16 (12-0-1)

- #1 ALL-AMERICANS: 53 PLAYERS
- #1 HEISMAN AWARD: 1 PLAYER
- #1 OUTLAND AWARD: 2 PLAYERS
- #1 ALL-BIG TEN: 128 PLAYERS
- #1 BIG TEN MVP: 6 PLAYERS

- #1 ALL-TIME ALL-BIG TEN: 2 PLAYERS
- #1 COLLEGE FOOTBALL HALL OF FAME: 13 PLAYERS, 3 COACHES, 1 TRAINER
- #1 GOPHERS TO ENTER THE COLLEGE FOOTBALL HALL OF FAME FOR SERVICES RENDERED AT OTHER SCHOOLS AFTER THEIR PLAYING DAYS AT MINNESOTA: 1 PLAYER, 4 COACHES
- #1 NATIONAL FOOTBALL FOUNDATION GOLD MEDAL AWARD: 1 PLAYER
- #1 20TH CENTURY COLLEGE RECORD FOR MOST POINTS SCORED IN A SEASON: 725 IN 1904

- #1 NATIONAL LEADER FOR HIGH SCORING IN A GAME FOR 1904: 146 AGAINST GRNNELL
- #1 NATIONAL LEADER OF FIELD GOALS FOR 1907: GEORGE CAPRON WITH 11
- #1 THE ONLY PLAYER IN HISTORY TO BE NAMED ALL-AMERICAN AT TWO POSITIONS AT THE SAME TIME: BRONKO NAGURSKI AT FULLBACK AND TACKLE IN 1929
- #1 NATIONAL LEADER IN INTERCEPTIONS FOR 1939: HAROLD VAN EVERY WITH 8
- #1 NATIONAL LEADING TEAM IN KICKOFF RETURN AVERAGE FOR 1940: 36.4 YARDS
- #1 NATIONAL LEADER IN YARDS GAINED FOR 1944: WAYNE "RED" WILLIAMS RUSHED 911 YARDS IN 136 CARRIES; RETURNED PUNTS 242 YARDS; RETURNED KICKOFFS FOR 314 YARDS AND AVERAGED 163 YARDS PER GAME FOR A TOTAL 1467 YARDS
- #1 NATIONAL LEADER IN PUNT RETURNS FOR 1953: PAUL GIEL WITH 17 RETURNS FOR 288 YARDS AND A 16.9 YARD PER RETURN AVERAGE
- #1 NATIONAL LEADING TEAM IN RUSH DEFENSE FOR 1962: 52.2 YARDS PER GAME
- #1 NATIONAL RECORD FOR MOST RUSHES IN A GAME: 57 BY KENT KITZMANN AGAINST ILLINOIS IN 1977
- #1 NATIONAL RECORD FOR LONGEST KICKOFF RETURN: 100 YARDS BY RICK UPCHURCH AGAINST WISCONSIN IN 1974 AND BY BOBBY WEBER AGAINST OHIO STATE IN 1977
- #1 NATIONAL RECORD FOR MOST YARDS GAINED BY A FRESHMAN FOR THE FIRST GAME IN HIS CAREER: 205 YARDS BY DARRELL THOMPSON AGAINST BOWLING GREEN IN 1986
- #1 BIG TEN RECORD FOR FEWEST TEAM PASS ATTEMPTS IN A GAME: 0 IN 1940 AGAINST OHIO STATE.
- #1 BIG TEN RECORD FOR MOST YARDS RETURNED ON KICKOFFS IN A GAME: 203 YARDS BY RON ENGEL AGAINST MICHIGAN IN 1951
- #1 BIG TEN RECORD FOR MOST YARDS RETURNED IN A GAME BY INTERCEPTION: 140 BY WALTER BOWSER AGAINST MICHIGAN STATE IN 1970.
- #1 BIG TEN RECORD FOR MOST YARDS RETURNED IN A SEASON BY INTERCEPTION: 203 YARDS BY WALTER BOWSER ON 5 INTERCEPTIONS IN 1970
- #1 BIG TEN RECORD FOR FEWEST TEAM FUMBLES IN A SEASON: 8 IN 1976
- #1 BIG TEN RECORD FOR MOST SCORES IN A GAME BY SAFETY: 2 VS. INDIANA IN 1981
- #1 BIG TEN RECORD FOR LONGEST RUN FROM SCRIMMAGE: 98 YARDS BY DARRELL THOMPSON AGAINST MICHIGAN IN 1987
- #1 BIG TEN RECORD FOR GAINING OVER 1000 YARDS BY RUSHING IN EACH OF HIS FIRST TWO YEARS OF PLAY: DARRELL THOMPSON IN 1986 (1240 YARDS) AND 1987 (1229 YARDS)

National Champions... by Year

1883	YALE
1884	YALE
1885	PRINCETON
1886	YALE
1887	YALE
1888	YALE
1889	PRINCETON
1890	HARVARD
1891	YALE
1892	YALE
1893	PRINCETON
1894	YALE
1895	PENNSYLVANIA
1896	PRINCETON
1897	PENNSYLVANIA
1898	HARVARD
1899	HARVARD
1900	YALE
1901	MICHIGAN
1902	MICHIGAN
1903	PRINCETON
1904	PENNSYLVANIA
1905	CHICAGO
1906	PRINCETON
1907	YALE
1908	PENNSYLVANIA
1909	YALE
1910	HARVARD
1911	PRINCETON
1912	HARVARD
1913	HARVARD
1914	ARMY
1915	CORNELL
1916	PITTSBURGH
1917	GEORGIA TECH.
1918	PITTSBURGH
1919	HARVARD
1920	CALIFORNIA
1921	★CORNELL
1922	★CORNELL
1923	ILLINOIS
1924	NOTRE DAME
1925	DARTMOUTH
	ALABAMA
1926	STANFORD
	ALABAMA
1927	ILLINOIS
1928	GEORGIA TECH.
	SOUTHERN CAL.
1929	NOTRE DAME
1930	NOTRE DAME
1931	SOUTHERN CAL.
	NOTRE DAME
1932	SOUTHERN CAL.
	MICHIGAN
1933	MICHIGAN
	OHIO ST.
	SOUTHERN CAL.
1934	★MINNESOTA
	ALABAMA
1935	★MINNESOTA
	SOUTHERN METH.
	PRINCETON
	LOUISIANA ST.
1936	★MINNESOTA
	LOUISIANA ST.
1937	PITTSBURGH
	CALIFORNIA
1938	TEXAS CHRISTIAN
	TENNESSEE
	NOTRE DAME
1939	TEXAS A&M
	SOUTHERN CAL.
	CORNELL
1940	★MINNESOTA
	★STANFORD
	TENNESSEE
1941	★MINNESOTA
	TEXAS
1942	OHIO ST.
	WISCONSIN
	GEORGIA
1943	NOTRE DAME
1944	ARMY
1945	ARMY
1946	ARMY
	NOTRE DAME
	GEORGIA
1947	●MICHIGAN
	NOTRE DAME
1948	MICHIGAN
1949	NOTRE DAME
1950	★OKLAHOMA
	TENNESSEE
1951	★MICHIGAN ST.
	TENNESSEE
	MARYLAND
1952	★MICHIGAN ST.
1953	NOTRE DAME
	MARYLAND
1954	UCLA
	OHIO ST.
1955	★OKLAHOMA
1956	★OKLAHOMA
1957	OHIO ST.
	MICHIGAN ST.
	AUBURN
1958	LOUISIANA ST.
	IOWA
1959	SYRACUSE
	MISSISSIPPI
1960	◆MINNESOTA
	MISSISSIPPI
	IOWA
	WASHINGTON
1961	ALABAMA
	OHIO ST.
1962	SOUTHERN CAL.
	MISSISSIPPI
1963	TEXAS
1964	MICHIGAN
	ALABAMA
	ARKANSAS
	NOTRE DAME
1965	MICHIGAN ST.
	ALABAMA
1966	NOTRE DAME
	MICHIGAN ST.
1967	SOUTHERN CAL.
	NOTRE DAME
	TENNESSEE
1968	OHIO ST.
	GEORGIA
1969	TEXAS
1970	NEBRASKA
	TEXAS
	OHIO ST.
1971	NEBRASKA
1972	SOUTHERN CAL.
1973	NOTRE DAME
	ALABAMA
	OKLAHOMA
1974	OKLAHOMA
	SOUTHERN CAL.
1975	OKLAHOMA
	OHIO ST.
1976	PITTSBURGH
	SOUTHERN CAL.
1977	▼NOTRE DAME
1978	ALABAMA
	SOUTHERN CAL.
	OKLAHOMA
1979	ALABAMA
1980	GEORGIA
	OKLAHOMA
1981	CLEMSON
	PENN ST.
1982	PENN ST.
	SOUTHERN METH.
1983	MIAMI (FLA.)
1984	BRIGHAM YOUNG
	FLORIDA
1985	OKLAHOMA
1986	PENN ST.
	OKLAHOMA
1987	MIAMI (FLA.)
1988	●NOTRE DAME
1989	MIAMI (FLA.)

★ TEAMS COACHED BY FORMER MINNESOTA PLAYERS – GILMORE DOBIE (1921,22), BERNIE BIERMAN (1934,35,36,40,41), CLARK SHAUGHNESSY (1941), BUD WILKINSON (1950,55,56) AND BIGGIE MUNN (1951,52)

◆ TEAM COACHED BY MURRAY WARMATH (1960)

● TEAMS COACHED BY FORMER MINNESOTA COACHES – FRITZ CRISLER (1947) AND LOU HOLTZ (1988)

▼ TEAM COACHED BY MINNESOTA-DULUTH ALUMNI AND HALL OF FAMER DAN DEVINE (1977)

THERE IS A LOT TO ARGUE ABOUT IN CROWNING A NATIONAL CHAMPION. NINE POLLS* WERE USED IN LISTING THE ABOVE TEAMS. NINE WERE USED ON THE CHANCE SOME MAY BE RIGHT.

THE LONGEST STRING OF CHAMPIONS WAS CHOSEN BY THE HELMS FOUNDATION OF LOS ANGELES. THOUGH THEY STARTED THEIR SELECTIONS IN THE 1930'S, THEY RETROACTIVELY DETERMINED TEAMS GOING BACK TO 1883. THEY ENDED PICKING TEAMS IN 1982.

---

*RANKINGS: ASSOCIATED PRESS; DICKINSON; DUNKEL; FOOTBALL WRITERS ASSOC. OF AMERICAS GRANTLAND RICE AWARD; HELMS ATHLETIC FOUNDATION; LITKENHOUS; NATIONAL FOOTBALL FOUNDATION & HALL OF FAME; UNITED PRESS INTERNATIONAL COACHES; WILLIAMSON

...by Titles

Titles	School	Years
16	NOTRE DAME	1924, 29, 30, 31, 38, 43, 46, 47, 49, 53, 64, 66, 67, 73, 77, 88
11	YALE	1883, 84, 86, 87, 88, 91, 92, 94, 1900, 07, 09
11	SOUTHERN CAL.	1928, 31, 32, 33, 39, 62, 67, 72, 74, 76, 78
10	OKLAHOMA	1950, 55, 56, 73, 74, 75, 78, 80, 85, 86
9	ALABAMA	1925, 26, 34, 61, 64, 65, 73, 78, 79
8	PRINCETON	1885, 89, 93, 96, 1903, 06, 11, 35
8	OHIO ST.	1933, 42.54.57, 61, 68, 70, 75
7	HARVARD	1890, 98, 99, 1910, 12, 13, 19
7	MICHIGAN	1901, 02, 32, 33, 47, 48, 64
6	MINNESOTA	1934, 35, 36, 40, 41, 60
5	MICHIGAN ST.	1951, 52, 57, 65, 66
5	TENNESSEE	1938, 40, 50, 51, 67
4	PENNSYLVANIA	1895, 97, 1904, 08
4	CORNELL	1915, 21, 22, 39
4	ARMY	1914, 44, 45, 46
4	TEXAS	1941, 63, 69, 70
4	PITTSBURGH	1916, 18, 37, 76
4	GEORGIA	1942, 46, 68, 80
3	LOUISIANA ST.	1935, 36, 58
3	MISSISSIPPI	1959, 60, 62
3	PENN. ST.	1981, 82, 86
3	MIAMI (FLA.)	1983, 87, 89
2	ILLINOIS	1923, 27
2	GEORGIA TECH	1917, 28
2	CALIFORNIA	1920, 37
2	STANFORD	1926, 40
2	MARYLAND	1951, 53
2	IOWA	1958, 60
2	NEBRASKA	1970, 71
2	SOUTHERN METH.	1935, 82
1	CHICAGO	1905
1	DARTMOUTH	1925
1	TEXAS CHRISTIAN	1938
1	TEXAS A & M	1939
1	WISCONSIN	1942
1	UCLA	1954
1	AUBURN	1957
1	SYRACUSE	1959
1	WASHINGTON	1960
1	ARKANSAS	1964
1	CLEMSON	1981
1	BRIGHAM YOUNG	1984
1	FLORIDA	1984

...by Conference

IVY LEAGUE

(NO LONGER IN DIVISION I-A)

- 11 YALE
- 8 PRINCETON
- 7 HARVARD
- 4 PENNSYLVANIA
- 4 CORNELL
- 1 DARTMOUTH

35

BIG TEN

- 8 OHIO ST.
- 7 MICHIGAN
- 6 MINNESOTA
- 5 MICHIGAN ST.
- 2 ILLINOIS
- 2 IOWA
- 1 CHICAGO
- 1 WISCONSIN

32

PACIFIC TEN

- 11 SOUTHERN CAL.
- 2 CALIFORNIA
- 2 STANFORD
- 1 UCLA
- 1 WASHINGTON

17

INDEPENDENTS

- 16 NOTRE DAME
- 4 ARMY
- 4 PITTSBURGH
- 3 PENN ST.
- 3 MIAMI (FLA.)
- 1 SYRACUSE

31

BIG EIGHT

- 10 OKLAHOMA
- 2 NEBRASKA

12

SOUTHEASTERN

- 9 ALABAMA
- 5 TENNESSEE
- 4 GEORGIA
- 3 LOUISIANA ST.
- 3 MISSISSIPPI
- 1 AUBURN
- 1 FLORIDA

26

SOUTHWEST ATHLETIC

- 4 TEXAS
- 2 SOUTHERN METH.
- 1 TEXAS CHRISTIAN
- 1 TEXAS A&M
- 1 ARKANSAS

9

ATLANTIC COAST

- 2 GEORGIA TECH
- 2 MARYLAND
- 1 CLEMSON

5

WESTERN ATHLETIC

- 1 BRIGHAM YOUNG

1

A SYSTEM KNOWN AS THE DICKINSON RANKINGS BEGAN IN 1924. THE INVENTOR OF THE SYSTEM WAS PROF. FRANK DICKINSON OF ILLINOIS. IT WAS BASED ON MATHEMATICAL EQUATIONS WHICH HAPPILY TURNED OUT TO APPROXIMATE THE "EXPERTS'" OPINIONS.

IT WAS FROM THIS SYSTEM THE FIRST-EVER NATIONAL CHAMPIONSHIP TROPHY WAS CREATED. THE ROTATING TROPHY WAS PERMANENTLY GIVEN TO NOTRE DAME FOR HAVING WON IT THREE TIMES. A SECOND TROPHY WAS THEN INSTIGATED AND CAME IN PERMANENT POSSESSION OF MINNESOTA IN 1940. THE HISTORICAL RANKING SYSTEM ENDED AT THAT POINT.

THE MOST RECOGNIZED RANKINGS OF TODAY WOULD BE THE A.P. AND U.P.I. POLLS WHICH BEGAN IN 1936 AND 1940 RESPECTIVELY.

Postgame Credits

- GEORGE B. WRIGHT'S MAP OF MINNEAPOLIS, LITHOGRAPHED AND PUBLISHED BY RICE & CO. ST. PAUL, MINNESOTA (1873 ?)
- THE DAVIDSON MAP OF MINNEAPOLIS, C. WRIGHT DAVIDSON, PUBLISHED 1881
- ARIEL, (U OF M PUBLICATION) 10-26-1882, 10-3-1884, 11-2-1886, 11-30-1888
- 1883-84 MINNEAPOLIS DIRECTORY
- 1886 MINNEAPOLIS DIRECTORY
- UNIVERSITY OF MINNESOTA "GOPHER" YEARBOOKS FROM THE YEARS 1888-1962 AND 1964-1966
- DAVISON'S ATLAS MAP OF MINNEAPOLIS, HENNEPIN CO., MINNESOTA 1888
- ATLAS OF THE CITY OF MINNEAPOLIS, MINNESOTA, C.M. FOOTE PUBLISHING CO., 328 NICOLLET AVE. MINNEAPOLIS, MINNESOTA, © C.M. FOOTE 1892
- 1895 ST. PAUL DIRECTORY
- UNIVERSITY OF MINNESOTA GAME PROGRAMS: 9-19-1903, 10-17-1903, 10-1-1927, 10-6-1928, 11-17-1928 10-27-1934, 10-30-1948, 10-7-1950, 9-24-1955, 10-20-1962, 11-17-1962, 9-24-1966, 10-1-1966, 11-12-1966 9-27-1969, 10-4-1969, 10-18-1969, 10-25-1969, 11-8-1969, 11-22-1969, 9-25-1971, 10-7-1972, 11-18-1972, 9-14-1974, 11-18-1978, 9-13-1980, 10-27-1984, 9-28-1985
- THE MINNEAPOLIS TRIBUNE, 10-28-1903, 10-31-1903, 11-22-1903, 11-11-1906, 3-2-1907, 11-22-1908, 11-21-1909, 11-5-1916, 11-16-1924, 11-25-1928, 11-25-1936, 10-4-1942
- THE MINNEAPOLIS JOURNAL, 11-1-1903, 11-3-1903, 11-4-1906, 11-11-1906, 11-22-1908, 11-5-1916, 11-16-1924, 11-6-1927, 11-24-1928, 11-25-1928, 11-24-1931, 11-10-1935, 10-21-1936
- FOOTBALL AT MINNESOTA, THE MINNESOTA ALUMNI WEEKLY, 11-9-1914, VOL. XIV NO. 9
- UNIVERSITY OF MINNESOTA GENERAL ALUMNI CATALOGUE, UNDER DIRECTION OF W. J. MAXWELL 1916
- HISTORY OF MINNESOTA FOOTBALL, EDITED BY MARTIN NEWELL, THE GENERAL ALUMNI ASSOCIATION OF THE UNIVERSITY OF MINNESOTA, 1928
- THE MINNEAPOLIS STAR, 11-1-1936, 11-2-1941, 10-4-1942, 12-1-1942, 11-29-1943, 10-16-1949, 12-2-1967, 12-2-1968
- DR. HENRY L. WILLIAMS, A FOOTBALL BIOGRAPHY, BY STAN W. CARLSON, EDITOR & PUBLISHER-STAN W. CARLSON, MINNEAPOLIS, MINNESOTA © 1938
- THE ST. PAUL PIONEER PRESS, 11-10-1940
- DICKINSON'S FOOTBALL RATINGS FROM GRANGE TO HARMON, © FEB. 1941 BY FRANK G. DICKINSON, WHAT'S WHAT PUBLISHING CO., 26TH & PRATT STREETS, OMAHA, NEBRASKA
- WHO'S WHO IN MINNESOTA ATHLETICS, EDITED BY RICHARD CHARLES FISHER, PUBLISHER WHO'S WHO IN MINNESOTA ATHLETICS, 1941
- THE MINNEAPOLIS TIMES, 12-11-1941
- LOOK MAGAZINE, 12-1-1942
- CHEERLEADING, BY NEWT LOKEN AND OTIS DYPWICK, A.S. BARNES & CO., INC. © 1945
- A.A. STAGG GRAND OLD MAN OF FOOTBALL, BY FRANCIS J. POWERS, C.C. SPINK & SON, ST. LOUIS, MO 1946
- THE NEW ENCYCLOPEDIA OF SPORTS, FRANK G. MENKE, A.S. BARNS & CO., NEW YORK, N.Y. 1947
- SPORTS QUIZ, BY LYLE BROWN, POCKET BOOKS, INC., NEW YORK, N.Y. 1954
- UNIVERSITY OF MINNESOTA FOOTBALL "PRESS GUIDE" ISSUES FROM 1954-1983 AND 1987-1989
- GOLD GLORY, RICHARD RAINBOLT, RALPH TURTINEN PUBLISHING CO., WAYZATA, MN 1972
- GOLD COUNTRY REVIVAL, BY JOHN O'NEIL, MINNESOTA DAILY, VOL. 75, NO. 22, SEPTEMBER, 1973

- NCAA FOOTBALL RULES COMMITTEE CHRONOLOGY OF 100 YEARS 1876-1976, BY JOHN WALDORF, © 1975 BY THE NATIONAL COLLEGIATE ATHLETIC ASSOCIATION
- BIG TEN FOOTBALL, BY MERVIN D. HYMAN & GORDON S. WHITE, JR., MAC MILLIAN PUBLISHING CO., INC. 866 3RD AVE., NEW YORK, NY 10022, COLLIAR MAC MILLIAN, CANADA LTD. 1977
- 100 YEARS OF GOLDEN GOPHER FOOTBALL, EDITED BY RALPH TURTINEN, MENS INTERCOLLEGIATE ATHLETIC DEPARTMENT OF THE UNIVERSITY OF MINNESOTA 1981
- FOOTBALL RANKINGS, COMPILED BY LOWELL R. GREUNKE, JEFFERSON & LONDON: McFARLAND BOX 611, JEFFERSON, NORTH CAROLINA 28640 © 1984
- MINNESOTA FOOTBALL-THE GOLDEN YEARS 1932-1941, BY JAMES P. QUIRK 1985
- HOW THE WAR IN FRANCE CHANGED FOOTBALL FOREVER, BY WILLIAM BARRY FURLONG, SMITHSONIAN, SMITHSONIAN ASSOCIATES, 900 JEFFERSON DRIVE, WASHINGTON D.C. © FEB. 1986
- 1987 NCAA FOOTBALL, EDITED BY MICHAEL V. EARLE, NALL AVE. AT 63RD ST., PO BOX 1906, MISSION KA 66201 JULY 1987
- BIG TEN 1987 FOOTBALL YEARBOOK, 1111 PLAZA, SUITE 600, SCHAUMBURG, IL 60173-4990
- SOUTH ST. PAUL CENTENNIAL 1887-1987, THE HISTORY OF SOUTH ST. PAUL, MINNESOTA, PRODUCED BY THE SOUTH ST. PAUL AREA CHAPTER OF THE DAKOTA COUNTY HISTORICAL SOCIETY, 1987
- 1988 NCAA FOOTBALL, © 1988 NCAA, EDITOR MICHAEL V. EARLE, COMPILED BY STEVE BODA, JR. AND JAMES M. VAN VALKENBURG
- ON TO NICOLLET, BY STEW THORNLEY © 1988, NODIN PRESS, 525 N. 3RD ST., MINNEAPOLIS MN 55401

- BIG TEN OFFICES
- CLEMSON UNIV. SPORTS INFORMATION DEPT.
- DAKOTA COUNTY HISTORICAL SOCIETY
- HAMLINE UNIV. NEWS BUREAU
- HENNEPIN COUNTY HISTORICAL SOCIETY
- INDEPENDENCE BOWL
- MATTHEWS COMMUNITY CENTER
- MINNEAPOLIS PUBLIC LIBRARY
- MINNESOTA HISTORICAL SOCIETY
- NATIONAL FOOTBALL FOUNDATION HALL OF FAME
- SAINT PAUL PUBLIC LIBRARY
- SHATTUCK HIGH SCHOOL
- STANFORD UNIV. SPORTS INFORMATION DEPT.
- UNIV. OF ILLINOIS SPORTS INFORMATION DEPT.
- UNIV. OF MINNESOTA ARCHIVES AND LIBRARIES
- UNIV. OF MINNESOTA SPORTS INFORMATION DEPT.
- UNIV. OF PENNSYLVANIA SPORTS INFORMATION DEPT.
- UNIV. OF WISCONSIN BAND
- YALE UNIV. SPORTS INFORMATION DEPT.

Honorable Mention

THE FOLLOWING ARE INDIVIDUALS WHO HELPED MAKE THIS BOOK POSSIBLE. THEY LOANED THEIR KNOWLEDGE, TIME, BOOKS, PHOTOS, STORIES AND ADVICE. WITH THEIR ASSISTANCE THE LONG TASK OF CREATING THIS BOOK WAS MADE A PLEASANT EXPERIENCE.

- MYRTLE ALLEN
- MARIE ANGLE
- BOB BEEBE
- JACK WM. BROWN
- MARILYN BROWN
- OTIS DYPWICK
- BILL GARNAAS
- K.C. GILLMAN
- LOUIS GROSS
- ROSEMARY HANNAH
- ROBYN KANNAS
- JANE LEE
- MARY LACROIX
- FRANCIS 'PUG' LUND
- MILLIE MARPLE
- MURIEL McEACHERN
- GARY McVEY
- MARETTA MUXLOW
- BRONKO NAGURSKI
- ELLEN OLIVER
- DONITA PAPAS
- JACK PAPAS
- JEFF PAPAS
- JON W. PAPAS
- BOB PATRIN
- K.C. POEHLER
- MILLIE SMITH
- GEORGE SVENDSEN
- LT. COL. ROGER SYVERUD
- JAMES WALKER
- JEFF WARD
- DICK WESTBY
- KAREN ZWACH